LINCOLN CHRISTIAN UNIVERSITY

P9-DET-996

Anti-Bias Education
for Young Children and Ourselves

Louise Derman-Sparks
&
Julie Olsen Edwards

*With acknowledgement of the Anti-Bias Curriculum Task Force,
whose work and thinking were the foundation for the original edition*

National Association for the Education of Young Children
Washington, DC

naeyc®

National Association
for the Education
of Young Children
1313 L Street NW, Suite 500
Washington, DC 20005-4101
202-232-8777 • 800-424-2460
www.naeyc.org

NAEYC Books

Director, Publications and
Educational Initiatives
Carol Copple

Managing Editor
Bry Pollack

Design and Production
Malini Dominey

Editorial Associate
Melissa Hogarty

Editorial Assistant
Elizabeth Wegner

Permissions
Lacy Thompson

Through its publications program, the National Association for the Education of Young Children (NAEYC) provides a forum for discussion of major issues and ideas in the early childhood field, with the hope of provoking thought and promoting professional growth. The views expressed or implied in this book are not necessarily those of the Association or its members.

Correction

In previous printings of this book, a citation to Francis Wardle's work was inadvertently omitted. Our sincerest apologies to our colleague, Dr. Francis Wardle, a pioneer in thinking and writing about multiracial children and their families.

— LDS and JOE

Permissions

The poem "I Am Freedom's Child," by Bill Martin, Jr, is reprinted with permission of Michael Sampson. © 1970.

Excerpts from *Kids Like Us: Using Persona Dolls in the Classroom* (107–10, 140, and 142–44), by Trisha Whitney (St. Paul, MN: Redleaf Press, 1999), are adapted with permission. © 1999 by Trisha Whitney.

Excerpt from "The Garden Song," by David Mallett, is reprinted with permission. © 1975.

Excerpts from *What If All the Kids Are White? Anti-Bias Multicultural Education with Young Children and Families* (84–85, 119–20, 145–46, and 148–49), by Louise Derman-Sparks and Patricia Ramsey (New York: Teachers College Press, 2006), are adapted with permission of the Publisher. © 2006 by Teachers College, Columbia University. All rights reserved.

Excerpt from "Finding a Voice" in *In Our Own Way: How Anti-Bias Work Shapes Our Lives* (32–34), by Linda Irene Jiménez (St. Paul, MN: Redleaf Press, 1999), is adapted with permission. © 1999 by Linda Irene Jiménez.

Excerpt from "Myths about Men Who Work with Young Children" (16–18), by Bryan G. Nelson (Redmond, WA: Child Care Exchange, 2004), is adapted with permission from *Exchange* magazine. Visit www.ChildCareExchange.com or call (800) 221-2864. Multiple use copy agreement available for educators by request.

Excerpt from "Happy Adoption Day," by John McCutcheon, is reprinted with permission. © 1993.

Photo Credits

Harry Cutting Photography Inc: 1; *Mary Duru*: 29; *Larry Garf*: 20; *William K. Geiger*: 147; *Rich Graessle*: 110; *iStockphoto*: 70, 112, 117, 125, 145, back cover; *Jean-Claude Lejeune*: 85, 90; *Susan Lum*: 129; *Elisabeth Nichols*: 132, 149 (bottom left); *Karen Phillips*: 11, 135; *Ellen B. Senisi*: cover (top left, bottom left, bottom right), 149 (top left); *Shutterstock*: 55; *Bill Sparks*: iii (top); *Subjects & Predicates*: cover (top right), 32, 77, 149 (top right); *Elaine M. Ward*: 101; *Carol Whitehill*: iii (bottom)

Additional Credits

Additional text/photo editing: Lisa Cook and Natalie Klein Cavanagh

vii—From *Killing Rage, Ending Racism* by bell hooks. © 1995.

1—From *Child Honoring: How to Turn This World Around* by Raffi Cavoukian and Sharna Olfman. © 2006.

20—From an interview with Jim Clay; from an interview with Rita Tenorio.

32—Online: www.childpeacebooks.org/cpb/Protect/help.php#Making.

135—From an interview with Rita Tenorio.

157—From *Temple of My Familiar* by Alice Walker. © 1989.

158—Quote by Margaret Mead, source unknown.

160—From the poem printed on the cover of the constitution of the American Miners' Association, 1864. Author unknown. Online: http://labornotes.org/node/892.

Anti-Bias Education for Young Children and Ourselves

Copyright © 2010 by the National Association for the Education of Young Children. All rights reserved. Printed in the United States of America. Second printing 2012.

Library of Congress Control Number: 2009938138
ISBN: 978-1-928896-67-8
NAEYC Item #254

About the Authors

Louise Derman-Sparks is an internationally respected anti-bias educator. Author (with the ABC Task Force) of *Anti-Bias Curriculum: Tools for Empowering Young Children*, the original edition of the current volume, she has coauthored additional books with Dr. Carol Brunson Day and Dr. Patricia Ramsey. She speaks throughout the United States and abroad. Louise has a lifelong commitment to building a more just society for all people. Her children, Douglass and Holly, now grown, were her inspiration. A Pacific Oaks College faculty member for 33 years—when its mission and pedagogy reflected anti-bias education principles—Louise is retired. She served on the NAEYC Governing Board during 1997–2001.

Julie Olsen Edwards began her early childhood education career working as a family child care provider as a way to stay home with her new baby. She went on to work for Head Start, teach in private and public preschools and parent cooperatives, and teach kindergarten and reading in elementary schools, and work with community teen mother programs. For 38 years, Julie was on the faculty of Cabrillo College's early childhood education department, served as program chair, and was founding director of the campus Children's Center. A lifetime activist for children and families, she continues to write, teach, and consult on issues of equity, diversity, and anti-bias; emerging literacy; and family life and empowerment. She served on the NAEYC Governing Board during 2003–2007.

128600

Contents

Voices from the Field

At intervals throughout the book are short pieces we call "Voices from the Field" in which anti-bias educators contribute their insights in their own areas of experience and expertise.

A Renewed Sense of Hope

by Carol Brunson Day

What if someone told you that you could contribute in a small but significant way to making the world a better place? Would you want to do it? Of course you would. Then read on, because that is what this book offers—a chance to make the world fairer and more humane for everybody. And it offers the chance to achieve that grand goal from a place where you have already chosen to be—in your daily work with children and families.

Recalling (as I do) the sense of hope for change in society that filled the air during the 1960s, I feel the same now in what these authors are challenging us to do. Their emotion is as driven by hope for change as it is by commitment to the cause of equity.

In the descriptions of their and many others' work with young children, families, and teachers, what Louise Derman-Sparks and Julie Olsen Edwards convey to us here is certain to be cutting edge. This book's predecessor, *Anti-Bias Curriculum,* initially hit the early childhood education field of 1989 like a bombshell and has remained vital and provocative for 20 years. Similarly, this new edition will jar us, as it, in a way, chronicles our accomplishments and at the same time re-launches us into perilous psychological terrain. I expect *Anti-Bias Education* to generate both contentious debate and penetrating growth.

The key to what I anticipate will be its success is its approach and delivery. It is filled with stories about real experiences of real teachers with real children and real families, simply and honestly told. Be prepared to be drawn into the interactions. But also be prepared to be asked to think for yourself and be reflective. Your role won't be to just read and recall information. No. You must think about your own experiences and reflect on your own thinking. You must interact with the text.

Also be prepared to work hard, for the authors are demanding. They repeatedly ask you to try, and try again, when you don't get things quite right. They offer cautions to help you avoid the simple mistake ("simple" in that it is what we might be inclined to do because we are well intentioned). But they are not satisfied for you to remain on the surface of things. You must go deeply into issues such as class bias, and they won't be satisfied until you push yourself past your point of comfort and ease. Yet they are also gentle, offering reassurance along the way. Especially at the most precarious points, they provide scenario after scenario, telling you what to say and when to say it, capturing and explaining the subtleties of this "anti-bias" work through concrete examples. They illustrate, too, the value of making mistakes and assure us that repetition yields greater skill if not perfection.

Becoming a strong anti-bias educator is a journey; and with this book, Louise and Julie are inviting each and every reader to join the caravan. No matter how much you might already know about this topic, there's more provided here to learn, more to master. . . . And should you choose to fully engage in the journey, your reward will be a renewed sense of hope that by your own hand, things really can change.

A Few Words About This Book

Beloved community is formed not by the eradication of difference but by its affirmation, by each of us claiming the identities and cultural legacies that shape who we are and how we live in the world. . . . We deepen those bondings by connecting them with an anti-racist [anti-bias] struggle.

—bell hooks

Since the publication by NAEYC of *Anti-Bias Curriculum: Tools for Empowering Young Children* (Derman-Sparks & the ABC Task Force 1989), early childhood teachers across the United States and internationally have embraced anti-bias education as a central part of their work. This second edition, *Anti-Bias Education for Young Children and Ourselves*, builds on that original. Its underlying intentions remain the same—to support children's full development in our multiracial, multilingual, multicultural world and to give them the tools to stand up to prejudice, stereotyping, bias, and eventually to institutional "isms." As was said in the first edition, to achieve this for children means that as educators "it is not sufficient to be nonbiased (and also highly unlikely), nor is it sufficient to be an observer" (3). Rather, we are called upon to integrate the core goals of anti-bias education in developmentally appropriate ways throughout children's educational journey.

Continuity and change

Anti-Bias Curriculum: Tools for Empowering Young Children was grounded in the work of a group of dedicated early childhood teachers from the Pacific Oaks Children's School in Pasadena, California. They were joined by two additional teachers, one from the Los Angeles public school district and one from the Corinne Seeds University Elementary School at UCLA. The names of this group—collectively, the ABC (Anti-Bias Curriculum) Task Force—appear on page viii. Their work continues to be fundamental to this second edition.

Anti-Bias Education for Young Children and Ourselves now draws upon an even broader pool of experience and knowledge, which comes from the 20 years of anti-bias education practice that has occurred throughout the United States and abroad since the publication of the first edition. To gather this new information, research assistants Nadiyah Taylor and Meg Thomas worked with Louise to hold in-depth interviews with anti-bias educators working with children and adults from a range of backgrounds in communities throughout the United States. These interviewees, too, are listed on that contributors page.

These interviews resulted in a wealth of insights, perspectives, and experiences that greatly informed our writing. Many of the conversations are excerpted explicitly throughout the text. In addition, a number of experienced educators wrote features pertaining to specific arenas of anti-bias work, and these "Voices from the Field" appear at the end of related chapters. To all these collaborators, we send a heartfelt thank you, for your wisdom and your generosity in sharing. Your contributions make this a far better and richer book.

While some people have argued that the term *anti-bias* is "too negative," during our writing in the late 1980s the ABC Task Force and I (Louise) saw it as a proactive, positive term. We saw it as reflecting the reality that racism and other forms of injustice hurt children, and that if we want all children to thrive in a diverse, interconnected world, then all forms of bias and discrimination must end. Those original reasons for using the term still hold.

Original Anti-Bias Curriculum (ABC) Task Force

ReGena Booze
Cory Gann
Cheryl Greer
María Gutiérrez
Francois Polifroni
Lissa Peterson Samuel

Mary (Molly) Scudder
Marjorie Shore
Bill Sparks
Sharon R. Stine
Kay Taus
Mae Varon

Contributing Writers

Bonnie Aldridge
Julie Bisson
Margie Brickley
Carol Brunson Day
Tarah Fleming
Aimee Gelnaw
Janet Gonzalez-Mena
Luis A. Hernandez
Eric Hoffman

Lisa Lee
Diane Levin
Merrie Najimy
Bryan G. Nelson
Bj Richards
Louise Rosenkrantz
Nadiyah F. Taylor
Rita Tenorio

Contributors to:

Anti-Bias Education for Young Children and Ourselves

Interviewees

Chris Amirault
Nancy k Brown
Luz Cardona
Claire Chang
Hedy Chang
Regina Chavez
Jim Clay
Vicki Coffis
Betty Cohns
Carol Cole
Lupe Cortes
Marion Cowee
Ismael Mayo Cruz
Jill Golsh
Arlae Gomez
Catherine Goins
Deborah Hampton
Robin Hasselen
Josephine Hernandez
Linda Irene Jiménez
Eddie Jobe
Suzanne Jones
Chris Lamm
Lee Lesser
Lupe Marks
Mary Pat Martin
Rheta Negrete-Karwin
Jerlean Osbourne
John Nimmo
Norma Alicia Pino
Bryn Potter
Deborah Ravaçon
Kathy Roberts
Brian Silveira
Nancy Spangler
Anne Stewart
Stacy Thompson
Ellen Wolpert

Focus Groups:
Pacific Oaks College
   alumni in Oregon
ECE students of Chris
   Lamm, Fullerton College
Members, National
   Association for Family
   Child Care

Types of Programs

Campus child care
College lab school
Community college
Faith based
Family child care home
Head Start
Private
Professional organization
Public elementary school
Public nonprofit
Research facility
State preschool
University

Types of Work

Adult educator
College faculty
ECE program director
ECE teacher
Executive director
Family child care provider
Infant/toddler teacher
Parent educator
Primary school principal
Primary school teacher
Special education teacher
Staff development specialist

Racial/Ethnic Identities

(as people chose to identify themselves)
African American
Arab American
Asian American
Biracial
Chicano
Chinese American
Filipino
Japanese American
Latina/Latino
Lebanese American
Mexican American
Puerto Rican
   American
White
White Jewish

To Brad Chambers, whose life work inspired and guided.

Three changes to the title clarify the nature of anti-bias work today. Substituting *education* for *curriculum* and dropping "Tools for Empowering" highlight that true anti-bias education is an underlying perspective for *all* aspects of early childhood teaching—not only a tool chest of anti-bias materials and activities. Adding the phrase "and Ourselves" highlights that the adults who work with children also grow and empower *themselves* through their anti-bias teaching. In anti-bias education we can gain the self-awareness, skills, and confidence to join with others to ensure that early childhood education offers children of all backgrounds the best possible start to becoming successful members of our society.

Each chapter in this second edition builds on the work of the original. Several new chapters address additional issues that teachers have asked about over the years. All chapters now include Stop & Think questions for self-reflection. Whenever you encounter one of the Stop & Think prompts, we strongly encourage you to accept its invitation to consider how specific anti-bias issues apply in your own life. Ultimately, the most important curriculum tool you have to give to children is your own self. Deeper understanding of your own experiences strengthens your ability to work effectively with children and families from all backgrounds.

A word on terminology and usage

There are a variety of terms in use today for naming the many aspects of diversity and equity (or inequity) in the world; to complicate matters, the same terms have a variety of definitions. Moreover, people have different preferred terms for themselves, even people within the same social identity group. Consequently, no one can really proclaim that "This is the only right word or definition." Nor can any book's terminology and style satisfy everyone. As have other authors, we had to decide which terms and definitions made the most sense to us. The list of key terms following this prologue will help you understand how we, the authors, define words that are at the heart of this book. We suggest you copy the glossary and keep it in front of you as you read (and that teachers using the book urge their students to do the same).

How to use this book

This second edition is for veterans of anti-bias work *and* for newcomers unfamiliar with its goals and pedagogy. If you were a user of *Anti-Bias Curriculum,* we hope you will find in *Anti-Bias Education* a richness of new ideas to consider, questions to ponder, and strategies to use in your work. If this is your first experience reading about anti-bias education, do not expect to learn everything all at once. Over the years, many people who used *Anti-Bias Curriculum* have spoken about how they repeatedly went back to various sections to refresh and deepen their understanding. So do not be discouraged. And you are not really starting from scratch. As an early childhood professional, you already have many of the tools and skills you need, because anti-bias education uses the same developmentally appropriate basics as other aspects of quality early childhood practice.

The sequence of chapters will enable you to go from a conceptual overview of an anti-bias education approach (chapters 1 and 2), to basic teacher tools (chapters 3 and 4), and then to specific curriculum ideas for the various anti-bias topics (chapters 5 through 11). We urge you to follow this sequence as you read, so that you get a sense of the whole picture of anti-bias work before turning to study its various specific parts.

We invite you to interact with the ideas and exercises in this book. We hope that you will then use the many activity suggestions in ways that fit the specific group of children, families, and staff with whom you work. We also hope that you will add your experience and knowledge to the ongoing work of creating early childhood education programs that make it possible for *all* children to develop to their fullest promise.

A word of thanks from Louise

Writing a book is, at once, a deeply lonely and a social process. It takes a village of colleagues, friends, and family to provide the nurturance and encouragement to keep going—and the feedback to keep the writing grounded. Julie Olsen Edwards, my coauthor in this second edition, played a vital role in the revision process. As a former family child care provider and preschool teacher, the founder and director of Cabrillo College's

Children's Center, and a member of its early childhood faculty since 1971, Julie brought years of anti-bias education experience with children, families, and college students to her work on this book. She always kept me anchored in the realities of what happens in the daily life of early childhood programs and the needs of early childhood teachers and teachers-in-preparation.

Nadiyah and Meg, my two research assistants, both experienced anti-bias educators themselves, contributed their time, energy, and wisdom to the revision. They conducted many of the interviews and reviewed research published since the original publication.

A special shout-out to my two grown children—Douglass and Holly Sparks—who are a big part of my motivation for doing anti-bias education work, and to the friends and colleagues who supported me through this revision—Carol Brunson Day, Catherine Goins, Mary Pat Martin, Deborah Menkart, Patty Ramsey, Bill Sparks, Anne Stewart, Ruth Tavlin, and my "overseas sisters" Babette Brown, Glenda MacNaughton, Colette Murray, and Anke van Keulen. Special thanks also to all the early childhood teachers who, over the years, have told me their stories, given me feedback, asked good questions, and shared their dedication to creating a better world for children.

Finally, appreciation to the Bernard van Leer Foundation (The Netherlands), and in particular Huub Schreurs and Yolanda de Haan, for the grant that supported the interviews and provided honorariums to the invited "Voices" authors.

And a word from Julie

Like many working-class women, I entered the world of early childhood education by running a family child care home as a way of staying home with my babies. I had no idea where the early childhood journey would take me; and now, 45 years later, I am so grateful for the opportunities that brought me here.

I had another part-time job at that time— teaching remedial reading to illiterate adults, mainly women in their 40s and 50s for whom the world had become narrow and limited and who saw themselves as failures in our society. How, I wondered, did this happen? These women had started out life like the toddlers I took care of at home, filled with curiosity, flushed with confidence, convinced the world was theirs for the taking. What forces had limited and shamed them and had shut down their great capacity to learn and explore? And what did we need to do to protect children from those forces? Those questions still haunt me today—and are at the heart of my lifetime work in anti-bias education.

Writing this book with Louise has been a gift, a wonderful way to bring together what thousands of teachers and children have shown me over the years. We have tried to fill it with real stories about the exciting (and confusing and frustrating and satisfying) work that providers and teachers are doing with real children and families every day. It is deeply hopeful work that looks to a future where children are able to claim and use all the promise they are born with. This anti-bias work calls on us to recognize and stand up to the forces in the world that would deny any child the opportunity to flourish.

Thank you, wonderful Louise, for inviting me in. Thank you to all the students, teachers, parents, and children who have taught me so much. Every word I contribute reflects the prodding, questioning, and insights of the amazing women and men I worked with at Cabrillo College. Embraces to Rebekah and Toby, my children, my motivation, and my best teachers—and to Rob, my friend, colleague, and sweetheart since we were teenagers.

My parents, Jack and Tillie Olsen, taught me that there was joy in working to right a wrong. They lived and taught that respect, belief in justice, and especially the power of ordinary people organized to act together, are a force that can change the world. I dedicate this book to their memory. Their work goes on.

Key Terms

As awareness and social conditions change, so do the meanings of terms. The definitions below reflect our (Louise and Julie's) meanings and are the terms we and many other people who advocate for social and economic justice use.

Ableism (or Ableist): An attitude, action, or practice of an individual or institution, backed by societal power, that undermines human and legal rights, accessibility, or economic opportunities of people defined as having a disability.

Ally: A person who stands up against unjust treatment of members of an identity group other than his or her own. An **alliance** is when people from two or more identity groups act together to stop inequitable treatment of either or both groups.

American: Commonly used to refer to residents of the United States. However, because people in Canada, Central America, and South America also live in the Americas, the term "U.S. American" is sometimes used for greater clarity.

Bias: An attitude, belief, or feeling that results in and helps to justify unfair treatment of a person because of his or her identity.

Biracial; Multiracial; Multiethnic; Mixed heritage child: A child whose parents are from two or more different racial/ethnic groups. These terms cover a wide range of racial identity and ethnic combinations. A **biracial or multiracial family** may be a family in which the parents are racially or ethnically different from each other, or a family in which one or more parents identify as mixed heritage. See also *transracial.*

Blended family: Parents and children from two or more previous families that have combined into a new family.

Classism (or Classist): An attitude, action, or practice of an individual or institution, backed by societal power, that gives preferential treatment to or treats as superior those with more economic resources or higher social status and treats as inferior or denies access to those with fewer economic resources or less social status.

Conditionally separated family: A family in which a member is absent through a situation such as distant employment, military service, incarceration, or hospitalization.

Cultural continuity/discontinuity: The degree to which a person does or does not experience a match between his or her own culture's ways of doing things and another culture's ways; a clash between a child's home culture and his early childhood program's culture is an example of cultural discontinuity.

Discrimination: Action by an institution or individual that denies access or opportunity to people based on their social identity (such as gender or racial identity). Outcomes of such actions, rather than their intent, are the basis for use of the term.

Disability: A physical, cognitive, or emotional challenge, such as a vision or hearing impairment, dyslexia, cerebral palsy, or developmental delay. (This book uses the wording "child with a disability" to identify a child's humanity before his or her particular disability, as in "a child with autism spectrum disorder" rather than "an autistic child.")

Dominant group/culture: The *dominant group* within a society has greatest power, privileges, and social status. It may or may not be the majority of the population. In the United States, the dominant group has historically been White, Christian, affluent, and male. A dominant group achieves its position by controlling economic and political institutions, communications/media, education and health institutions, the arts, and business. The *dominant culture* is the way of life defined by the dominant group as "normal" and right.

Economic class: The financial conditions in which a person or family lives, which determine access to social institutions and financial security. Across a person's lifespan, he or she may live in different economic circumstances (e.g., grow up in poverty, become middle class, then return to a very low income level through divorce). This book uses terms such as *lower-income*, *upper-income*, or *working-class* rather than *lower-class* and *upper-class*, which imply value judgments.

Equity (or Equitable): Treatment that is fair and just, taking into account the capacities of individuals, while not discriminating because of racial identity, ethnicity, gender, religion, ability, or any other aspect of their identity. The concept of *equity* goes beyond **equality**, the latter implying identical treatment of individuals or groups despite their differing needs.

Ethnic group: A sizable group of humans whose members identify with one another through a common heritage derived from where their ancestors lived (e.g., Puerto Rico, Ireland, India). **Ethnicity** refers to the identification of group members based on such shared heritage and distinctiveness that make the group into a "people."

Extended family: Family members beyond the immediate family unit of parents and their children (e.g., grandparents, aunts, and uncles), especially when these relatives have major roles in a child's upbringing.

Family partnership: An approach to working with families that presumes that families have as much to teach early childhood professionals about their children as professionals have to teach families. This two-way connection contrasts with **parent education**, which implies a one-way flow of information and expertise from professionals to families.

Foster family: A household in which a child is a temporary member, with formal or informal guardianship passed to the new family. This "temporary" period might be as short as a few days or as long as an entire childhood. A **kinship care family** is a foster family in which there is a legal or informal arrangement for one of the parent's relatives, such as the child's grandparent, to care for the child.

Gender (or Sex): The biological state of being anatomically male or female.

Gender constancy: The understanding that people's gender does not change even if they change their behavior or dress (an understanding usually developed by age 7 or 8).

Gender identity: The awareness and acceptance of one's own gender.

Gender role: The behaviors, attitudes, and appearance that a particular society or culture defines as "masculine" and ascribes to males, or as "feminine" and ascribes to females.

Heterosexism (or Heterosexist): An attitude, action, or practice of an individual or institution, backed by societal power, that assigns legal, social, and cultural advantages to people who are heterosexual, while denying those same advantages to people who are homosexual. In contrast, **homophobia** is about individual feelings and behaviors that reflect the above.

Internalized oppression: Belief in societal negative misinformation about oneself and one's social identity group(s) that leads one to engage in self-restriction, self-limitation, and self-hate.

Internalized privilege: Belief in the entitlement and superiority of oneself and one's social identity group(s), based on societal myths and misinformation. This leads to the justification of mistreatment of groups outside the entitled group.

Intersex; Transgender: *Intersex* refers to people who are born with anatomy that is not unambiguously that of one gender or the other. *Transgender* refers to people whose self-perception of their gender identity does not match their gender anatomy.

"Isms": The many forms of institutionalized prejudice and discrimination based on social identities such as ability/disability, culture/ethnicity, economic class, gender, sexual orientation, racial identity, and others. (The resultant isms are ableism, ethnocentrism, classism, sexism, racism, and the like.)

Nationality; Citizenship: *Nationality* is the status of belonging to a particular nation by origin, birth, or naturalization. *Citizenship* is the legal status of being a citizen of a country. The term **national** includes both citizens and noncitizens.

Nuclear family: A married man and woman and their children.

Overt; Covert: Explicit and direct social messages (*overt*), in contrast to those that are hidden, indirect, and subtle (*covert*). Covert messages have a very strong impact on children, in part because they are not discussed, analyzed, or evaluated.

People of color: A socially created category referring collectively to the groups that have historically been and currently are targets of racism in the United States—for example, African Americans, Asian-Pacific Americans, Latino Americans, Native Americans, and Arab Americans. (Use of the inclusive term *people of color* in this book is not intended to deny the significant differences within this group.)

Prejudice: An attitude, opinion, or feeling formed without adequate prior knowledge, thought, or reason. Prejudice can be prejudgment for or against any person, group, or gender.

Pre-prejudice: Beginning ideas and feelings in very young children that may develop into real prejudice if reinforced by societal biases. It may be based on young children's limited experience and developmental level, or it may consist of imitations of adult behavior.

Race: A social construct that fraudulently categorizes and ranks groups of human beings on an arbitrary basis such as skin color and other physical features. Historically, it has been used as a rationale for colonization of other peoples' lands, enslavement, and war and oppression by one group against another. The scientific consensus is that *race* in this sense has no biological basis in the human species.

Racial identity: How one is classified by other people and by social institutions. In addition, it includes how one comes to understand and feel about one's racial group membership.

Racism (or Racist): An attitude, action, or practice of an individual or institution, backed by societal power, that undermines human and legal rights or economic opportunities of people because of specific physical characteristics, such as skin color. **Cultural racism** is the imposition of one racial group's culture in such a way as to withhold respect for, demean, or destroy the cultures of other groups.

Sexual orientation: The direction of one's sexual interest: **heterosexual** (to the opposite sex), **homo-**

sexual (to the same sex), **bisexual** (to both sexes), **asexual** (not attracted to either sex). A **lesbian** is a woman attracted to women, and a **gay** man is attracted to men.

Sexuality: The state of being sexual and the choices individuals make about how to live their sexual lives. Choices may include: sexual partner only within marriage, one partner for life, one partner at a time, multiple partners (in the same period of time), celibacy, alternating periods of sexual activity and celibacy. People of all sexual orientations make choices about the above.

Shared-custody family: Parents share legal responsibility for their child(ren), who may alternate living with each parent or may live with one parent and regularly see the other. Sometimes called **joint custody**.

Social identities: As compared with individual identities, this denotes memberships in groups that are defined by society, are shared with many other people, and have societal advantages and disadvantages attached to them. These identities include gender, economic class, racial identity, heritage, religion, age group, and so on.

Stereotype: An oversimplified generalization about a particular group, which usually carries derogatory implications.

Transnational family: A family who live part of each year in a different country. Children may be cared for by different people in each country, or the whole family may move together.

Transracial adoptive family: A family in which the racial identity group(s) of the parents differs from that of their adopted child.

Typically developing: Children whose development occurs within the age ranges commonly accepted as usual in human growth and development. ("Children who are typically developing" is preferred to terms such as "normal children" or "regular children," which imply that other children are defective rather than different.)

Whites: A socially created "racial" group who historically and currently receive the benefits of racism in the United States. The category includes all the different ethnic groups of European origin, regardless of differences in their histories, ethnicities, or cultures.

The Four Core Goals of Anti-Bias Education

ABE Goal 1
Each child will demonstrate self-awareness, confidence, family pride, and positive social identities.

ABE Goal 2
Each child will express comfort and joy with human diversity; accurate language for human differences; and deep, caring human connections.

ABE Goal 3
Each child will increasingly recognize unfairness, have language to describe unfairness, and understand that unfairness hurts.

ABE Goal 4
Each child will demonstrate empowerment and the skills to act, with others or alone, against prejudice and/or discriminatory actions.

What Is Anti-Bias Education?

1

We find these joys to be self-evident: That all children are created whole, endowed with innate intelligence, with dignity and wonder, worthy of respect. The embodiment of life, liberty, and happiness, children are original blessings, here to learn their own song. Every girl and boy is entitled to love, to dream, and belong to a loving "village." And to pursue a life of purpose.
— Raffi, "A Covenant for Honouring Children"

Early childhood educators have deep faith in the principle that all people deserve the opportunities and resources to fulfill their complete humanity. Moreover, we have a unique role in making this principle real, in promoting all children's chances to thrive and to succeed in school, in work, and in life. A basic principle in early childhood work is that when educators treat children as if they are strong, intelligent, and kind, children are far more likely to behave in strong, intelligent, kind ways. They are more likely to learn and thrive and succeed.

But what happens when children receive messages about themselves of disapproval, of disdain, of dislike? What happens when children do not see themselves or their families reflected and respected in their early childhood programs? When adults do not actively guide children's thinking about diversity, how do children make sense of information—accurate *or* biased—about people who are different from themselves?

"I don't want to sit next to her. She talks funny," comments a 3-year-old, regarding a new teacher who speaks English with a strong accent.

"I don't want to!" defiantly states a 4-year-old from a single-mom family when the teacher announces they are making cards for Father's Day.

"You can't be the princess! Princesses have blond hair!" announces a White 4-year-old to an African American friend.

"No girls allowed. No girls allowed. We're big. We're superheroes. No girls, no girls," chant three 5-year-old boys from the top of the climbing structure.

"This is supposed to be a happy painting. Why are you using all that black paint?" observes a teacher to a young child at an easel.

"Martin's daddy is going to drive on our field trip. He's going to bring his new car! Isn't that wonderful? It's blue and shiny and brand new!" announces a teacher at circle time.

Each of these statements, whether made by teachers or children, sends a negative message about self-worth—evidence of harmful lessons learned about oneself or about others. In an anti-bias classroom, teachers intervene with immediate and follow-up activities to counter the cumulative, hurtful effects of these messages. In an anti-bias classroom, children learn to be proud of themselves and of their families, to respect human differences, to recognize bias, and to speak up for what is right.

"Don't say 'No way, José; it will hurt José's feelings," explains a 4½-year-old to a 4-year-old in a preschool where teachers carefully teach not to use hurtful language about another's identity.

In a preschool where the teacher engages children to examine stereotyping and omissions in their books, a 5-year-old writes in awkward printing, "This book is irregular. It doesn't have any women in it."

Why teachers do anti-bias education

Anti-bias work is essentially optimistic work about the future for our children. Anti-bias teachers are committed to the principle that every child deserves to develop to his or her fullest potential. Anti-bias work provides teachers a way to examine and transform their understanding of children's lives and also do self-reflective work to more deeply understand their *own* lives.

Teachers' accounts of what drew them to anti-bias education in their practice illustrate their determination to make life better for children and also the deep hopefulness of this work. Perhaps you will hear your own "voice" in theirs:

Lupe Marks, a Head Start teacher:

> I remember that many adults put me down when I was a child, like saying, "Oh, she is just a little Mexican." These comments really affected how I felt about myself, and I vowed I wouldn't do the same to someone else. As a teacher, I wanted to break the cycle.

Lee Lesser, a preschool teacher and community college instructor:

> Hearing children say disturbing things, to which I did not know how to respond, was one big reason anti-bias curriculum attracted me. One European American girl told an Asian American boy, "You're stupid." When I asked her why she said that, she said, "Because he doesn't know how to talk." Another time an African American parent asked me for advice. Her light-skinned daughter didn't want to play with a Black Barbie doll and had told her that a Latino boy whose skin was about the same shade as hers wouldn't want to marry her because she was too dark for him. These events had a big impact on me and made me realize I needed support in my anti-bias journey.

Merrie Najimy, a primary school teacher:

> I think everyone who does anti-bias education has a turning point in their life that makes them pick up the work. As a Lebanese Arab American child, I was invisible in school curriculum and materials. Now I see my responsibility as a teacher to make sure that students of color in my classroom do not have that same experience. At the same time, I have to figure out how to get White kids to expand their thinking to understand that they are not the only people in the classroom, the school, the town, the country, the world.

Mary Pat Martin, a community college instructor:

> The anti-bias education approach put into words everything in my life that I always thought was right about equality and justice. It gave me the tools to put into practice what I always knew was the right way for me to do early childhood education.

Brian Silveira, a preschool teacher:

> Anti-bias curriculum changed the way I looked at child development and the world. I probably wouldn't be such an activist today without it. We *are* creating a better world.

The vision of anti-bias education

The heart of anti-bias work is a vision of a world in which *all* children are able to blossom, and each child's particular abilities and gifts are able to flourish. In this world:

● All children and families have a sense of belonging and experience affirmation of their identities and cultural ways of being.

● All children have access to and participate in the education they need to become successful, contributing members of society.

● The educational process engages all members of the program or school in joyful learning.

● Children and adults know how to respectfully and easily live, learn, and work together in diverse and inclusive environments.

● All families have the resources they need to fully nurture their children.

● All children and families live in safe, peaceful, healthy, comfortable housing and neighborhoods.

This vision of anti-bias education also reflects the basic human rights described in the United Nations (1989) Declaration of the Rights of the Child:

● The right to *survival*.

● The right to *develop to the fullest*.

● The right to *protection* from harmful influences, abuse, and/or exploitation.

● The right to *participate fully* in family, cultural, and social life.

In order for children to receive all these rights, their society, their families, and those responsible for their care and education must work to provide everything that each child needs to flourish. A worldwide community of educators shares the vision toward which anti-bias education strives. They adapt its goals and principles to the needs of children and families in their specific contexts.

Because of societal inequities, too many children still do not have access to the "basic human rights" due them. Imagine a world of justice and equal opportunity for *all*.

■ What would that world look like for each of the children you work with?

■ What would that world look like for the program you work in?

■ What would *you* add to the "vision of anti-bias education" list?

Bias is built into the system

Early childhood teachers want children to feel powerful and competent. They strive to welcome children and to show respect to their families as best they know how. However, beyond individual teachers' hopes, beliefs, and actions is a society that has built advantage and disadvantage into its institutions and systems. These dynamics of advantage and disadvantage are deeply rooted in history. They continue to shape the degree of access children have to education, health care, security—in a word, access to the services necessary for children's healthy development. These dynamics also greatly affect the early childhood education system, despite whatever values individual teachers may have.

Inequity of resources, and the biases that justify that inequity, have an enormous impact on children's lives. *It is important to remember that it is not human differences that undermine children's development but rather unfair, hurtful treatment based upon those differences.*

One major dynamic of advantage and disadvantage that especially affects early childhood practice is that of the "visibility" or "invisibility" of certain kinds of people and cultures in a program. Too many early childhood materials focus on children and families who resemble the stereotypes of American culture as it is most commonly depicted—middle-class, White, suburban, able-bodied, English-speaking, mother-and-father (nuclear) family—as if these were the only types of children and families we work with. Books that accurately and positively depict children from low-income or rural families are few in number. While there are increasing numbers of authentic and respectful books about children of color, they do not yet cover all of America's many ethnic groups and cultures. Only a handful of toys, pictures, songs, posters, and the like, depict the full range of family structures, such as shared-custody families; single-parent

families; foster families; gay/lesbian-headed families; families with a parent or other family member with a disability or who is homeless, unemployed, or incarcerated; newly arrived immigrant families; families separated by military duty; and on and on. This invisibility or visibility in the classroom's physical environment undermines some young children's positive sense of self, while teaching other children that they are specially deserving.

Given the continuing societal inequities into which children are born, anti-bias education raises these questions for early childhood educators:

● How does living in a highly diverse and inequitable (unjust) society affect children's development?

● What do children need in a diverse but inequitable society to grow up healthy and strong?

● What do early childhood educators (and families) need in order to respond to this challenge?

This book looks at these three questions and provides a set of strategies for teachers who want to see themselves as champions for *all* children and their families. Anti-bias education is needed because children live in a world that is not yet a place where all of them have equal opportunity to become all they could be. We know children need to feel safe and secure in all their many identities, feel pride in their families, and feel at home in their early childhood programs. We also know that children need tools to navigate the complex issues of identity, diversity, prejudice, and power in their daily lives so that they may learn, thrive, and succeed.

Rita Tenorio, an experienced early childhood educator, puts it this way:

> Racism and other biases are part of our society and part of what children have to learn to deal with, to become savvy about. They have to be ready to take what is their right to have: respect, decent jobs, a decent education. What we are about in education is preparing children for the future—giving them what they need to be successful. We need to give children a critical perspective and appropriate tools. Those they will need no matter what they become in life.

The four goals of anti-bias education

Anti-bias education has four core goals, each of which applies to children of all backgrounds and influences every arena of our programs. As illustrated in the box "Gears," each goal interacts and builds on the other three. Together, they provide a safe, supportive learning community for all children. Effective anti-bias education happens when all four goals are part of your program.

Goal 1

Each child will demonstrate self-awareness, confidence, family pride, and positive social identities.

This is the starting place for all children, in all settings. A basic goal of quality early childhood education work is to nurture each child's individual, personal identity. Anti-bias education adds to that goal the important idea of nurturing social (or group) identities. Goal 1 strengthens social, emotional, and cognitive development. As children develop a strong sense of both individual and group identity, they also develop more tools for success in school and in life.

Guidelines for teaching Goal 1

● Build on self-concept activities you already do by also exploring the children's various social identities (e.g., racial, cultural, gender, economic class). Each of chapters 5 through 11 offers many ideas for how to do this in each arena. You may also want to read *What If All the Kids Are White?* (Derman-Sparks & Ramsey 2006) for further ideas about social identity issues and activities.

● Remember that respectfully making visible and supporting *all* of the children's families is an essential element in nurturing a positive sense of self for each child. (See chapter 9 for more information on families.)

● Support children fully in the social identity aspects of Goal 1 before you move on to any of the other goals. This is essential. As Bill Martin (1970) says in his poem "I Am Freedom's Child": "As I learn to like the differences in me, I learn to like the differences in you."

Goal 2

Each child will express comfort and joy with human diversity; accurate language for human differences; and deep, caring human connections.

In an anti-bias approach, encouraging children to learn about how they are different from other children and learn about how they are similar go hand in hand. These are never either/or realities because people are simultaneously the same and different from one another. This is at the heart of learning how to treat all people caringly and fairly.

From infancy on, children notice and are curious about all kinds of differences among people. They also develop their own (often surprising) explanations for the differences that they observe and experience. By preschool, children have already developed ideas about many aspects of human diversity—including ideas that may seem quite strange to adults. Moreover, many children already have begun to develop discomfort about or even fear of specific kinds of differences.

Some teachers and parents are not sure they should encourage children to "notice" and learn about differences among people. They think it is best to teach only about how people are the same, worrying that learning about differences causes prejudice. While well intentioned, this concern arises from a mistaken notion about the sources of bias. Differences, in and of themselves, do not create the problem. *Children learn prejudice from prejudice*—not from learning about human diversity. It is how people respond to differences that teaches bias and fear.

Gears

At a conference in Berlin, Germany, on early childhood anti-bias education, teachers from 31 child care centers, participants in a national initiative organized by Projekt Kinderwelten (a nonprofit, nongovernment organization), displayed storyboards documenting their work. One center had a wonderful way to show the relationship among the four anti-bias education goals. They made four wooden, interlocking gears—each representing one goal. When you moved any one of the gears, the rest also moved.

Goal 1 . . . moves Goal 2 . . . moves Goal 3 . . . moves Goal 4

Moreover, a difference-denial approach, which ignores children's identities and family cultures, runs the risk of making invisible the many children who do not have the social identity of the dominant group.

Guidelines for teaching Goal 2

● Strike a balance between exploring people's similarities and differences. We share similar biological attributes and needs (e.g., the need for food, shelter, and love; the commonalities of language, families, and feelings) *and* we live these in many different ways.

● Developmentally, it is best to teach children by beginning with what they already know and have experienced. Therefore, it is important to explore the many kinds of diversity present among the children in the group, even when they come from similar racial, cultural, economic class, and family backgrounds. This will set the stage for learning about diversity in their larger communities beyond the classroom.

● Further broaden children's knowledge of diversity by acquainting children with groups of people who live and work in their larger neighborhood and city. Preschoolers learn best about people as individuals, not as representatives of groups or countries.

● Avoid a "tourist curriculum" approach to diversity, as described later in this chapter.

Goal 3

Each child will increasingly recognize unfairness, have language to describe unfairness, and understand that unfairness hurts.

Children cannot construct a strong self-concept or develop respect for others if they do not know how to identify and resist hurtful, stereotypical, and inaccurate messages or actions directed toward them or others. Developing the ability to think critically strengthens children's sense of self, as well as their capacity to form caring relationships with others. Furthermore, being able to think critically about the world is a skill important for later school success.

Guidelines for teaching Goal 3

● Assess children's misconceptions and stereotypes. First, find out their thinking and feelings about a particular kind of diversity (e.g., a person who is deaf, a person who is White or American Indian, a person who is homeless). Note comments children make in informal conversations or play (see the box "Dealing with Misinformation"). Hold planned conversations to draw out their ideas; use a picture, a question, or a book to spark their insights.

● Plan activities that help children learn how to contrast inaccurate, untrue images or ideas with accurate ones.

● In the same activities, build children's budding capacities for empathy and fairness.

● Support critical-thinking activities, which pave the way for their learning to take action to make unfair things fair.

Taking into account the social background of children as we make plans for teaching them helps to make education equitable and fair. For example:

> In an inclusive kindergarten classroom in a public school, the teacher does a unit with the children about "handicapped" parking spaces. They look at photos of these spaces and at the signs that people put in their cars so they can park there. When they find out that some teachers are inappropriately parking in their school's handicapped parking spaces, the children make "tickets" to put on those cars, and the inappropriate parking soon stops—thus moving naturally into Goal 4.

Goal 4

Each child will demonstrate empowerment and the skills to act, with others or alone, against prejudice and/or discriminatory actions.

This fourth building block of anti-bias education is about helping every child learn and practice a variety of ways to act when:

● another child behaves in a biased manner toward her or him

● a child behaves in a biased manner toward another child

● unfair situations occur in the center/classroom

● unfair situations occur in the children's immediate community

Children's growth on Goal 4 strengthens their growth on the other three goals. If a child is the target of prejudice or discrimination, she needs tools to resist and to know that she has worth (Goal 1). When a child speaks up for another child, it reinforces his understanding of other people's unique feelings (Goal 2). When children are helped to take action, it broadens their understanding of "unfairness" and "fairness" (Goal 3).

Biased behaviors among children such as teasing, rejection, and exclusion based on some aspect of a child's identity are a form of aggressive behavior and are just as serious as physical aggression. The old saying "Sticks and stones may break my bones, but

Dealing with Misinformation

Overhearing a child telling classmates that adopted children were "thrown away" by their "real parents," I knew I needed to deal with this misinformation immediately. I told the children that two doll "classmates" had told Rachel (one of our persona dolls) that "she had been thrown away by her real parents because she was a bad baby." I invited the children to explore Rachel's feelings of hurt, sorrow, and anger. One of the kids said Rachel might feel afraid that she would be "thrown away" again if she did something bad.

I then asked the children what they knew about adoption. "What do you think? Were those [doll] kids right about adopted kids being thrown away?" Only one child, herself adopted, knew something true about adoption. I acknowledged her information and reassured her: "Barbara knows some real information about adoption. That's right, Barbara."

The next step was asking about where to get correct information: "Rachel needs to find out the truth about adoption right away. How do you think she can get real information? Whom could she ask?" The children had several ideas: "Her mom." . . . "Her Bubbe [grandmother]." . . . "Maybe her teacher knows." . . . "A book about being adopted." I supported their ideas.

Then I added to the story, telling how the doll got reliable information, and I related an accurate explanation about adoption. (Remember that if you need to do some research to be sure you have the correct information in a similar situation, tell the children you need to collect the true information and will talk with them about it the next day.) We ended by my asking, "Are there other things you would like to know about adoption? Who has a question?" I answered a few more questions and ended the discussion.

Source: Adapted from T. Whitney, *Kids Like Us: Using Persona Dolls in the Classroom* (St. Paul, MN: Redleaf, 1999), pp. 107–10. Used with permission.

---

names will never hurt me" does not apply. Children's developing sense of self *is* hurt by name-calling, teasing, and exclusion based on identity. And children who engage in such hurtful behaviors are learning to be bullies. An anti-bias approach calls on teachers to gently but firmly intervene, support the child who has been hurt by the biased behavior, and help children learn other ways of interacting. Anti-bias education is a necessary partner of conflict-resolution education.

Guidelines for teaching Goal 4

● Be alert for unfair practices that directly affect children's lives. You may be the first to identify the problem, or the children may bring a problem to your attention.

● Engage the children in dialogue about their feelings and ideas regarding the specific situation. Provide information about the situation, as appropriate.

● Consider the interests and dynamics of your group of children. Do they care about the problem? What kind of actions would help them appropriately address the issue?

● Consider the children's families. Learn how each family teaches their child to handle being the target of discriminatory behaviors. Explain why you believe it is important for children to learn several ways to respond. Incorporate diverse strategies based on what families do.

● Plan and carry out an action to address the problem (see the example below and the box "Children Figure Out What Actions to Take"). If one action works, great! If it does not, try again with a different activity.

A teacher in a Midwest college child development center helps children address the problem of racial bias in a calendar sent to them in which all the children in the pictures are White. After carefully looking at the pictures and discussing their observations, the children decide the calendar is not fair because it does not show many kinds of children. They dictate a letter to the company, but do not receive a response. Their teacher then helps them create a petition using the words from their dictated letter. The children collect a hundred signatures from the college students on their campus. The company replies to the petition, promising the next calendar will show many kinds of children.

Chapters 3 and 4 will help you to understand how to go about putting these four goals into practice. Chapters 5 through 11 will help you focus on the various specific aspects of identity for which children need support.

Educational principles for putting anti-bias goals into action

Now that you have a grasp on what anti-bias education hopes to accomplish, here are some principles for using the four anti-bias education goals.

● **The four anti-bias education goals are for everyone, and everyone benefits.**

Social inequities and biases undermine healthy development in *all* children, in one way or another; and *all* children benefit from being made visible and equitably included in daily classroom activities. Some people wonder how White children fit into an anti-bias approach, thinking that diversity issues only really affect children of color. However, the continued realities and messages of inequity in our society and world also negatively affect White children's sense of self and attitudes toward others. Nurturing White children's healthy identity and their positive attitudes toward others is an essential part of anti-bias education.

Conversely, some people wonder whether anti-bias education is primarily for White children. Carol Brunson Day offers her insights about this question:

> People of color often have the feeling that anti-bias education is work that Whites need to do, because the sources of racism come from White history and culture. They question its relevancy for children of color, for whom they believe empowerment is the key issue.
>
> White children definitely need anti-bias education. So, too, do children of color, although the specific work differs from that with White children. Education to prevent internalized oppression by fostering strong personal and social identities and to counter prejudices about *other* groups of color are two essential tasks that are part of the larger anti-bias work. We also need to create alliances to achieve our shared ultimate goal of a more equitable society.

● **Anti-bias education activities pay attention to the realities of children's lives.**

The four anti-bias education goals create a framework for teaching all children, but a one-size-fits-all curriculum is not effective in anti-bias work any more than it is effective for any other aspect of early childhood education that is developmentally (culturally) appropriate. There are different kinds of inequity and power issues connected to each area of diversity, and each one affects children's development in a somewhat different way.

Some children need support to resist social messages of racial or cultural inferiority, which undercut their positive identity; others need guidance to develop a positive self-concept without absorbing social messages of superiority. Children of wealthy families need help resisting the message that material accumulation defines their worth; children of poor families need teachers who make them visible and respect their lives. Some girls will need extra support to develop their math and science abilities; some boys will require help to develop skills for having nurturing, cooperative interactions with their peers.

Anti-bias educators also design their work based on the specific cultural backgrounds of the individual children and families they serve. Here is some useful advice from African American anti-bias educator Anne Stewart:

> As teachers, we know that developing strong self- and group identity, being rooted in home culture, and having skills to resist messages that undermine confidence enable children to succeed in school and afterward. Ask yourself, "What is already in the culture to which we can tie ABE goals?" For example, African American families understand that kids must have pride in themselves to do well in school and in the world. Families, however,

Children Figure Out What Actions to Take

At circle time, the teacher explains that a group of the doll boys were playing Fort with the outdoor climbing equipment. Jamie, a girl persona doll, wanted to join in, but the boys declared, "Only boys can play in this fort. You do not know how to play."

Teacher: How do you think Jamie felt? Has this ever happened to you? Can girls play that game too? What could Jamie do?

Children: She could tell him he hurt her feelings. . . . I would climb into that fort anyway. . . . I'd go find someone else.

Teacher: You have many good ideas. Jamie has many choices of what she can do. It depends on how she feels. She could try to work it out, or tell the boys to let her in, or she could go find someone else to play with. What could she say if she wanted to try to work it out with them?

Children: "Girls can too!" . . . "How would he like it?"

Teacher: Those are all great ideas. What if she wanted some help? Where could she find help?

Children: Her friends; she could go get 'em. . . . Maybe the teacher? . . . Make her own fort.

Teacher: What if she's feeling bad? What could you do or say to help her feel better?

Children: I'd give her a hug. . . . "Don't listen to him. He's wrong!" . . . "I'll play with you. I like you."

Teacher: We could also make a sign that reminds everyone that everyone can play where she or he wants. What should we write?

Children: "Girls can play where they want to. So can boys." . . . "Don't hurt kids' feelings." . . . "Friends can help you."

The teacher makes up the sign and posts it where the children can read it. Later, when incidents occur among them to which their "rules" apply, she reminds the children of what the sign says.

***

Source: Adapted from T. Whitney, *Kids Like Us: Using Persona Dolls in the Classroom* (St. Paul, MN: Redleaf, 1999), pp. 142–44. Used with permission.

may not make the connection between school success and children learning to change the world in which they live—even though the connection is real and there is a long history of African Americans acting on it.

● **Anti-bias education is developmentally appropriate.**

As in all other areas of early childhood curriculum, teachers tailor and scaffold anti-bias education materials and activities to each child's cognitive, social, and emotional developmental capacities. They plan and choose learning experiences that stimulate children to explore the next step of new ideas and skills and allow each child to apply new understandings and behaviors in his or her daily life.

Principle 8 of NAEYC's position statement on developmentally appropriate practice—"Development and learning occur in and are influenced by multiple social and cultural contexts"—makes explicit that anti-bias education is developmentally appropriate. So, too, does the principle of "Creating a caring community of learners." As the position statement explains,

> Because early childhood settings tend to be children's first communities outside the home, the character of these communities is very influential in development. How children expect to be treated and how they treat others is significantly shaped in the early childhood setting. In developmentally appropriate practice, practitioners create and foster a "community of learners" that supports all children to develop and learn. (NAEYC 2009, 16)

● **Anti-bias planning uses both child- and teacher-initiated activities.**

Children's questions, comments, and behaviors are a vital source of anti-bias curriculum. They spark teachable moments as well as longer-term projects. However, it is not sufficient to do anti-bias activities only when a child brings up a relevant issue.

Teacher-initiated activities are also necessary— be they intentionally putting materials in the environment to broaden children's awareness or planning specific learning experiences around issues or areas that matter to families and the community. Teacher-initiated activities open up opportunities to uncover and help children explore ideas. We do not wait for children to open up the topic of reading or numbers before making literacy and numeracy part of our daily early childhood curriculum. Because we have decided that these understandings and skills are essential for children, we provide literacy and numeracy discussions and activities in our classrooms. The same is true for anti-bias.

A balance between child-initiated and teacher-initiated activities is as vital in anti-bias education as in any other part of the early childhood curriculum.

● **Anti-bias learning does not happen in one lesson or one day.**

Anti-bias education is not just a set of activities for occasional use (although that is often how new anti-bias educators begin). It is a focus that permeates everything that happens in our program. All learning proceeds unevenly and requires many lessons on the same topic. Children need multiple ways to think about and experience the ideas and skills of anti-bias work, too.

As children first begin to talk about identity and fairness issues, they may make more, rather than fewer, biased comments than before. But such comments are a natural part of the anti-bias process—it takes many attempts before they learn a new way of thinking about difference, so children need to be free to ask questions and share their ideas.

● **Anti-bias education calls on teachers to know themselves.**

As you saw in the quotes from teachers early in this chapter, teachers themselves are on a journey as they work with children, families, and colleagues on the four anti-bias education goals. Broadening our understanding of ourselves is both a challenge and a reward of being anti-bias educators. (See chapter 3 for further discussion of this topic and suggestions for getting-to-know-yourself activities.)

Anti-bias education work is a journey with many paths and rhythms; each person chooses her or his own (see the box "What Do the ABE Goals Mean to Me?"). Some teachers focus on their own growth and the changes they make in their own work. Others move on to conversations with other adults— colleagues, families, friends. Many anti-bias educators also decide to engage in change work beyond their classroom.

● **Anti-bias education avoids the pitfall of tourist curriculum.**

One of the most common mistakes teachers new to anti-bias work make when incorporating diversity activities into their program is to do "tourist curriculum." Tourist curriculum, a superficial educational approach, does not make diversity a routine part of the ongoing, daily learning environment and experiences. Instead it is curriculum that "drops in" on strange, exotic people to see their holidays and taste their foods, and then returns to the "real" world of "regular" life. That "regular" daily learning environment is shaped by the cultural norms, rules of behavior, images, and teaching and learning styles of the dominant U.S. groups (middle-class, White, suburban, able-bodied).

Several teaching behaviors signal a tourist curriculum, including *tokenism, trivializing, misrepresenting,* and *stereotyping.* (See the section "Tourist Curriculum Is Hazardous to Growing Children" in chapter 4 for an explanation of these practices.) The most frequently seen example is when a teacher does activities about "other" cultural groups as part of a holiday/special unit, and then the group disappears from the curriculum until the same time the following year.

This kind of teaching about diversity communicates messages (even if unintentionally) that undermine respect for different ways of living. One message is that the dominant way of life must be the "normal" or "right" way, as it is the daily experience of school. Another message is that because "other" cultural groups are only occasionally part of the curriculum, they must be less important than the dominant groups. Through these messages, tourist curriculum in essence undermines the core goals and values of anti-bias education.

● **Anti-bias education rests on strong relationships among staff and between staff and families.**

Many teachers find that raising issues of diversity and inequity with other adults is more challenging for them than working with children is. This is not surprising. A kind of "emperor's new clothes" syndrome in our society (i.e., thinking it's better to pretend not to see what is in front of our eyes) keeps many of us silent about anti-bias issues. However, collaboration has the benefit of providing more effective anti-bias education for the children and a richer, more complex, and more effective experience for the adults.

What we do matters

Anti-bias education work in early childhood is shaped by a deep-seated belief in the importance of justice, the dream of each child being able to achieve all he or she is capable of, the knowledge that together human beings can make a difference. Listen to the voices of children who have experienced anti-bias education at school or at home. They give us hope and direction.

> Several 3-year-olds (Asian, White, and Latino) are at the art table playing with small mirrors while they paint on paper ovals. As they look at their eyes, Jesse starts crooning to himself: "Oh, pretty eyes, pretty eyes. Lots of different eyes, pretty eyes, pretty eyes. Brown and blue, pointy, round. Pretty eyes, pretty eyes."

> Two preschool girls are playing Indians by whooping and pretending to have tomahawks. Miriam (age 4) stops them by saying, "Stop! That isn't like real Indians. Mrs. Cowell is Cherokee, and you will hurt her feelings!"

A kindergarten teacher shows the children a magazine picture titled "Brides of America." All of the women pictured are White. She asks, "What do you think of this picture?" Sophia, whose family is Nicaraguan, responds, "That's a silly picture. My mom was a bride, and she doesn't look like that."

A mother relates the following anecdote: "When I picked Jonah up from kindergarten the other day, he said, 'Mom, Kevin had tears in his eyes and his face looked sad and he told me that a bigger kid pushed him off the bars at recess. So Zena and I went to go find the boy and ask him why he did it. We couldn't find him, but then we found him on the field. We're not allowed to go on the field, but we *had to* because we had to save Kevin.' After he told his story, I reflected, 'Wow. You are a really good friend, Jonah.' He said, 'Yeah, when I see something unfair, Mom, I change it.'"

Why do we do anti-bias education work? We do it because we live in a world that is not yet a place where all children have equal opportunity to become all they are. A worldwide community of educators shares the vision toward which anti-bias education strives, adapting its goals and principles to the specific needs of the children and families they work with.

We invite you to be a part of this community, and we hope this book will provide some beginning maps for your journey.

"What Do the ABE Goals Mean to Me?"

Consider the four core anti-bias education goals as they apply to your own daily life and work. How do you assess yourself on each? (You can do this exercise by yourself or with your learning partners.)

1. (ABE Goal 1) To what degree, or in what ways, do I nurture construction of a knowledgeable, confident self-identity and group identity in myself?

2. (ABE Goal 2) How do I promote my own comfortable, empathetic interactions with people from diverse backgrounds?

3. (ABE Goal 3) In what ways do I foster my critical thinking about bias?

4. (ABE Goal 4) Under what circumstances do I cultivate my ability to stand up for myself and for others in the face of bias?

5. What are the challenges to achieving these goals in my life?

6. What might be ways for me to develop each of these goals in my work? in my personal life?

Source: Adapted from C. Lamm, "Anti-Bias Perspective Seminar," unpublished manuscript (ECE Department, Fullerton College, CA, Spring 2007). Used with permission.

The Vital Connection between Anti-Bias Education and Peace Education

by Diane Levin

For children to become truly responsible and caring members of a global community in which diverse people cooperate and resolve conflicts without violence and war, the foundation needs to be laid early. Doing this well requires taking into account how understanding similarities and differences affects children's development and learning. From birth onward, children's attention is often drawn to what they don't know—to the novel and different rather than to the familiar. Children naturally use similarities and differences among people, objects, and events to help them define and understand their world—a parent or familiar caretaker from a stranger, a bottle from a breast, or a rattle from a pacifier.

As children try to relate what is different to what they already know, they learn new lessons about the world. These lessons can contribute to their reacting to differences with trust and tolerance or with fear and violence. The lessons set the tone for how children will deal with differences among people throughout life—differences in how they look, act, and think. The lessons also influence how children deal with differing points of view during conflicts. For instance, if two children want to play with the same ball, a conflict can result from their differing ideas about who should have the ball. Children who have learned to deal with conflicting ideas by working differences out justly and peacefully are more likely to find a way to share the ball than are children who view differences with suspicion and threat.

We play a vital role in how children learn to think about and deal with similarities and differences. It is by helping children begin to develop positive attitudes, values, and skills about diversity when they are young that they will learn what it means to respect and stand up for themselves and others in the face of injustice, and come to a just and comfortable relationship with diversity among people as they grow up. Our efforts will help children develop the strategies they need to break the cycle of violence in their own lives and in the wider society.

Source: Adapted from D. Levin, *Teaching Young Children in Violent Times: Building a Peaceable Classroom,* 2d ed. (Cambridge, MA: Educators for Social Responsibility; Washington, DC: NAEYC, 2003), Chapter 6: Anti-Bias Education.

Children's Identity Development

2

I like me, no doubt about it. I like me, can't live without it,
I like me, let's shout about it, I am Freedom's child.

You like you, no doubt about it. You like you, can't live without it,
You like you, let's shout about it. You are Freedom's child.

We need all the different kinds of people we can find to make Freedom's dream come true,
So as I learn to like the differences in me, I learn to like the differences in you.

I like you, no doubt about it. You like me, can't live without it,
We are free, let's shout about it. Hooray for Freedom's child!

—Bill Martin, Jr., "I Am Freedom's Child"

Throughout our lives, we all actively construct our identities in a continually evolving understanding of ourselves and others. From birth on, "development and learning occur in and are influenced by multiple social and cultural contexts" (NAEYC 2009, 13). As with all other aspects of human growth, this process of identity and attitude development

> requires viewing each child within the sociocultural context of that child's family, educational setting, and community, as well as within the broader society. These various contexts are interrelated, and all powerfully influence the developing child. For example, even a child in a loving, supportive family within a strong, healthy community is affected by the biases of the larger society, such as racism or sexism, and may show some effects of its negative stereotyping and discrimination. (13)

Understanding how young children construct their personal and social identities, how they think about differences and absorb messages about prejudice and social advantage or disadvantage, is the foundation of effective anti-bias education.

Adults sometimes ask: Aren't prejudice, discrimination, and anti-bias adult issues? Why bring children into it? In one sense, these *are* adult issues. Adults have the power to create, to teach, to maintain bias—and to eliminate it. In another sense, because the realities of prejudice and discrimination begin to affect children's development early, it *is* developmentally appropriate to address them in our work with young children.

Young children need caring adults to help them construct a positive sense of self and a respectful understanding of others. They need adults to help them begin to navigate and resist the harmful impact of prejudice and discrimination. A person's early childhood years lay the foundation for a developmental and experiential journey that continues into adulthood. With appropriate adult guidance, this foundation will be a strong one, providing the base for the next stages of healthy development and the skills a person needs to thrive and succeed in a complex, diverse world.

What children are like

Here are some characteristics of children's development that are important to consider when planning anti-bias activities and fostering children's understanding.

● **Young child curious about their own and others' physical and cultural characteristics.**

From their first year of life, children begin to notice differences and similarities among the people who surround them. They use these observations to construct their self-identity and their concepts about others. As young as 6 months, infants demonstrate that they notice differences in skin color (Katz & Kofkin 1997). Toddlers begin to notice and comment on gender and racial differences. By age 2, children are using appropriate gender labels (*girl, boy*) and learning color names, which they begin to apply to skin color (Ramsey 2004).

By age 3, children begin asking questions about their own and others' attributes, including racial identity, language, gender, and physical disabilities. For example:

Why is that man's skin dark?

Why is that lady getting pushed in a chair?

Why does she talk funny?

My skin looks like yours, Mommy.

Why do I have freckles?

I have the same thing as Daddy.

By age 4, they begin to show awareness of family structure and economic class differences (Tatum 2003). For example:

Why does Susie have two mommies? Does she have a daddy?

I want to have Nike shoes like Matthew has.

Between ages 3 and 5, children become very curious about what parts of themselves are permanent and will stay the same and what parts will change (Ramsey 2004). For example:

If I like to climb trees, do I become a boy?

If I like to play with dolls, do I become a girl?

Why is my skin this color? Can I change it? ... Can I make my skin [pink, brown, like Eric's]?

Will I always need a prosthesis in place of my arm?

● **Children begin to construct a personal sense of self and multiple social identities.**

All people have a personal identity and multiple social identities—all of which contribute to our sense of self (Cross 1991). Our *personal identity* includes factors such as our name, our specific family, age, place in the family, personality, and talents and interests. These attributes are what give us our sense of individuality. Our *social identities*, by contrast, refer to the significant group categorizations assigned to us by the society in which we grow up and live and which we share with many others. These include our racial, ethnic/cultural, gender, and religious identities, as well as economic class, geographic identities, and so on.

For example, one child's personal identity might include being a twin, being shy and artistic, and preferring to play alone or with his twin. His social identities might include being male, East Coast urban, African American, Christian, and from a two-parent, middle-class family. Another child's personal identity might include being the oldest child in her family, being outgoing and playful, loving music, and being very athletic. Her social identity might include being female, European American, rural, Buddhist, and from a working-class, grandparent-led family.

Personal identity is what most early childhood teachers think about when they are planning ways to nurture children's positive self-concepts—and the early childhood field knows a great deal about how to do this essential part of our work. Much of the research about children's formation of identity and attitudes also traditionally focuses only on the personal aspect of identity.

However, the pioneering research of people such as William Cross contributes important new insights about both personal *and* social identities. (Cross [1991] uses the term "group reference identity" for what we call social identity.) Such research is especially useful to anti-bias education work and is why we are elaborating on the concept of social identity here. Chapters 5 through 11 of this book describe dynamics in children's development of several specific social identities (e.g., racial, gender, economic class) and address ways we in the early childhood community can respond.

All people are born into specific social identities and may acquire others as adults (e.g., work, marriage status, parenthood), or may even change some (e.g., economic class, gender). Learning what our various social identities mean is a lifetime journey that begins in toddlerhood. Among the earliest ones that children pay attention to are gender ("Am I a girl or a boy?") and racial identity (comparing skin color). From childhood on, we may also feel differently about our various social identities—proud of some identities and downplaying or denying others—depending on the circumstances and contexts in which we find ourselves.

Social identity categories generally carry legally specified definitions, rights, and limitations—which may change over time—along with stereotypes, biases, prejudices, and discrimination. It was not so long ago, for example, that women and people of color did not have the right to vote. It has been even more recently that children with disabilities got the legal right to attend public schools with their typically developing peers. Even today, people who are homosexual do not have many of the legal and civil rights afforded to people who are heterosexual. Advantages and disadvantages connected to various social identities do change over historical time—usually because of the persistent actions of many people who work to eliminate the disadvantages.

These social realities either support or harm children's beliefs about their families, about others, and about themselves. While our social identities do not singly determine our happiness or success in life, they significantly open up or undermine our access to opportunities and resources. Our social identities also influence our beliefs about our own capacities and limitations, and they make successful life outcomes easier or harder to attain. Families and educators who understand the role of both personal and social identities in children's development (as well as in their own lives) are better prepared to support children's healthy development and to teach children how to resist bias that may undermine any aspect of their ability to thrive.

● **Children learn about their own and others' social identities through both overt and covert messages.**

Learning about our social (and personal) identities begins in our family. However, messages from the larger society soon filter in and become another critical influence. These messages are both overt and covert and come from many places: from children's family members, friends, movies and television, books and advertising, and of course, from early childhood programs.

Some of what children learn about their own and others' social identities comes from *overt* lessons. For example, people explicitly declare their ideas about boys and girls: "Boys don't cry." . . . "Be careful. She's a girl. She can get hurt." . . . "You're a little flirt!" . . . "What a strong boy you are!" Some people explicitly declare their attitudes about children with disabilities: "I do not want my son in the classroom with *that* child in the wheelchair. She will take up all of the teacher's time." Or about same-sex parents: "Children can't have two daddies."

However, much of what children learn about their social identities comes from *covert* messages.

These are indirect messages that are like "social trace contaminants"—tiny or unseen messages that accumulate over time to create harm (Pierce 1980). One type of covert lesson comes from a lack of diversity in the lives of families and communities. For example, children may hear overt messages that "People are all alike" and that we should "Treat all people with respect," yet they may never see their family develop friendships with people different from themselves or even interact with other social groups in their day-to-day life. Another message like a "social trace contaminant" comes anytime the children's family is treated poorly, receiving slow service in stores or restaurants, for example, or encountering rudeness from social agency personnel.

A third type of covert message is the "double message"—when the behavior of family, teachers, religious leaders, or the media conflicts with overt messages from these same sources. For example, a teacher may do a "Who We Are" unit each year to support children's self-concept, yet call a child a name other than her given one, because the teacher finds the child's real name too hard to pronounce. Or children may hear adults say, "Looks aren't important," yet they are regularly praised for their looks and clothing. Another quite common example is hearing that "Skin color doesn't matter," while television and movie bad guys are all dark-skinned.

● **Young children are learning about who is and isn't important.**

Invisibility erases identity and experience; visibility affirms reality. When children see themselves and their families reflected in their early childhood setting, they feel affirmed and that they belong. When children's identities and families are invisible, the opposite happens. Children feel that they are unimportant and do not belong. *These lessons from societal visibility or invisibility are among the most powerful messages children receive.*

Messages of invisibility and visibility also communicate who matters and who does not. When young children look at the books or posters in a classroom and find only two-parent families, they may learn that this is the "right" kind of family and that all other kinds of families are wrong. When the dolls in the classroom are all White, or the pictures on the classroom walls show only White children, children may learn that White is "normal" and other colors of human skin are "less than" or bad. When they see positive images in their early childhood programs or the media portraying people only in "white collar" or professional jobs, they may conclude that other kinds of jobs are not okay. If they live on farms yet see puzzles and books showing only urban children and adults, they may think that farmers must not be important enough to be part of school lessons.

When children and their families are visible, children are more likely to feel that they are all right. Conversely, when they and their families are invisible, children may develop a sense of shame about who they are.

The lessons of societal visibility and invisibility come from many sources: what children see and do not see in movies, television, books, toys, learning materials, and what they observe in the people who teach them, provide medical care, lead religious rituals, and so on. Children absorb these messages every day, often without the adults in their lives even knowing what the children are learning.

Stop & Think: What did you experience about *your* social identities?

- Make a list of all the various social identities you have now (e.g., related to your appearance, work, economic status, family statuses). Which social identities have brought you rewards? Which ones brought you prejudice and discrimination or limited your access to societal institutions? Which have been more difficult for you?

- What did your family teach you about your various social identities? What messages were overt and which covert?

- How did schools help or hurt you in your various social identities? Did you feel that you and your family were visible and/or invisible in the learning materials and curriculum?

- What overt and covert lessons might young children get from their favorite TV programs? Who is visible? Who is invisible? About which groups are there positive or negative messages?

● Children try to make sense of all that they see and hear.

As in all other areas of learning, young children try to make sense of their world by organizing what they observe and experience into "theories." This is true for how they explain their observations of skin color, gender, culture, disabilities, and so on. It is useful to listen to these child-generated explanations because it helps us understand how young children are trying to make sense of great complexity. For example:

After hearing about *melanin* and skin color, Robin asks, "If I eat melon will my skin look brown like Leticia's [Robin's best friend]?"

Peter looks at both sides of his hand and tells his mom, "This part is my Black part and this side is my White part."

"When I grow up I'm going to have three babies grow inside me," says David, whose mother is pregnant. His friend Tad objects, saying only girls can have babies inside them. "That's okay," David says cheerfully, "I'll tell my mommy to reborn me and I'll be a girl when I'm grown up."

"I want a button [hearing aid] like Bonita has," says English-speaking Shavon. When asked why, she replies, "So I can hear her Spanish words and talk to her."

While young children's theories about difference are often charming, they are also often incorrect. Listening to their ideas helps us pick up where they are confused and suggests how we can make their understanding more accurate. While working with children to expand and correct their ideas, it is also important to be respectful of the intelligence that underlies their attempts to make sense of what they experience. (See the section "Responding to Their Questions and Comments" in chapter 4.)

● Young children develop pre-prejudice as they absorb negative attitudes, misinformation, and stereotypes about various aspects of human diversity.

Children's inexperience and limited cognitive skills are not the only influences on their thinking. From early on, young children also show signs of absorbing whatever societal norms, stereotypes, and biases surround them concerning various aspects of their own and others' identities. They pay close attention to how the important people in their lives feel about human differences and similarities. Children notice subtle cues and draw conclusions about issues adults do not talk about, as well as formulate ideas after picking up on emotional tension from adults.

As a result, they learn incorrect ideas, stereotypes, and attitudes about a wide range of human dimensions including racial identity, economic class, culture, sexual orientation, and abilities/disabilities. Consider these comments, overheard by teachers and parents:

At home, after bathing, a 2½-year-old Asian American child tells his mother, "Now my hair is white because it is clean."

A 4-year-old boy, wanting to take over the wheel of a pretend bus, tells the child already there, "Girls can't be bus drivers. They have to cook." Conversely, a 4-year-old girl tells a boy classmate, "You can't be the nurse. Only girls can."

"Chelsea can't play with us. She's a baby," a 3-year-old tells her teacher. Chelsea, 4 years old, uses a wheelchair.

"You can't have two mommies," says one 4-year-old to a child who does. "That's bad," she continues.

Two 5-year-old White boys are playing in the sand. A Vietnamese American boy asks to join them. "Nah, nah, you can't play with us, you Chinese," they chorus, pulling their eyes into a slant.

Two boys playing with hoses and fire hats: "He don't got new boots like I do! So he can't be fire chief."

Pre-prejudice can usually be easily addressed at this early stage if adults are paying attention. But such ideas and feelings are also seeds that can grow into prejudice if a child's family or other important people in the child's life ignore or reinforce them. Even though many adults like to think that young children do not notice differences and are unaware of prejudice, research shows that this is not so. For example, a year-long study of preschoolers' conversations and play in a racially diverse preschool showed that children quickly learned racial terminology, used racial language to describe themselves and others, and used racial terms as negatives when teasing or excluding children from play (Van Ausdale & Feagin 2001).

● **Children begin to construct their own versions of who belongs in their country.**

As children observe their family and the world around them, they form understandings about the status of different groups in the broader society. For example, Glenda MacNaughton's research using persona doll stories with Australian 4-, 5-, and 6-year-olds uncovered unexpected early ideas about citizenship and diversity. Here are two examples of how the children thought about the citizenship of the indigenous people (or Aborigines) of Australia (who have lived there for 60,000 years), and about Vietnamese Australians, a recent immigrant group (2004, 69):

Researcher: These dolls all live in Australia. I was wondering, do you live in Australia?

James: I was born in Australia.

Researcher: Do you think all of these dolls were born in Australia?

James: No.

Researcher: Could you tell me [why]?

James: (interrupts and points to Shiree, the "Aboriginal" doll) That is an Aboriginal, isn't she?

Researcher: That is right. So, was she born in Australia? (James shakes his head)

Researcher: No? Where do you think she was born?

James: In Aboriginal.

Researcher: In Aboriginal land? And can you tell me about Australia? What it means to live in Australia?

James: That you all have a white skin.

Several children commented during their interviews that "Willy," the Vietnamese Australian doll, also was "not Australian." Their explanations included:

"Willy couldn't be Australian because he was born in Australia, but he still is Vietnamese."

"Willy and Shiree are not Australian because they've got different faces."

"Willy and Shiree must ask God if they want to be Australian; God might allow Shiree to be Australian but not Willy."

Based on her analysis of the data, MacNaughton (2004, 70) wrote that,

Bringing children's knowledge to the fore using the dolls and simple questions taught us two things:

• that colonial "othering" of "race" and culture was still part of how young Anglo Australian children were constructing a sense of self;

• that it was possible for some children to move beyond these understandings to more post-colonial understandings of "race" and culture.

Anti-bias educators need similar research in the United States to know what ideas young children here have about citizenship and racial/ethnic identity. As our population becomes increasingly diverse, this is information becomes more and more essential.

Stop & Think: Learning about differences

■ What is your earliest memory of realizing that some people were different from you and/or your family? (Differences of economics, religion, racial identity, language, disability?)

■ How did you feel about yourself in relationship to the "others"? How did you feel about them as compared with you?

■ When you were a child, how might you have described an "ordinary" person? What family structure would the person have? What color skin? What home language? What would be their work and economic class? Where and how would they have lived?

■ What stereotypes and negative messages did you learn from home, school, religious settings, and/or media about people whose identities were different in some way from yours?

■ What, if anything, changed your mind regarding any of these ideas or attitudes? Do you remember how old you were when such changes occurred?

■ What do you know about how the children you teach perceive their various social identities? other children's social identities?

● **Children begin to be aware of the power dynamics linked to social identities.**

Children quickly absorb messages about power relationships in their world. They pay attention to who is "in charge," "the boss," and "the person who gets to make decisions." They are very sensitive to who is considered okay and safe and who is not. This beginning awareness may plant seeds that grow into internalized oppression and internalized privilege.

Internalized oppression is a set of hurtful, inaccurate beliefs about oneself in relation to one's social identity group(s) that results in behaviors such as self-limitation, self- and group rejection, shame, and even self-hate. *Internalized privilege* is a set of hurtful, inaccurate beliefs about oneself in relation to one's social identity group(s) that result in a sense of entitlement. Internalized privilege is born out of the belief that one's identity group is the "norm" and is therefore entitled to advantages and benefits more than and regardless of the cost to others. The idea also serves to justify the mistreatment of those not in the privileged group.

Early ideas that seed internalized privilege and internalized oppression often form as young children try to make sense of what they see and hear in their daily experiences. For example (Derman-Sparks & Ramsey 2006, 39):

> During the ride home from his preschool, which maintains two separate and unequal programs—one for affluent, mostly White children, which is better resourced, and another for low-income, mostly children of color—a 4-year-old suddenly says to his mother: "Mommy, I'm really glad that I'm White."

We want White children to feel good about their racial identity, and it is logical to be glad to be in a program with more equipment. However, making the connection between Whiteness and having better services is also a seed that can blossom into a sense of entitlement based on racial identity. Without guidance from family and teachers, ideas such as this can become a sense of internalized privilege as a child gets older and observes and experiences more and more examples of why he should be "glad that I'm White."

Consider a few other examples of the beginnings of internalized privilege, this time about gender and economic class:

> Ishmael and Molly are playing in a "truck" they have made from the big blocks and cardboard boxes. "I'm driving," Ishmael announces firmly. "I want to drive!" protests Molly. "I'm the Daddy Man, so I drive!" he replies—and after a moment of thought, Molly moves over into the passenger seat.

> "How come we got a new car and Arlae's mommy brings her on the bus?" asks Karen on the way to school. "Your daddy and I worked hard to buy this car," her mother replies a little defensively. "Oh, I didn't know," Karen says quietly. "I'll tell her mommy to work harder."

Here is an anecdote from Louise's family, illustrating the seeds that might grow into internalized oppression:

> "I don't want to be Black anymore," my 4-year-old son announced at dinner one evening. In response to our question about why, he said, "I want to be like the people on *Emergency!* when I grow up." (*Emergency!* was a TV program in the 1970s about paramedics and firefighters, none of whom was Black.)
>
> It became clear that this was not an issue of personal self-concept—my son was not saying he didn't like himself. Rather, it seemed to us that he was trying to figure out what to do with a media message about his racial identity. We immediately responded, "You can be a firefighter when you grow up if you want to. There are already many Black firefighters." (We also did follow-up activities to reinforce this message—visiting a fire station with an African American firefighter and buying a puzzle showing dark-skinned firefighters.)

If a child comes to a similar conclusion about the need to change his racial identity to become what he wants to be when he grows up and no adult intervenes, what might be the eventual outcome for his sense of self?

Sometimes young children may show the beginning of internalized oppression by rejecting their home language when it is not English. When early childhood programs don't support a child's home language, they convey the message (intentionally or not) that English is the more important language.

> Apple, a 4-year-old girl from a Cambodian, Khmer-speaking family, enters speaking no English. As she slowly picks up the new language, she firmly refuses to speak in Khmer when her mother comes to pick her up. When her mother speaks to her in their home language, Apple firmly places her hand over her mother's mouth.

Trying to uncover a child's underlying reason for such rejection is important, although children cannot always articulate their rationales. Regardless of the reasons, unless adults teach children to honor their home language and encourage their ability to speak both it and English, we run the risk of children going silent, being ashamed of their home language, even losing their ability to communicate with some family members (see chapter 5 for a fuller language discussion).

The roots of internalized oppression or internalized privilege either are fed or dry up depending on children's experiences in the larger world. Here is an example from Julie's family of how internalized oppression and internalized privilege can take root:

> When my son was tiny, he had that wispy, white, "dandelion" hair sticking up all over his head. Sometimes children at the nursery school teased him about his hair, which hurt his feelings and took some intervention from the teacher and support from us. A few years later, my foster daughter, who is African American, came to live with us. She, too, got some teasing for her large, fluffy "Afro" hair, and again, the teacher and our family intervened.
>
> However, during his preschool years, my son's hair became blond, straight, and very much like the hair he saw in books and movies. By the time he was 5, hair was no longer an issue for him. Indeed, others saw him as an "all-American boy," and the many images of boys like him in school, in the media, and so on, reinforced the message. My foster daughter, however, picked up all the messages about "good hair versus bad hair" and the covert messages from movies and books about who is beautiful and who is not.
>
> Such social messages repeatedly reinforced the early teasing, and try as we might we were unable to protect her from coming to think of herself as "funny looking." It was not until we moved to a community where there were many other African American people, and a favorite teacher with a wondrous Afro, that she began to see her own beauty.

Both internalized privilege and internalized oppression derive from misinformation about one's social identity groups (e.g., being "less than" or "more than" other groups) and from the societal realities and messages (both overt and covert) about power differences between groups. While young children do not yet understand the full implications of the power and resource differences they observe around them, seeds of ideas about power and social identity do plant themselves and come to flower more fully in later childhood and young adulthood. Internalized oppression and internalized privilege eventually become so deeply learned that their messages come to feel like "just the way it is."

We will return to the topic of internalized privilege and internalized oppression in chapter 3.

Anti-bias education and the whole child

One of the fundamental premises of early childhood education, grounded in human development theory, is that the first five years of life are critical to children's healthy neurological growth, as well as to laying the foundation for the development of human empathy and connectedness. Furthermore, cognitive, emotional, and social development are inextricably intertwined. As Jack Shonkoff, director of the Center on the Developing Child at Harvard University, says,

> Emotional well-being and social competence provide a strong foundation for emerging cognitive abilities. Together they are the "bricks and mortar" of the foundation of human development. . . . The brain is a highly integrated organ. Social development and regulation of behavior are as much a part of development as cognitive learning. (2007)

Anti-bias education is an integral part of the "bricks and mortar" of emotional well-being and social competence, as well as an emotional foundation upon which children fully develop their cognitive capacities. A healthy sense of self requires that children know and like who they are without feeling superior to others. Understanding and liking one's own personal and social identities open up the possibilities of building caring connections with others. Thinking critically about stereotypes, prejudice, and discrimination takes away barriers to comfortable and respectful interactions with a wide range of people and gives children a tool to resist negative messages about their identities. Strong cognitive development is also enhanced when children develop curiosity, openness to multiple perspectives, and critical-thinking skills.

Anti-bias education thus strengthens the possibilities for early childhood care and education programs to implement the profession's commitment to foster the development of the *whole* child. It supports children in developing a fuller, truer understanding of themselves and the world and strengthens their sense of themselves as being capable and empowered to make "unfair" things "fair." In turn, these social, emotional, and cognitive abilities increase the likelihood that children will be able to navigate the larger worlds of school and their communities constructively and effectively, regardless of the experiences they have there.

Keeping the Promise: A Mother's Story

by Nadiyah F. Taylor

Families depend on their school to put into practice its educational philosophy. People from traditionally oppressed groups hope to find a place where their children experience encouragement and support to love all the parts of who they are. Families also look to anti-bias education as a method to begin to right the wrongs of our turbulent society and begin anew with a younger generation. I believe that directors and teachers who work in a program that claims to do anti-bias education also understand and believe in the hope inherent in this approach. However, do they understand the frustration and pain that comes when a program falls down on its promises?

My son is 4 years old. He has dark brown hair with rich red and golden brown highlights. It is big, bouncy, and full of curls that spring this way and that and seem to move with a wind that comes from within. He wears his hair in braids, twists, ponytails, and cornrows, and his favorite style is "my curls, Mom." He enjoys it and receives lots of positive feedback from others about it.

One Sunday night I braided my son's hair in loose cornrows. He ran to the mirror to admire the hairdo and expressed excitement about the way it looked and that it would keep his hair from falling into his face while he practiced his newfound skills on the high bar at school. However, sometime between arriving at school with his father at 7:30 a.m. and his classmates' arrival at 9:00 a.m., my son concluded that, "Even though it made me sad, Mommy, I needed to take out my braids so [one of his classmates] wouldn't tease me." My husband, who saw him later that morning, described the devastated and shamed look on my son's face as he explained that he needed to change himself to protect himself from teasing. One child teased that he had "puffy" hair and was a "barnacle head." Some other children thought he looked like a girl.

During the following week, my son decided that it was safe to wear his hair in curls, but that he could add no other adornment and definitely could not have braids or ponytails. During that same period, he also started to talk to me about how he thought *my* hair was puffy and looked a little weird. It was devastating for me to watch my son deciding he needed to change who he was and what he loved about himself because his classmates had teased him about the one thing that made him different.

What made me more upset, if that was possible, was that my son was attending a school with one of the most comprehensive, well written anti-bias statements I have seen. Yet his sweet, honest, overwhelmed teacher told me she had no idea where to start or what resources to draw upon. As a result, my beloved son was not the only one hurt: All of the children lost out because of the teacher's and director's inaction. The school failed to educate their teachers, and they, in turn, failed the children.

Anti-bias education is personal for me and for the well-being of my child. I am a Black woman in an interracial relationship and have a beautiful biracial son. I am also an educator of children and adults and believe that anti-bias education is fundamentally important to a child's development. How can we in early childhood education say we educate the whole child if we overlook the racial/ethnic, gender, and ability aspects of children's identities? Despite the fact that my son's teachers know the importance of being culturally sensitive, culturally competent professionals, they still don't have the skills to create an environment that addresses the needs of all children, and my son still struggles with his identity as a result.

Can you imagine what it felt like for me to see some of my son's sparkle diminish that day, and what might have been different had his teachers, and his school, followed through on their anti-bias promise? I encourage *all* programs to look at their curricula to find ways to include anti-bias principles in all areas on a consistent basis. However, I also ask that programs promising anti-bias education regularly assess—honestly—what they are actually doing.

PS: I did talk with my son's teacher about what had happened, and I saw a dramatic change in her. She reached out to me and others for information and support and began to educate herself. She renewed her commitment to serve all children. To my great delight, she is now one of the leaders in anti-bias education at the school. This gives me much hope that more and more early childhood educators and programs will understand and truly carry out their promise to do anti-bias education.

Beginning to Begin

Something happens . . .

● You see a group of children laughing at a new classmate who speaks with an accent.

● You listen in on three girls (all White) playing in the costume corner, and one says, "I get to be princess 'cuz I've got blonde hair," and the other girls agree without comment.

● You hear a child insist to her friend, "She's not your *real* mommy!"

● You watch a child refuse to play with another, "Because he's too fat!"

● You hear a staff member refer to a family on public assistance as "those kinds of people."

● You have a parent ask you to remove his child from the snack group of the only teacher of color on the staff.

You recognize the harmful effects of misinformation, stereotypes, biases, prejudice, and fear on young children. And because you care about children, about helping them live proudly and joyfully in a diverse world, you feel you have to do *something*. The question is: What to do? If you keep silent, you leave the children alone to make sense of a hurtful world. If you wait until you are completely sure of yourself, until you know "enough," the moment will pass, and the children you work with will have more deeply learned negative attitudes toward themselves and others. Sometimes you just have to begin.

So you take a deep breath. You think about *all* the players in the incident. What was each one trying to accomplish? What misinformation did they have? How can you help them see the world in a new way? You make a plan, determined you will not let this opportunity pass.

But what if you tried to open a discussion and instead froze and said nothing? What if you said something and it was the "wrong" thing? What if you offended someone? What if the children or the adults ignored you? That's okay. Remember that it takes time to learn any new behavior. You, as a developing professional, have the right to learn, too. If the interaction didn't go the way you hoped, revisit it later. Remind yourself that your action didn't *create* the problem. The problem, the hurtful behavior, happened, and you responded to it. Don't let yourself believe that your intervention "made things worse." Your intervention put words to the moment, and made it possible for everyone to keep thinking and learning. Remember that even if your voice shook, you still modeled to the children or the adults that people can speak up when something is wrong. You modeled courage. You have begun a dialogue. You are engaging in anti-bias education.

People often say that doing something new is scary and that change is difficult and frightening. Sometimes that can be true. But change is also exciting and enriching and, often, deeply satisfying. When you begin doing something you believe in, something you know will address a hurtful area for children—it can be a proud and fulfilling experience.

Here is one more suggestion: Celebrate! Call a friend and let someone know. You took a risk. You stood up for children's right to live in a world without bias. You began a new journey toward a better world. Bravo!

Becoming an Anti-Bias Teacher: A Developmental Journey

3

This work helps you to be a whole human being. It is a kind of redemption. It opens your eyes and makes you whole.

—Jim Clay

This work is as much about changing your own perspective as a teacher as it is about the activities you do in the classroom. If you're not willing to make a commitment to the four anti-bias education goals yourself, the rest is not useful.

—Rita Tenorio

Anyone who desires to can learn to be a skilled anti-bias educator. But it takes making a personal commitment. The more passion you have about the need for creating a world of justice and peace for children, the more you will be able to make it a priority in your work. Once you make that commitment, learning to do anti-bias education is a developmental journey. You start wherever you are right now. You go through many stages as you learn and practice ways to translate the four core goals of anti-bias education into practice with actual groups of children and families. You will have your own rhythm, speed, resting points. A verse from a children's song—"Inch by inch, row by row, gonna make this garden grow"—captures the reality of this journey. As Lupe Cortes, an early childhood teacher explains:

> Anti-bias work constantly pushes me to do self-reflection, to do the personal work that is necessary to be the best teacher I can be at that moment. I have to ask myself, "Why is this so big for me? Why am I being so reactive to what the parent or child said?" I do get discouraged sometimes that there is still so much work to do with myself, that I have all sorts of stumbling

blocks, that the onion has too many layers. However, I end up growing from the experiences—and they keep my work fresh. There is still so much to learn, and the meaning of the work makes it worth all the struggle and risks.

As you persist through the challenging times and see the fruits of your work, eventually anti-bias education becomes a part of everything you do. It becomes a way of life.

Stop & Think: Being an anti-bias teacher

- Why do you want to do anti-bias education? What do the anti-bias goals mean to you?

- What do you hope anti-bias education will do for the children you teach? If your hopes are realized, how will it benefit them?

- What do you hope anti-bias education will do for their families? How will it benefit them?

- What anxieties and concerns do you have about doing anti-bias education in your setting?

- Where will you find support for doing anti-bias education within or outside of your program?

Ongoing learning about yourself, as well as about the children and families you serve, makes it possible to effectively decide what to say, what to do, when to wait, and when to act in many different kinds of settings. It also will help you understand why some changes come easy, and others are hard for you, as this teacher did:

> I do child care at my church on Sundays and have always done an Easter curriculum, with eggs and spring flowers and baskets as well as telling the story of Jesus rising. I knew I couldn't do the religious part of the curriculum at the public preschool I was hired at, but I thought the eggs and baskets would be wonderful. I was so surprised that there were families who were offended! (Jewish families, Adventist families, and some Christian families who thought the eggs and baskets were pagan.) And I have to admit, I was pretty hurt. I hadn't realized how important those symbols are to me.

The better you know yourself, the better you can understand your own responses to the children and families you work with. For example, if you were raised to believe that being prompt is a sign of responsibility and respect, and your family always had a car, then it might be hard for you to comprehend the experience of low-income families who chronically drop their children off late because they must get to school by unreliable buses. Once you recognize how your own experiences have limited your viewpoint, you can see past your perspective and work on understanding the contexts of those families.

All of us have learned biases about our own and others' groups. Those biases act as filters that keep us from accurately seeing who we are and what is happening in front of us. In the following real-life example, a student teacher faces an important learning moment concerning how her biases had resulted in an incorrect and unfair interpretation of certain children's behavior:

> The student teacher had been videotaped doing circle time. The circle had fallen apart, with children getting up, running away, and refusing to participate. That evening the class discusses what happened. The student teacher complains about the disruptive behavior of two African American boys who had "ruined" the circle. Then the teacher plays the tape. Everyone is shocked to see that the real disruption had come from two White boys, that one of the African American boys had joined in later and the second had been almost entirely a bystander. "But I remembered it as Alec and William!" the student teacher says in tears, "How could I have been so wrong?"

Becoming an anti-bias educator has a learning curve, as does acquiring any new skill or understanding. Just as you had to learn how to hold children's attention in a circle time or set up a rainy day activity that really worked, it takes time, practice, and opportunities to do anti-bias education effectively. It is not realistic to try to make many changes all at once, even if you wish you could. Expect that not all will go smoothly, that you will stumble, that you will make mistakes and learn from them. But each small step you take will change your understanding of yourself and deepen your effectiveness with young children and their families.

Begin by identifying a support person

It is possible to begin doing anti-bias education by yourself, alone with your own group of children. But having colleagues and families who support and join with you makes the journey to becoming an anti-bias teacher richer and helps you "keep on keeping on." We all need the diverse perspectives and honest feedback of peers to expand our understanding of ourselves. We need others to help us uncover and change our learned biases or discomforts.

Goals for the Anti-Bias Teacher

• You will increase your awareness and understanding of your own social identity in its many facets (gender, racial, ethnicity, economic class, family structure, sexual orientation, abilities/disabilities) and your own cultural contexts, both childhood and current. (ABE Goals 1 & 2)

• You will examine what you have learned about differences, connection, and what you enjoy or fear across lines of human diversity. (ABE Goal 3)

• You will identify how you have been advantaged or disadvantaged by the "isms" (racism, sexism, classism, ableism, heterosexism) and the stereotypes or prejudices you have absorbed about yourself or others. (ABE Goal 3)

• You will explore your ideas, feelings, and experiences of social justice activism. (ABE Goals 3 & 4)

• You will open up dialogue with colleagues and families about all these goals. (ABE Goal 4)

The goals above are very similar to the ones the anti-bias teacher will set for children. Being open to learning and growing is fundamental to becoming a capable anti-bias educator.

When we have other people to talk with, it makes it easier to decide what to keep, change, or add to make our teaching more effective. It also strengthens our skills and confidence for talking about anti-bias issues. Perhaps most important, having support while we try out anti-bias activities means we have someone to share in our successes, to learn from what didn't work well, and to help us plan next steps.

Stop & Think: Identifying support people

- Whom do you know who cares about what happens to children's identities, self-concepts, and attitudes toward diversity? about prejudice, bias, and institutional isms?

- Whom do you know who respects and likes you and might be willing to support you in becoming a better teacher?

- What would stop you from calling that person/people and asking for support?

To get started becoming an anti-bias teacher, you may need some other teachers to talk and share ideas with—to help each other figure out what went well, what needs work, and where to go next. Ideally, you will find people at your program who also want to do this work. If not, find a colleague outside your work site who shares your belief in the importance of children learning to live with strength and skill in a diverse and inequitable world. Some teachers communicate by phone or email if their anti-bias partner is farther away.

Set up a regular, weekly or biweekly time to meet or talk. Agree to share the time together equally. One of you talks, the other listens and supports, then trade—so the speaker becomes the listener and the listener, the speaker. After you have both had an uninterrupted turn to tell your stories, you can help each other examine the issues, feelings, and attitudes that emerge.

Be sure to call each other to celebrate victories, even small ones! Each step you take matters. What we do *right* is rarely seen as important to acknowledge; talking about what we did well is often seen as bragging. But just as children need words to support their learning successes, we adults need to put into words how well we do things and to get recognition for our hard work.

Become aware of your feelings and beliefs

Ultimately, the most important thing we bring to our teaching is who we are. Deepening our understanding of who we are now and how we came to *be* that person is at the heart of becoming a strong anti-bias teacher. The Stop & Think reflection questions throughout this book invite you to bring to the surface—maybe for the first time—what you think, feel, and believe, as well as how the world and your experiences in it may have shaped your understandings. For example, Flora, a toddler teacher enrolled in a college anti-bias class, wrote:

> "I was really surprised how 'wrong' it felt to me to hear young children address adults by their first name. In this class I've come to realize there are a lot of different ways that children are taught to show respect for adults. The way my family does it is just one way, not the 'right' way."

Reflection questions are always easier to address honestly in the company of others who are struggling with the same process of personal and professional growth. Sharing your answers with others deepens everyone's understanding. The contrasts between people illuminate and inform and help us to make sense of our own experiences. (See the box "Guidelines for Heart-to-Heart Listening" for a helpful technique you can use.) It also makes for fascinating and enriching staff and family meetings!

Thinking about your many social identities

As described in the previous chapter on children's identity development, each of us has a *personal identity*—our name, age, place in the family, personality, interests, talents, and so on—which makes us an individual. But each person also has many *social identities* related to our racial identity, gender, culture, language, economic class, family structure, sexual orientation, abilities and disabilities, religion, and the like, which connect us as members of multiple specific groups. Social identities derive from the social-political and economic systems of the society in which we live, as well as being a part of who we are. Our social identities play a significant role in how others see us and treat us, and they affect our access to the society's institutions (e.g., education, health, legal). Consequently, how we feel about our various social identities is at once individual, familial, and societal.

When one or more of our social identities are shared with many of the people around us (and when we see our identities reflected in the media, etc.), we may be unaware of having been shaped by those identities. The attributes and behaviors we absorb from those identities seem just to "be" and to feel "normal" or "regular." Often it is easier to become aware of our identities when we think back about the ways we did *not* belong or the ways some doors were closed to us based on those identities.

Guidelines for Heart-to-Heart Listening

Listening partners can use the Heart-to-Heart technique to tell each other stories that explore who and where they are in relation to the many anti-bias issues discussed in this book. Draw from the many Stop & Think questions in this chapter and others. Be sure that you create a safe environment for yourselves. Respect each other's stories. Don't judge, and don't interpret each other's experiences.

When you are the speaker:

• Speak from your heart. Don't worry about getting the "facts" right; tell your story the best you can. Provide enough details so that what happened and what you feel are made clear.

• It is okay to cry, laugh, shake, yawn, or whatever, while you are telling your story.

• This is your time, so take it! The more you are honest with yourself, the more you will learn and grow.

When you are the listener:

• Totally respect the speaker's confidentiality.

• Listen as a believer (that is, listen to hear why the story is true from the speaker's point of view, even if you see there are alternate perspectives).

• Stay out of the speaker's story; no questions, interruptions, distractions, advice, or recommendations. (Wait until *after* you both have had your talking and listening turns, then you can explore themes and issues that arise from your stories.)

• If strong feelings come up for the *speaker* while you are listening, remember that you do not need to come to the rescue. Your job as listener is to stay present and attentive and be confident that your partner can work through his or her feelings.

• If strong feelings come up for *you* while you are listening, remember that the feelings are about *you*—not about the speaker. They are useful information for you to have about yourself.

People who carry deep injuries from experiencing prejudice and discrimination related to one or more of their social identities may be reluctant to think and talk about this subject out of fear of reopening old wounds. Some people may find it hard to examine their social identities that connect them to unfair treatment of others (e.g., White mistreatment and economic exploitation of people of color). Even so, it is essential to becoming effective anti-bias educators that we examine each aspect of who we are, in order to understand fully how our identities influence how we relate to people today. Understanding these dynamics in your life will strengthen your awareness of, sensitivity to, and empathy for the personal and social identity development of the children and families you serve.

Uncovering your learned stereotypes, discomforts, and biases

We all become aware of and start learning about the similarities and differences among people very early. Positive and negative attitudes and feelings toward difference begin to develop in infancy. Examining what you have learned over the years will be a little like eating an artichoke: You have to peel off the layers to get clearer about your experiences and assumptions now.

No one escapes learning stereotypes and misconceptions about various aspects of human diversity. These lessons begin when we are very young, taught initially and most powerfully by our family and then by the larger world around us. And all of us still carry inaccurate and negative messages—even if we no longer believe they are true—that can keep us from seeing each person as a unique, whole person fully deserving of our respect.

Stop & Think: Understanding what you were taught

■ What memories do you have of what your family taught you about various kinds of diversity among people? Was their behavior consistent with what they said?

■ What do you remember from childhood about how you made sense out of human differences? What confused you?

■ What did you learn in school about whom you should and shouldn't be friends with? What were you taught about how and why people were different? Were the same messages taught at home?

■ What childhood experiences did you have with peers or adults who were different from you in some way (racial identity, culture/ethnicity, family structure, economic class, religion, gender role, sexual orientation)? Were these experiences comfortable? Why or why not?

■ As an adult, in what ways do you agree or disagree with your parents' views about the various groups? If you disagree, how did you develop your own, different ideas?

It is important to remember that as children, we *did not have a choice* about receiving these lessons. But it is essential that now, as adults, we uncover and eradicate the stereotypes and misinformation we were taught, and any biases and prejudices that may have grown from them, as they keep us from nurturing and teaching all children equally and fully.

Racism, sexism, heterosexism, and the other isms are ugly, so facing the possibility that we are capable of perpetuating them can generate pain, shame, guilt, or anger. Do not let these strong feelings stop you. Acknowledge to yourself the feelings that arise, and remember that becoming more self-aware is an essential first step to undoing past learning. It clears the way for you to replace misconceptions with accurate information and to develop more positive attitudes and greater empathy for all children and families. Carol Brunson Day reminds us,

> We have to come to an understanding of self—and that how we see our own identity is related to how we see others. This requires being introspective and is necessary work for everyone to do, regardless of our racial, ethnic, or cultural identities.

There are many things you can do to deepen your understanding of self. Here is one exercise to help you better understand how stereotypes have shaped your thinking:

1. Make a list of all the stereotypes you have heard about the various racial/ethnic groups in the United States. Do this quickly! Don't censor yourself. Write these down regardless of whether or not you believe them.

2. Examine your list and try to figure out from where or whom you heard those stereotypes, and at what age each came into your life. Be honest with yourself about which ones you believe. You cannot change your thinking unless you first identify what you need or want to change.

3. What kinds of behaviors of boys make you uncomfortable? of girls? Where do these two sets overlap and where are they different? From where or whom did you learn your differing gender expectations?

4. What feelings come up when you work with families with very low incomes? who are homeless? have a family member in jail? with very high incomes? Do you prefer to teach children from a particular economic class? What or who are the sources of your feelings?

5. What feelings come up when you work with gay/lesbian-headed families? What messages have you received about such families? about gays and lesbians? What or who are the sources of your feelings?

6. What kinds of disabilities make you feel comfortable? uncomfortable? Which kinds of disabilities in children make your teaching most challenging? What or who are the sources of your feelings?

Further, use the many Stop & Think reflection questions in chapters 5 through 11 in this book to uncover and examine the many messages and experiences you have had about specific kinds of difference and to rid yourself of stereotypes, misinformation, and biases you may not realize that you hold.

Examine institutional advantages and disadvantages

Uncovering, examining, and eliminating our own personal prejudices and discriminatory behaviors are necessary tasks in the journey of becoming an anti-bias teacher. Another critical task is to understand how the *institutional* forms of prejudice (the isms)—racism, sexism, classism, ableism, and the others—negatively affect early childhood education and the lives of the families and children we serve.

What is an ism?

An ism is about the institutional advantages and disadvantages people experience due to their membership (or perceived membership) in certain social identity groups. An ism is systemic, meaning it is found throughout a society and its institutions, such as education, health, law, housing, employment, and media. An ism is much more than a matter of people being nice or not nice to each other. Isms are expressed in laws, in organizational policies, and in regulations, as well as in the thinking and actions of people who carry out the policies.

Isms can be overt or covert. *Overt* isms are explicit, direct, and spelled out. Some forms of overt, legal discrimination do still exist. For example, laws in many states prohibit a same-sex partner from getting custody of the couple's children if the biological parent dies. Some neighborhoods still have ordinances that prohibit selling or renting houses to people from certain age groups.

Covert isms are indirect, subtle, and hidden. We detect them through the outcomes or consequences of laws, organizational policies, and regulations and in people's actions and attitudes. Today, the more likely form of most isms is covert, although their outcomes continue to create disadvantage for some and advantage for others. Some examples of covert isms in early childhood education include the invisibility of certain kinds of children and families in classroom materials; teaching methods that do not take into account cultural learning styles; a publishing industry that solicits and produces teaching materials focused mainly on the dominant groups in the culture; and who is and isn't represented on the faculty in teacher-training programs.

Individuals and isms

It is important to understand that as individuals we carry out the dynamics of institutional advantage and disadvantage—whether or not we had anything to do with creating them in the first place. Some people do this intentionally and proudly because they really believe that some groups are less worthy or deserving than others. But many people implement acts of institutional advantage and disadvantage without their realizing or even wanting to. Regardless, what matters are the consequences of our behavior, not simply our intentions.

For example, you may believe in the importance of having materials that reflect all of the children in your class. However, if the administrator of your early childhood program does the ordering, or if you are told as a teacher which companies you must order your materials from, then you may end up with a material environment that makes some of the children invisible. Unless you find a way to change this situation, you are reinforcing advantage and disadvantage to different children. Kathee Lyda, a White, Japanese American student teacher, writes about the impact on her of covert lessons about her identity from her family and school:

> I never gave a name to who I am. My father's insistence that my sister and I were "real Americans" was like a locked trunk that hid my experiences of being the only person who looked like me anywhere in my school. I was always aware of physical differences between humans—but somehow just knew (I guess this was a "covert lesson") that I shouldn't talk about it. Now I listen to children talking about shapes of eyes, teachers talking about how people are different, and I can't believe how much I needed those conversations.

Uncovering and examining institutional advantages and disadvantages is often more challenging to do than is uncovering personal misinformation and prejudices. Begin by thinking through the Stop & Think questions below. Talk about your ideas with friends and colleagues and listen to theirs. Read more about how institutional isms work. (See the epilogue for more things you can do.)

Stop & Think: What have you experienced about institutional inequity?

- Describe your own and your family's experiences with institutional isms on the basis of racial identity, culture, ethnicity, language, learning disabilities, religious beliefs, family structure, gender, economic class, or other arenas of social identity. What was the impact on you? How do these experiences influence your work with children and families today?

- Think about your interactions with various social institutions such as school, health care, transportation, media, law, employment, and the like. In what ways did your social identities ease or hamper your access to these institutions?

- To what degree did you see your family reflected in the books and other classroom materials in your school while you were growing up?

- What happens now when you get learning materials for your classroom or program? Can you find diverse and nonstereotyped materials? What, if anything, do you and others on the staff do to ensure that every child and family is made visible?

- Is the staff where you work broadly diverse across all the lines of human difference? If it is, how has that happened? If it isn't, what would it take to make it change?

Internalized privilege and internalized oppression

Institutional isms convey advantages and disadvantages to groups of people. But they also create psychological dynamics that can affect our individual sense of self and undermine our healthiest and fullest development as human beings. These dynamics are internalized privilege and internalized oppression. When a teacher acts out of unexamined internalized privilege or internalized oppression, that teacher runs the risk of unintentionally undermining children's development.

Internalized privilege

The dynamic of *internalized privilege* (sometimes termed "internalized superiority") describes the psychological consequences for people whose social identities—that is, their membership in one or more privileged groups—bring them economic, social, and cultural advantages. Those advantages (or "privileges") encompass a whole series of rights, expectations, and experiences that function as the grease that can make daily life easier, smooth access to institutions, bring economic success, and provide social supports. Internalized privilege, then, is a feeling or belief that what are actually advantages over other people are merely "natural" and "ordinary" circumstances.

Internalized privilege functions as a set of lenses, making it more difficult for an advantaged person who has internalized this sense of privilege to see that not everyone is so lucky as he is. These lenses lead the person to wrongly assume that everyone else has his same opportunities for smooth access to institutions and acceptance and that people who are unsuccessful in society had his opportunities but were not smart enough or didn't work hard enough to make use of them. For example, it rarely occurs to men to think that being able to stand at a bus stop late at night without fear of rape is a form of male privilege. Most Whites assume that a police officer will pull them over only if they have actually done something wrong, which is a form of advantage that some racial groups do not get. And heterosexuals don't have to worry whom they might upset if they put up a picture of their partner in their workspace.

The lenses of internalized privilege result in members of privileged groups having incomplete and inaccurate pictures of what is going on around them—in their own lives, in their communities, and in the lives of others (see the box "Recognizing Privilege"). They may even result in members of privileged groups believing they have earned or are more deserving of those group advantages than is someone whose group memberships bring economic, social, and cultural *dis*advantages.

Internalized oppression

By contrast, *internalized oppression* (sometimes termed "internalized inferiority") describes the psychological consequences for people who belong to one or more social identity groups who experience any of the many faces of institutionalized prejudice and discrimination, such as limited access to opportunities or resources and constant negative messages about their groups. Internalized oppression is a feeling or belief that the negative messages are true. It is learned behavior that is a response to institutionalized racism, sexism, classism, and the other isms, which have undermined the sense of self.

For example, when adolescent girls self-select out of math classes, it feels to them like a free choice, but they may well have come to believe the social messages that "girls just aren't good at math" and "thinking mathematically isn't feminine." Or when children from low-income families absorb the social message that intellectual careers are not for them, that they just aren't smart enough for academic work, they believe they are accurately assessing their potential.

Internalized oppression can look like *self-hate* (that is, prejudice or hostility toward members of one's own group). Internalized oppression might include behaviors such as rejecting one's natural physical characteristics, name, language, cultural traditions, or values. It can mean believing stereotypes about one's own group, or identifying with a different (usually the dominant) culture's worldview and accepting its standards as accurate and true. For example, people who have internalized oppression might adopt the dominant culture's standards of beauty regarding hair color, eye shape, body size, or skin tone as being "better" than their own group's standards. They may try to change their own appearance to meet the other group's standards. They might unconsciously give more value to children or seek friends only among people whose looks are closer to the dominant culture's standard of beauty.

Jose Rocha, a early childhood teacher taking an anti-bias class, wrote about learning internalized

---

Recognizing Privilege

by Bryn Potter, a preschool teacher

I have a BA degree and all the benefits that come with it. I got a good education and was taught that this was a right, deserved by and available to anyone. I went to public elementary school in a largely middle-class neighborhood. It seemed average to me, even lacking in programs compared with the public schools across town where the movie stars lived. But in fact, my school had enough funding to offer a very good education and GATE (gifted) programs, and I got to have these because of where I lived.

My high school offered GATE and Advanced Placement courses for those who were on track for college. This offered all kinds of advantages. My senior year, we wrote our entrance essays in English class, and I completed my college applications in Government class. I took all of this for granted as my high school's responsibility, when in fact I now know that many high schools do nothing to help students with college plans.

If I had been asked how I ended up on the college track at my school, I think I would have answered that I worked hard and that my family valued education. These statements are both true, but they evidence the blinders of internalized privilege that prevented me from seeing the advantages afforded me by my economic class. The experience of people without a degree or the means to get one was invisible to me. If someone didn't go to college, I assumed that they didn't want to (which is funny, because I never asked myself whether I wanted to go, or what I'd be willing to do to get there).

Source: Class assignment for Julie's anti-bias curriculum course. Used with permission.

oppression regarding economic class:

> If we are invisible at school, it determines the value of who we are and how we view others and how they view us. I grew up in a very poor family where money was an issue. I never had new clothes or new shoes. My parents would always shop at the flea market. Growing up was hard because I never had "cool clothes," and the other kids would make fun of me. Now I can say, "That was classism." I don't know why having a word makes it easier to think about, but it does! . . . I was always receiving misinformation about who I was. It was hard for me to construct my self-identity.

Stop & Think: What oppressive messages have you internalized?

- In your heart of hearts, do you believe some of the messages that declare members of your own social identity groups (racial identity, gender, economic class, ability, etc.) to be inferior in some ways?

- If so, what are these messages? Where did you learn them?

- How has internalizing these messages affected your life so far?

- How might your belief of these messages affect your work with children and families?

- What would it take to eliminate these messages from your thinking and behavior? If you did, what would be the result?

Unraveling our privileges and oppressions

Internalized privilege and internalized oppression are hard to escape, as this teacher in a toddler center found out:

> I was so excited when I found out our new director would be a man. It's very important to have men in early childhood programs. But then I heard myself saying, "Besides, men make better bosses." I couldn't believe what I had just said! I realized that, somehow, I believed that women could not be good bosses— that they would be gossipy and untrustworthy or pushy and aggressive. Once I said this out loud, I was shocked! In reality, the last two directors I had worked with had both been women and had been fine at their job. I guess this is an example of internalized oppression about women.

Because we all have multiple social identities, each of us contains a complex set of internalized privileges and oppressions, with differing balances between the two. For a revealing and interesting exercise used in many anti-bias courses, do the "My Social Identities Portrait" exercise, shown at the end of this chapter.

The degree to which any one of us absorbs the attitudes and behaviors associated with each aspect of our multiple social identities varies considerably. Factors such as our family's level of education, school

experiences, personal social and emotional experiences, and the political time in which we live all play a role. How we feel personally about our various social identities may stand in opposition to the social realities of advantage and disadvantage. For example, social discrimination and negative messages about being working class do not necessarily stop people from being personally proud of their working-class family background.

Go back to the "My Social Identities Portrait" exercise, this time reflecting on how you personally feel about each of your social identities. This is a good time to also think about which messages of internalized privilege or internalized oppression you would like to eliminate from your thinking and behavior, and decide what steps you will take down that path. (To help you think about this, see the box "How Might Internalized Privilege or Oppression Affect Your Relationships at Work?")

Unraveling our internalized privilege and internalized oppression frees us to be better teachers. It is an emotional as well as a cognitive developmental journey. Here are a few examples of how students in a class at Pacific Oaks College wrote about how the steps they experienced felt to them (Derman-Sparks & Phillips 1997):

- At the start of the journey:

> "Racism is tension. I recall every awareness of racism by the corresponding feeling of embarrassment or anxiety or shame or confusion." (55)

> "I'm not going to think about this [racism] anymore now. I have to go to work, play, bed, eat, etc. I have important things to think about. That's how I keep it safe." (55)

- Beginning to face the issues intellectually and emotionally:

> "This class is shattering my illusions, and it's hard to accept." (89)

- Beginning to do the necessary internal work:

> "It feels like I had this big closet to clean out . . . and was now trying to decide what stayed, what needed fixing, and what to throw out. It's a big job, but it feels great. I know I am going to be more of the person I want to be." (112)

- Later in the journey:

> "Tonight was our last class. I've been thinking why it affects people so much. I think it's because, in untying the knot, you're unraveling the web of lies that each of us has inevitably experienced, and racism is only a part of the false information each of us received while growing up. . . . There are many other parts that have taken their dehumanizing toll, and, in unraveling even a bit of the whole, we feel tremendously excited. We have only to unravel more of it to reclaim ourselves more completely." (137)

Explore social justice activism

Many people think of *activism* only as walking a picket line or joining protest demonstrations. While these kinds of activities have resulted in many important social justice changes, there are also many other types of activism. Activism often starts at the personal level. Reflecting on your own development is one key step. Incorporating anti-bias education into your work is another. So, too, are reflecting on your own development and assessing your work with children and families and with other staff (see chapter 4).

Your individual action matters. However, to be truly effective in creating more equitable education and other social systems, people also have to work together and in many different ways. For example,

> Several male teachers in one county form a support group and begin to make presentations to a directors group about the importance of men in early childhood education—resisting the isolation they all feel. The same group of men act as allies by providing child care for a group of mothers who were meeting about inequitable health care insurance.

Resisting and being an ally

Anytime a person stands up against poor treatment of themselves or members of their own group, that is a form of activism called *resistance*. Anytime a person stands up against poor treatment of members of another group, that is called *alliance*. For example, if at a staff meeting someone makes a racist joke about Latinos and you are Latino, when you speak up you are "resisting." If you are White and speak up, you are being an "ally."

Both forms of action are important, and it is useful to be clear which is which. When people are resisting poor treatment and you wish to be an ally,

---

How Might Internalized Privilege or Oppression Affect Your Relationships at Work?

Here are some questions to help you reflect on your interactions with children, families, and other staff. Think about whether you do the following behaviors "frequently" or "sometimes" or "rarely." Next, focus on those you answered with "rarely" and make a plan for how you will move to "sometimes" and eventually to "frequently." Keep in mind that reflecting on these questions and making plans for improving your practice should be an ongoing effort throughout the school year.

How do I interact with staff and parents?

• Do I treat other staff respectfully, recognizing and appreciating their unique cultural styles and belief systems? Do I ask about, openly talk about, and appreciate the differences between us? Do I model open and respectful listening?

• Do I work carefully to broaden gender roles among staff?

• Do I treat all staff as important contributors to the program (e.g., teacher assistants as well as teachers; the cook and cleaning people as well as the director)?

• Do I interact with families thoughtfully and respectfully, paying close attention to the basic power dynamics between us? Do I take responsibility for building and maintaining open and sensitive dialogue?

• Do I ask each family for information about their child? In the classroom, do I use what I learn about children?

• Do I work on overcoming any discomfort or biases I have about any specific aspect of diversity?

• Do I constructively talk with other staff about any actions that I think undermine respect for diversity?

• Do I support our efforts to identify biases and change practices that do not encourage fairness?

• Do I work with others to find ways to ensure a diversity of skin colors, languages, gender identities, and family structures among staff at all levels?

How do I interact with children?

• Do I recognize, understand, acknowledge, and respect each child's individual cultural and learning styles? Do I make provisions for children who prefer to play and work alone and for those who prefer being with peers?

• Do I invite children to try new ways of interacting with people and materials, while also supporting their preferred learning styles?

• Do I adapt my interactions with each child to use his or her family's style regarding encouragement? limit setting? behavior expectations? teaching of life skills? Where I must do things differently at school than what children are used to, do I help children feel comfortable about living in two worlds?

• Do I answer children's questions about human differences easily and directly; pay attention to children's interest in human differences; encourage them to express their feelings and questions; and help them to reflect on their own ideas about various aspects of diversity?

• Do I handle children's inappropriate behaviors (e.g., hitting, hurtful words, exclusion) in equitable ways? Or does my response differ based on the child's racial identity, gender, culture, ability, or economic class background?

it is essential you ask what they want you to do and how you can help, rather than presuming that you know how another group should proceed. If people in your own identity group are acting oppressively, it is important you act, at least to question the behavior.

There are many ways to take action with others. With colleagues you can organize a letter-writing campaign to publishing houses about the need for more books about specific types of children, or to state legislators urging increased funding for early childhood programs for low-income families. Teachers can work with colleagues through their professional organizations and unions. You can join with families to organize around issues in the early childhood program or in the children's neighborhood, such as convincing local stores not to group toys based on gender stereotypes or getting more playgrounds built with accessible equipment. Sometimes you will want to work with a broader group of people to bring up early childhood issues in local, state, and federal elections and legislation (see the epilogue for more on this and other avenues for action).

Imagine becoming active

If you haven't imagined yourself as an activist, here are some questions and activities to help you consider what may be getting in your way. You can reflect on them by yourself, as well as talk about them with your anti-bias learning partner or group:

● What images come to mind when you think about a social activist? Draw pictures of some. Where do you think your images come from: direct experiences? television or movies? newspaper accounts?

● What messages did you get from your family or in school about people's ability to make change? about people whom your family or teachers considered activists?

● Did any members of your family ever take action to improve the world? What kinds of action? How did the rest of your family feel about what they did? How did you feel?

● Describe an incident in which you experienced prejudice or were discriminated against. What did you do? Did anyone stand up for you, support you, or help you make sense of what happened?

● Describe an incident in which you observed prejudice or discrimination directed at someone else. Did anyone stand up for that person? What did you do? Then what happened? How do you feel today about what you saw and did?

● What is your worst fear about what might happen if you were to speak up when you saw or experienced prejudice or bias? How would you feel about yourself if you did nothing? If you did speak up, what is your best hope of what might happen?

● When did you first become aware that there were people in the world who were social activists? How did you hear about them? What kind of people did you think they were? How did knowing about them make you feel? How do you feel now about people who are social activists?

- Find out about the experiences of activists in your community who have worked to make change. Ask them: "What motivated or started you in doing activism? What supports you? What are your challenges? What have you gained personally? What keeps you going?"

Stand up as an anti-bias educator

What children call "fairness" and "unfairness," we adults know as issues of justice and injustice. One of the finest hopes we can have for our children is to give them a just world—a world that recognizes all people for the unique, fully human beings they are; a world where every child has equal access to the opportunities to become all he or she can be. Early childhood educators care deeply about what happens to children. Working to make the world that children live in a place where every one can flourish is an extension of that caring.

Many early childhood teachers are willing to risk taking on new, anti-bias education behaviors for the sake of children. It is when other adults are involved that our fears and anxieties can take over. Qualms about how other adults may react to our anti-bias work can keep us from getting started. "I might offend someone" is a fear that teachers becoming anti-bias educators must face and overcome if they are to do effective anti-bias work with children.

Sometimes, it is true, someone might take offense. Sometimes doing something in a new way or challenging an old way creates conflict. For example,

Some teachers at a campus child development center begin to examine their children's books for gender stereotypes. They are upset by how many books they find that portray boys as adventurous and active and girls as passive or as caregivers or ballerinas. They decide to put away the stereotype-filled books and make their own until they can raise money to purchase better ones. Other staff members and some of the parents are furious. They call the project "book burning" and "censorship," complaining that the teachers are just being "politically correct."

It takes many weeks of discussion to find a solution. The teachers listen carefully. They present a workshop on how they see the children being hurt by the stereotypes and encourage families to tell their own stories (and there are many). The teachers show the books they are concerned about and ask the families to talk about them. One of the fathers says, "I won't let my kids eat lots of sugar because I know it's bad for them, so I guess it makes sense to get rid of books that are bad for them, too."

In the end, everyone has learned a lot, and the parents are energized to fundraise for new books.

As experienced anti-bias educator Jim Clay explains,

I do not love having conflicts, but I have done anti-bias work enough that I have some confidence about the outcome. In the end, conflicts will resolve, and I will still be here.

Educators who do speak out, who take action in the name of anti-bias education, find that most times all parties share the same aim: to protect children from bias and prejudice. Often people who start out being surprised by, worried about, or angry at teachers for taking an anti-bias approach become delighted by and proud of such work happening in their children's program. Moreover, when teachers welcome these conflicts as an opportunity to learn with and from others, the positive connections and respect that can result are long-lasting and strong.

Your personal journey

Learning to be an effective anti-bias educator is a journey. Wherever we begin, there are always new paths to explore and knowledge to acquire. As you continue to grow and learn, you will want to know more (things to read, workshops to attend, professional connections to make), and in the epilogue we suggest several paths to help you "keep on keeping on."

This chapter focused on ways to engage in the self-reflection essential to the anti-bias education journey. While we strongly recommend *beginning* with some of the exercises in this chapter, we do not suggest that you do *all* of them before actually doing anti-bias work in your own program. Chapters 5 through 11 are filled with practical ideas for putting the anti-bias education goals into your work with children. Each idea you try will expand your understanding, along with that of the children.

You will have a unique path as an anti-bias educator. Keep in mind the following counsel (Alvarado et al. 1999) of educator-activists who have been on their journeys for many years:

- Each person's development as an anti-bias educator has its own pattern, pace, and timetable. The key is to keep going, keep moving, and keep committed.

- We must constantly reflect on our work, learn from our mistakes, expect that it will not all work smoothly, and keep trying.

- We must embrace disagreement and complexity as being fundamental to working with children, families, and staff from diverse groups and in changing times.

- We must celebrate each victory—acknowledge and share the small daily successes and the larger ones. This is what gives us the strength (and joy) to stay the course.

My Social Identities Portrait

Instructions: Circle those identities in columns 2 and 3 that apply to your life. Look at the pattern of circles in the two columns. Either with a talking partner or in writing, describe for each of the circled identities: *In what ways you have experienced either privilege and visibility or prejudice and discrimination? Which identities opened doors for you, and which ones made life harder?*

Social Identity	Which Identities Apply to Me?	
	Groups defined as the norm; recipients of societal advantages	**Groups that are targets of institutional prejudice and discrimination**
Race	White	People of color Bi- or multiracial people and families
Ethnicity/Heritage	European American "Melting pot"	All other defined or recognizable ethnicities
Language	English	Home language other than English
Gender	Male	Female, intersex, transgender
Economic class (in childhood, now)	Middle to wealthy	Poverty or working class
Religious beliefs	Christian or Christian tradition	Muslim, Jewish, Buddhist, Hindu, pagan, atheist, etc.
Age	Productive adults (ages 20–45 for women, 20–60 for men)	Children, adolescents, women over 45, men over 60
Sexual orientation	Heterosexual	Asexual, bisexual, gay, lesbian, transgender
Education	College degree Highly literate	High school or less Literacy struggles
Body type/size	Slim, fit Medium height for women, tall for men	Large, overweight Very short or very tall
Able self (physical, mental, emotional)	Healthy Functional, no apparent disability	Any form of disability (physical, mental, emotional stability; learning; behavior controls)
Family structure (in childhood, now)	Married Parent with 1–3 biological children	Unmarried Single parent; divorced; relative's children; adoptive, foster, or blended family

Creating an Anti-Bias Learning Community

4

Invisibility erases identity and experience.
Visibility affirms reality.

Creating a caring community of learners is fundamental to anti-bias education. As NAEYC's position statement on developmentally appropriate practice reminds us:

> The foundation for the community is consistent, positive, caring relationships between the adults and children, among children, among teachers, and between teachers and families. It is the responsibility of all members of the learning community to consider and contribute to one another's well-being and learning. (NAEYC 2009, 16)

This chapter will guide you through the process of creating the anti-bias environment that best fits the children and families in your program and local community. This is challenging and also exciting, satisfying work. Each teacher begins in a different way, but whatever his or her starting point, anti-bias teachers keep improving the learning community they create year by year.

Positive interactions with children

Children's daily interactions with their teachers and other adults are at the heart of anti-bias education. Children are very keen observers of adult behavior; they pay attention to even very subtle clues about how people feel and about what is and isn't considered acceptable behavior. Moreover, children are quick to notice double messages—what adults *do* teaches as least as much as what they *say*. Children also pay close attention to the interactions *among* the adults in a program.

Almost everything adults say or do around children carries messages about gender, economic class, racial identity, ability, and family culture. As we discussed in chapter 3 on becoming an anti-bias teacher, frequently adults have no idea when they are perpetuating stereotyped information and bias in their language and behaviors. The Stop & Think questions found in most of the chapters in this book will help you and your colleagues uncover and reflect on what messages children are receiving from you and your learning environment about the various topics of anti-bias work. We encourage you to take the time to think about these questions carefully.

What children ask, say, or do about any aspect of their own or others' identities and differences are the wonderful "teachable moments" of anti-bias education. How you respond to these opportunities is a central part of effective teaching with young children. When children make comments that reflect discomfort, stereotypes, or rejection of an aspect of diversity, they may stir up your own hurt or anger about prejudice and discrimination.

Most adults have had little experience talking about difference and bias with children. You may freeze or feel unsure about what to say. Even if you are unsure, teachable moments offer rich possibilities for you to discover what children think and feel about various diversity issues and to support their attempts to understand the world they live in. Use these moments: Pay attention, ask questions, listen carefully, and then respond as appropriate to the child and the situation.

Responding to their curiosity

"Why is my hair black and Whitney's hair yellow?" . . . "Why does Caleb have braces on his feet?" . . . "Why does Madison have two mommies?" . . . "Teacher, teacher! What makes that man so fat?"

The majority of children's questions about their own and others' various identities and appearance reflect their desire to make sense of the world. They are not necessarily signs of developing prejudice (see the discussion of "pre-prejudice" in chapter 2). However, silencing children ("Shhhh! We don't talk about that!") or avoiding real answers ("It's not important") can lead children to conclude there is something discomforting or fearful about being different. To understand the differences they see around them, children need language and accurate information. They rely on adults for matter-of-fact, developmentally appropriate responses to what puzzles them.

Here are some guidelines suggested by anti-bias educator Eric Hoffman for responding to children's curiosity:

● Just listen—Stay calm and interested. Don't make assumptions or judgments about the child.

● Figure out what the child wants to know—It may not be what the question appears to be on the surface.

● Listen for feelings behind the words—Does the question reflect mere curiosity or also discomfort of some kind? (If the latter, see the next section about pre-prejudice.)

● Answer matter-of-factly and simply—Use language appropriate to the child's developmental understanding.

● Always respond—If you do not know what to say, explain that you want to answer but must first think about what to say. Get back to the child with your response by the next day.

● Follow up—Decide whether a particular child's question warrants follow-up activities with all the children. One way to help you decide is to informally ask the rest of the children about their ideas in regards to the initial child's question. (See the section "Curriculum Planning, Including Persona Dolls" later in this chapter.)

Responding to pre-prejudice and discriminatory behavior

More than mere curiosity, sometimes children's questions, comments, or behaviors indicate an underlying stereotyped idea, discomfort, or rejection about human differences. Even if young children are making fun of a specific identity by repeating words or ideas they have heard from others without knowing what they fully mean, such language exploration still is pre-prejudice because it has the potential to turn into real prejudice.

Like their simple questions, these incidents are teachable moments for anti-bias education. But they almost always require more than a simple answer. Here's one example (you will find others throughout chapters 5 through 11) from teacher Eric Hoffman, who overheard four 4-year-olds talking and giggling and repeating a jingle that made fun of Chinese people. Although he was pretty sure their interest was in the silly sounds and their pleasure in playing together, he felt it was important to intervene:

"I hear you saying a rhyme that makes you laugh," I said. They started to repeat the words, but I stopped them. "Do you know what the word *Chinese* means?" They all shook their heads. I explained that it referred to "people who are Chinese" and that a Chinese person would be insulted by the jingle. They were taken aback. . . . I explained about Asia and China, but I could see that my geography lesson was beyond their comprehension.

Goals for the Classroom

To create an anti-bias learning community in which . . .

● Teachers will consistently interact with children in emotionally supportive, developmentally appropriate ways, including addressing identity, capacity, and bias. (ABE Goal 1)

● Families will feel welcome; be visible, respected, and informed; and contribute to classroom anti-bias activities. (ABE Goals 1 & 2)

● The physical learning environment will reflect the rich diversity of human beings, including through visual images and in all learning materials. (ABE Goal 2)

● Teachers will include anti-bias perspectives and strategies in all curriculum planning and approaches. (ABE Goals 3 & 4)

Then I added, "It looks like you're not trying to hurt anybody's feelings. So let's think of some rhymes that won't upset anyone." We came up with a great list of ridiculous rhymes that left them rolling on the floor with laughter. (Adapted from Derman-Sparks & Ramsey 2006, 119–20)

As Hoffman observes, whether a teachable moment arises from children's direct questions or more indirectly, as it did in this vignette, talking to young children about fairness and unfairness means taking abstract ideas about how the world works and translating them into concrete, "child-size" language. Says Hoffman, "That takes practice! Do not be discouraged if your first attempts do not work well. Children want to know more about diversity, unfairness, and how to make an unfair situation fair. They will give you plenty of opportunities to try again."

The teacher in the vignette above got another opportunity with the children in his classroom:

I felt good about how I handled the situation until later in the day, when I heard one of the children say to another, "You shouldn't say *Chinese*. That's a bad word." [I decided to use the persona dolls to explore the issue in greater depth.] I had one of the dolls talk about her loving Chinese family, and how much she hated being made fun of for her physical differences. The doll talked about how wonderful her family was and how much her feelings were hurt when people made fun of the way they looked. That opened the door for many classroom discussions about ethnic labels, places in the world, ancestors, and how much it hurts to have someone make fun of the way you look, speak, or act. (Adapted from Derman-Sparks & Ramsey 2006, 120–21)

Indicators of children's negative ideas about a particular human difference come in various forms. Say a child in your class excludes certain classmates from play because they don't speak English well, or insists to a peer, "You cannot have two daddies!" or makes a negative comment to a new child who comes to school wearing old or soiled clothes. What should you say and do?

First, it is essential to respond quickly and clearly. Ignoring comments and actions that indicate pre-prejudice gives the child permission to attack another's identity, and it leaves all children feeling unsafe in your classroom.

Second, follow through with the children involved—and often also with the rest of your group. In these situations, you want to teach children to respect and appreciate differences, to resist stereotypes and bias, and to stand up for themselves and for others against hurtful and unfair treatment.

Handling incidents of pre-prejudice

Here are some more strategies from Eric Hoffman:

● Stay calm.

● State what you observed—Putting what you see and hear into words helps everyone get a clearer sense of what the problem is without making anyone feel shamed or humiliated.

● Set limits—Firmly, yet calmly, remind the rejecting child that it is not okay to make fun of or to exclude others because of who they are. It is important that you set clear and firm limits anytime someone is being hurt physically or emotionally.

● Explore feelings—Provide emotional support to *both* children. Let the injured child know that she is wonderful in your eyes. Treat the rejecting child caringly, too, showing clearly that the problem is the behavior, not the child. Encourage *both* children to feel safe and express their feelings fully, which will help them calm down enough to think clearly and understand what has just happened. Listen carefully; what they say can guide you to underlying needs, questions, and desires.

● Go beyond no; try to figure out what underlies the rejecting child's behavior—Children do not learn much when they hear only *no*. Behind every child's inappropriate behavior is a feeling, question, or desire that deserves attention. Perhaps the child was looking for a way to meet her own needs (e.g., she wanted to be the doctor in dramatic play, she didn't want to share her best friend's attention) or ways to express frustration and anger (e.g., the other child took the truck she wanted to use). Or she may be expressing real feelings of discomfort, anxiety with a new person, or biases learned at home. Think about what might be motivating the behavior you are seeing, and try to put it into words. Then help her figure out how to get what she wants, but in positive ways. She will gradually come to see you as a valuable ally in her quest to meet her needs, including the need to figure out how the world works.

● Take action that respects children's developmental understanding and their culture's interaction style—Conflict-resolution methods are one way to do this (e.g., "Let's figure out what is happening"). However, that approach may not be appropriate for all children. For example, some might not feel okay about expressing their feelings. In that case, after your initial intervention of setting limits, you could invite the rejected child to play a game and then invite the rejecting child to join in. A follow-up approach might be to tell a persona doll story with a similar plot, engaging the children in talking about their feelings and what other dolls could do to help. (See the section "Curriculum Planning, Including Persona Dolls" later in this chapter for more.)

● Respect children's learning process—No one-time comment or intervention teaches anyone a new way of thinking. By itself, talk rarely changes beliefs. Children construct a positive view of human similarities and differences through many concrete experiences. Interacting with real people has the biggest impact, but useful experiences can also come through books and other media. Unlike adults, who often cling to their beliefs even in the face of contradictory evidence, young children will change their ideas when they discover better information. Despite this, the activities and conversations you start today may not have an impact for weeks.

Responding to patterns of discomfort or bias

Sometimes an expression of bias or discomfort is a passing thing, a brief moment when a child lacks appropriate language to express his or her ideas or is "figuring it out." If, however, you observe a *pattern* of behavior that indicates a child has passed beyond expressions of pre-prejudice to actually expressing negative opinions about any aspect of others' identities, it is important that you act. For example, even after you have intervened using the strategies discussed above, perhaps the child persists in refusing to play with a peer because "his skin is dark," or even escalates the behavior by telling other children not to play with him. Again, what should you do?

Talk with other staff

Your first step is to confirm that a pattern exists. To check your perceptions, talk with other staff. Tell them what you have observed and ask whether they have seen similar examples. If they have, together identify the contexts in which the child's behavior typically occurs. Identify what further information you need from the child (if possible) and from the child's family to get a picture of what factors might be triggering the behavior. In addition, carefully assess whether your classroom environment or curriculum might be reinforcing the prejudice, however unintentionally. For example, have you intervened with the child but not followed up with any class activities to explore children's ideas and feelings about skin color? (See chapter 6 for ideas about racial identity activities.)

Keep in mind that a child's discomfort or bias may have a variety of underlying sources, such as influences of media or peers, a dynamic in your program, wanting exclusive play with a particular child, simple fatigue, or beliefs taught in the child's family. Any of these influences may be interacting together and/or with the child's own developmental understanding.

Conference with the family

When there is an isolated incident (e.g., a child says, "Girls can't play on the climbing structure"), it is useful to mention it to the family during informal check-ins and conversations. Let them know how you handled the incident, and see whether the family has any information to help you think about their child.

When a *pattern* of incidents appears, however, it is essential that you plan a family-teacher conference. The goal for this longer meeting is to collaborate with the family to figure out how to promote the child's own positive identity and his or her capacity for interacting with others across various kinds of diversity in nonprejudiced, respectful ways.

● Schedule the conference at a time and place that makes it convenient for the family to attend.

● Always begin by letting them know how much you like their child and that you appreciate that they agreed to talk with you.

● Share your observations and concerns about the child; be specific, providing anecdotal data. Explain the reasons for your concern.

● Ask the family to share their observations about the child's behavior regarding the aspect(s) of diversity under discussion. If they have seen the same pattern, how did they respond? How do they feel about the child's behavior?

● What do they think might be influencing the behavior? What do they think about their child's experiences in your program? What stressful situations are going on in the child's life? Does the child get opportunities to interact with people who are different in the aspect(s) of diversity under discussion? What attitudes does the child hear from close family members? What does the child watch on television? What books and toys does the child have at home?

● Discuss the methods you are using (or plan to use) at school with their child to work on the issue. Find out whether the family members feel any of your ideas are inappropriate—either for their child or for them. Try to find strategies agreeable to everyone.

● Together develop strategies for intervention at home. Help the family decide what they will say when their child behaves in a biased way. Encourage making friends with children of different backgrounds.

Encourage additional ways to expand the child's experience of diversity, such as community activities and books that depict difference of various kinds. Encourage the family to carefully select TV shows, then watch with the child, reinforcing "fair" or "true" images and pointing out "unfair" and "untrue" images.

Support the targeted child

If a child's biased comments or behavior had a specific target, be sure to also work with the targeted child. Do not assume that the targeted child is unaffected, even if she is not obviously upset. If you want to address the issue with classroom follow-up activities, be sure to ask the targeted child's permission, as the teacher in this example did:

> Ben and Brandon, both 5-year-olds, are working on a table activity. "You act like a baby," Brandon angrily says. Their teacher intervenes. She puts her arm around Ben and asks Brandon why he feels that way. "He doesn't talk right and he scribbles and he doesn't even know how to write his name," replies Brandon.
>
> Turning to Ben, the teacher asks him, "Do you like that Brandon calls you a baby?" Ben shakes his head and says no. "Benjamin isn't a baby, Brandon. He is 5 years old, just like you, and can do many things. What have you seen him do?" Brandon thinks a moment: "He can ride a bike and play ball." "Yes," agrees the teacher, "and he can run and climb. Benjamin also can't do some things yet that you can do. He will be able to talk more clearly and draw and learn to write his name, but it will take him longer. Remember how long it took you to learn how to ride the two-wheel bike? You didn't like it when other children teased you. Benjamin needs a lot of time to learn, and I expect you to be a good friend to him."
>
> Later, the teacher sits down with Ben and asks him whether it is okay for her to tell the children a story about Racquel, the persona doll who uses a wheelchair and is learning how to write letters and numbers. Ben says yes. He sits next to the teacher when she tells the story. At the part where another doll, Carolyn, tells Racquel that "she is a baby," the teacher asks the children how they think Racquel feels and how her doll "classmates" could support her. The children have lots to tell: "She would feel bad." . . . "She would be angry with Carolyn." . . . "I wouldn't like it." . . . "They should tell Racquel that they like to play with her." . . . "They can tell Carolyn that Racquel is not a baby." The teacher affirms their ideas. Ben, looking sad at the beginning of the story, begins to smile and nod his head in agreement with his classmates' ideas.

It is as important to talk with the family of the child on the receiving end of biased behavior as it is to talk with the rejecting child's family. Explain what you have done to support their child's self-esteem. Describe how you handled the incident; do not blow it up bigger than it was or trivialize it. Be sure the family knows you have met with the other child's family, too. Ask the family how they teach their child to deal with prejudice. If they want your suggestions for how to follow up at home, come up with some ideas together. Assure them you will keep them informed in the coming weeks . . . then do so!

Responding to negative self-identity

What if the pattern of behavior indicates that a child has negative feelings about an aspect of his own identity? Again, it is essential to act. If the child is willing and able to talk with you about his feelings, try to find out what might be causing them. But keep in mind that most young children are unable to give reasons for how they feel. As before:

● Check your perception—Talk with other staff to find out their observations about the child's feeling about himself.

● Speak with the family—Describe your observations, focusing on the child's behavior, not analyzing or judging. For example, "I am seeing some signs that Timothy may be struggling with how he feels about himself. I would like to meet with you to discuss this further."

● Set up a family-teacher conference—Ask whether anyone in the family has noticed similar behavior at home. This is very important, because if they haven't, dynamics at school may be the source of the problem. Find out what and how his family is teaching him about the aspect(s) of identity under discussion.

● Make a plan—Depending on what you and the family have observed, try to figure out together what might underlie the problem. Plan what you can do at school and the family can do at home to build the child's self-awareness and self-esteem.

Positive relationships with and among families

Comprehensive approaches that integrate families as valuable and indispensable partners in the learning community are part of early childhood education's professional vision and responsibility. NAEYC's position statement on developmentally appropriate practice (2009, 23) explains that: "Practitioners work in collaborative partnerships with families, establishing and maintaining regular, frequent two-way communication with them. . . . [They] involve families as a source of information about the child . . . and engage them in the planning for their child. . . . Mutual respect, cooperation, [and] shared responsibility" inform these family-teacher relationships.

Building positive partnerships with families rests on our willingness to recognize families' areas of expertise. These include a family's expectations and hopes for their child, childrearing strategies, guidance methods, daily life rituals, language, and other aspects of their home culture. Educator and family advocate Lisa Lee explains,

> Families honor us with the care of their children. When I think of my anti-bias work, I go beyond the activities to the relationships. I recall the *popos* (grandmothers) of the children, enjoying sitting in the play yard and talking to the teachers in Chinese while their grandchildren played. I remember the father who came to school each year, after working an early morning shift at a restaurant, to help cook our Lunar New Year luncheon.
>
> What I learned from these relationships resulted in a shift in my perception of my role. Where once I benevolently helped families, who were appreciative in turn, I came to realize that I needed those families as much as they needed me. Where once I advocated on behalf of families, anti-bias work became about advocating together on things we both cared about on behalf of the children we cared so much about. In the end, what we did specifically together paled in comparison with how we were together as a community.
>
> Instead of seeing "deficits" and cultural differences as the problem, teachers who are allies appreciate the strengths and gifts that families bring to the learning experience. When we bring depth to implementing an anti-bias approach, we uphold their trust.

Yet, families too often are a neglected resource because teachers are not sure how to approach them. Some teachers may think it is impolite to ask families about their home life. Some may even discount information from families because they believe their own professional knowledge about development is more important. Sometimes teachers' personal experiences of school-family relations, both in their childhoods and as parents themselves, influence their ideas and comfort levels about the "right way" to connect with families.

Because strong family-teacher relationships are the foundation for an anti-bias education partnership, learning how to build one with each child's family is critical. Following in the next section are some key strategies for this work (for more good ideas, see Keyser 2006).

Stop & Think: What did you learn about school and family?

■ What are your earliest memories about how your family and your teachers related? Did anyone in your family visit school? Who? Why? What was that like for you?

■ What did you learn about teacher authority? Were you taught "the teacher is always right"? Did you ever talk to your family about troubles at school? If so, what was their reaction?

■ How did your school reflect or ignore your family's values, beliefs, and structure? How did you feel about that?

■ How have your early experiences shaped any assumptions you make today about family-teacher relationships?

Creating a secure and supportive environment for all families

Ensuring that every family feels welcome and comfortable creates a crucial foundation for mutually respectful relationships. It is an essential first step in an anti-bias classroom. As families develop trust that you care about and believe in their child, they come to feel that they, too, "belong" in your early childhood program. There are many ways to achieve this—not necessarily with new techniques, but by applying new context to old techniques.

● Have a school/family handbook—Make sure your school/family handbook clearly states the program's inclusive approach to all families. Carefully read all of the text to catch any references (in illustrations, anecdotes, and examples) that appear to acknowledge some kinds of family structures and not others (e.g., "Dear Parents" can imply that every family has two parents in the home). As needed, develop additional handbooks about your program in languages other than English. Use photos to show key ideas about your philosophy and the various activities in your program. Ask for help from family and community members to simply and briefly explain each photograph.

● Do an intake interview—At intake interviews, ask participants to describe their families, including extended family members and "significant others," so that you will know who is important to the child. Keep in mind that families will vary in how much information they choose to disclose to you at the beginning of the school year. Some information may feel too personal, such as their views about different aspects of diversity. Other information may feel unsafe to share. For example, a family may be homeless, living in a shelter or car, and may not want the teacher to know that they do not have a "permanent" address. An undocumented immigrant family may be fearful of deportation if the school has too much information about them. Parents in a gay/lesbian-headed family may not want to disclose their sexual orientation because they risk losing their jobs if they are open. If a family chooses not to answer a specific question, let it go for the time being. If you believe the information is essential to effectively teaching their child, return to it at another time after you have built up a relationship with the family. Be sure to have a bilingual staff member or interpreter present as needed.

● Create an equitable enrollment form—On enrollment forms, replace the usual labels *Mother* and *Father* with more open-ended and inclusive ones such as *Parent/Parents, Co-Parents, Guardians, Other Family Members, Significant Others,* or simply *Family*. Find out how the various families in your program refer to their immediate and extended members. Use parents' and children's correct surnames; they may not share the same ones.

● Send a welcome letter—Distribute a welcoming letter to new families communicating a philosophy of inclusion and respect for diversity (see the box "Family Welcome Letter" for an example). Be sure the letter is in all the home languages of your families. You may need help from the local community to do this, but most people and organizations addressing second-language issues are glad to assist.

● Provide a resource library—Create an inclusive family library of resources and referral materials: books, articles, and listings of support services and community advocacy organizations for all kinds of families and family circumstances. If families speak languages other than English, make sure there are materials in their languages.

● Make the classroom accessible—Evaluate whether your classroom is accessible to people with disabilities. Can a family member who uses a wheelchair come for a visit or a conference? Do you know of someone who can act as an American Sign Language translator?

● Arrange the physical environment thoughtfully—Create a comfortable space where families can talk with one another or with you. Have water, coffee, tea, juice, and simple snacks regularly available.

Build common ground

As a teacher, you already share the most important common ground with families—caring about their child. Wanting the best for the child underlies each person's beliefs about how to foster development and learning best. Take time to build this common ground

---

Family Welcome Letter

Dear Family,

   We want to welcome your family as the newest members of our early childhood community. Our philosophy is one that places a great deal of value on center/family partnerships. As a staff, we adhere to the following definition of family (borrowed from the Boston Children's Museum Exhibit on Family Diversity):

FAMILIES

We may be related at birth, adoption, or invitation.
We may belong to the same race or we may be of different races.
We may look like each other or different from each other.
The important thing is, we belong to each other.
We care for each other.
We agree, disagree, love, fight, and work together.
We belong to each other.

Please share your family with us so that we can include, validate, and celebrate each child's familial relationships as part of our day-to-day interactions with your child and all of our children. We welcome you all and look forward to developing a rich and supportive relationship with you and your child.

[names of staff]

Source: Aimee Gelnaw. Used with permission.

---

with each family. One way to show your interest is to tell families frequently about the progress and talents you see in their child, not just talking to them when an issue arises.

   Find ways to talk regularly with each family. Take time to find out what approach works best with each family. Both you and the families will benefit from regular one-on-one time. Make sure you talk about positive behaviors and successes and not just problems the child may have.

● At pickup/drop-off—Hold frequent, short, informal chats at the beginning and end of the school day. Before talking about their child, some families will want to engage in small talk, so teachers and family members get to know a little about each other as adults; others will want to go right to that topic. Some programs arrange staffing so that more than one teacher is on hand when children arrive. One teacher can focus on welcoming the child into the classroom and the other can focus on talking to each family—sharing details about what the child is doing at school and hearing what the child is doing at home.

● By phone/email—Try to get around to all of your families every two weeks through phone conversations or email. For families who can't communicate using these methods (e.g., a homeless family who doesn't have access to either) or do not feel comfortable with these methods (e.g., a family for whom English is difficult), intentionally make time for face-to-face conversation at drop-off or pickup times.

● Through a daily log—Keep a daily class log. Some families enjoy reading short anecdotes and summaries of their child's day.

● Through family-teacher conferences—Invite all the people involved in parenting a child to come to family-teacher conferences and participate in school. Encourage input and perspectives from each person involved. Sometimes teachers (often without realizing it) focus only on the mother rather than both parents, or they focus on whichever person they consider to be the "real" parent.

● In their home language—Being able to talk with families whose home languages you do not speak may take considerable work. There is, however, always a way, and families will appreciate your efforts. Some strategies include hiring staff members who speak those languages, asking another family member who speaks English to translate (it's usually best not to ask a child to interpret), recruiting community volunteers, or learning a second language yourself.

In the end, all these efforts pay off tenfold. Remember that the more frequently you can chat with each family, even for a brief time, the more your relationship will grow and the deeper the questions you can ask about family culture and life will become.

Pay attention to power dynamics

It is often difficult for educators to recognize that they have a position of a power in their relationships with families. Because of our role as teachers, families see us as being in a position to judge their child and their parenting. Also, parents bring to the classroom their own histories with school and professionals, which at times may add to their fears about teachers' attitudes.

In many cultures, a teacher is someone to be respected and obeyed. Some families wouldn't consider even raising issues of concern, much less challenging a school policy or a teacher's practice. This means that the responsibility for creating genuine dialogue lies with us. It is our job to listen and learn as well as talk, and to initiate the search for common ground and solutions to specific differences.

Collaborating with families

To form a caring learning community where all children can learn and thrive means forging a working partnership based on what families wish for their child and what you believe is important for children.

Stop & Think: What is your ideal for the family-teacher relationship?

■ How do you want children to feel about their family's connection to you and your program?

■ What worries you most about gathering information from families about their home cultures? What would help you overcome your concerns?

■ What strengths do you have for connecting and building partnerships with families? What traits might stand in your way? Who could help you overcome these obstacles?

■ How might you benefit from having mutually respectful relationships with the families in your program?

Promoting children's identity and anti-bias attitude development

The more families become part of a program of anti-bias education, the more their children are likely to develop anti-bias identity, knowledge, empathy, and skills.

● **Learn about each family's desires for their child's identity development.**

After you have begun establishing a relationship with each family, begin to ask about what and how they teach their child about aspects of his or her identities (racial, ethnic/cultural, gender, religious, or otherwise)—and what terms are used at home to describe these identities. Don't be surprised if some family members haven't given much thought to these issues or are not comfortable with or sure of the value of talking about them.

As the year progresses, another issue to explore with families is how they respond to their child's biased remarks or behaviors. Convey that you are not judging their child or them but are interested in helping the child develop more open ways of thinking.

Lots of small conversations bring more information than a structured interview will, and both tend to work better than a written questionnaire, which typically provides limited information—if a family responds at all. Inviting all the families to meet as a group is a way to open up discussion about their ideas and feelings about children's identities and attitudes toward others. Ask the group, "What do you want your child to know about who he is and about who his family is?" and "What do you want your child to know about people who are different from your family?" In a group discussion, people have the opportunity to hear different perceptions and may be more willing to communicate their own.

Families' ideas about some aspects of their children's identities may not agree with your understanding of identity development. Some prefer teaching about identity to happen only at home. Some families may believe that preschoolers are too young for such learning. Some may believe that the best way to raise an unbiased child is never to discuss human differences. Some White families have never developed language for their own racial identity and may want their child to think of herself only as "human." Some families of color may be skeptical that White teachers will use information from them in supportive, respectful ways.

Do not get discouraged. Remember that it takes a while to learn all the perspectives of families in your program.

● Approach differences in perspective as opportunities to build partnerships.

As you introduce and work with families on anti-bias topics, you may encounter a range of responses. Many families agree with or are open to the goals of anti-bias work. Others are not sure but are willing to learn. Some disagree, at least in some areas. Even among families who fully support anti-bias education, differences may arise over a specific topic or strategy. How you respond and whether you respect the disagreement are more important than the solution at which you arrive. If you see differences as opportunities for all parties to learn and grow, then you will be able to initiate productive conversations and find workable resolutions of differences.

Listening carefully to families' concerns, showing genuine interest in them and their dreams for their child, and respecting their perspective opened the door to finding a productive solution in this example:

> At Rosie's family child care home, the older boys are playing too roughly with the babies and toddlers. She begins a "Taking Care of Babies" curriculum, which includes a visit from a father who diapers his infant son and feeds him a bottle, reading books such as *William's Doll*, and opportunities for the children to bathe dolls. When Robbie's dad arrives to pick him up, he is very upset to see Robbie cradling a naked doll. His father is adamant, "No son of mine is going to play with dolls!"
>
> Rosie responds that she will honor his request, but that she needs to better understand why so that she and the family are working together. Robbie's dad reluctantly agrees to come back and meet with her. At the conference, Rosie listens carefully as he shares that his own dad roughed him up as a child for "not being tough enough" when he was bullied at school. He is very fearful that Robbie might be similarly bullied. After much listening on Rosie's part, Robbie's dad comes to feel that she really understands how much he loves his son and how much he wants to protect him.
>
> At this point, Rosie explains her curricular objec-

tives: to teach Robbie to play more gently with the little ones and help prepare him to become a good dad someday—goals the father agrees he can support. With some mutual understanding and trust established, the two agree that it is okay if Robbie cuddles and pretend feeds stuffed animals instead of dolls. This is not the entire solution Rosie wanted, but it is, she feels, a step in the right direction. And she is sure that supporting Robbie's dad as a good father is even more important than following the specific curriculum she had planned.

● Face up to disagreements.

Even within families there are often disagreements about the right way to care for children and about what children should (and shouldn't) be learning. The potential for disagreement grows as children are cared for outside their family, especially if they live in a diverse society (as most societies are!). All over the world, early childhood professionals work at bridging the disagreements between their views and those of families.

Dutch anti-bias educator and author Fuusje deGraff (2006) has written about how disagreements between teachers and families should be about negotiating and comprising. To find a solution, teachers first must recognize that they are dealing with a clash of values, not "deviating" behavior that needs adjustment. Teachers must consider the other person as an equal partner, without whom it is impossible to find an effective solution. They must also believe that any solution has to be mutual, with both parties possibly having to compromise. It is also vital to remember that a negotiation is an interaction during which *both* people exchange ideas to find common ground that does not violate fundamental values of either party.

This process takes place in three phases. The first phase requires figuring out your context (perspective, values, beliefs, experiences) in the situation. The second is learning these from the other person; deGraff advises teachers to stay open and curious, and not to rush the process. The last phase of dealing productively with clashes (conflicts) is finding a mutually satisfying solution. Rather than being a "quick fix," a reflection method takes time to gather needed information and explore solutions. Another great benefit of addressing clashes in this way is learning that there are multiple problem definitions and multiple solutions.

Staff often have to confront their own feelings about individualizing solutions based on family desires (e.g., respecting religious food restrictions). Teachers sometimes fear that having a different rule for one child in the group will lead to other problems, such as teasing or rejection from classmates.

Another common fear is that all the children will want to do the same thing. However, it is not hard to get preschoolers to accept such individualization. If it is common practice to talk about, empathize with, and respect similarities and differences, meeting the specific needs of each child becomes part of the classroom culture. Teachers can say, "This is what Jamal's family wants. It is one of the ways we are different from one another." Preschoolers tend to be quite open to this—they want to be helpful, too. Accommodating special requests only becomes a problem when children are not offered explanations. Then the practice becomes strange, mysterious, or uncomfortable.

This openness is one of the advantages of an anti-bias approach. When your program's overall message is "We are all the same; we are all different. Our differences are as valuable and interesting as our sameness," then children are open and easy with the idea that different families have different needs for their children.

Getting good at talking freely with families about their child's day-to-day routines makes it a little easier to address differences in perspective and potential conflicts. Keep figuring out what you are willing to change and what you are not, defining the line between what is workable and what could hurt the child or the program. For example, it is relatively easy and painless to grant a family's request that their child keep his shoes on even though you allow children in your program to take off their shoes. On the other hand, if a parent says, "I don't want my child to be around the Spanish-speaking children," agreeing to the parent's request would violate the basic values of respecting diversity.

What if a family exhibits prejudiced views?
Sometimes teachers must work with a family who request support or accommodation in the classroom for their prejudices toward a specific group. What would you do if (as many teachers have already encountered) a family member tells you . . .

> "I do not want my child sitting next to or playing with any Arab children."

> "I want you to tell Trudy that a lesbian/gay-headed family is not a real family."

> "I don't want my daughter playing with a Black doll. I know she's only 4, but that can lead to interracial dating and marriage later."

> "My children are not to hear stories or songs in Spanish."

> "You'd better make sure that kid with cerebral palsy doesn't get more of your attention than my Antonio."

The easiest (and often most tempting) response is to assert immediately that "In this classroom, we encourage all the children to sit and play with everyone, and we respect all kinds of families. If this is not acceptable to you, then you can decide if you want to take your child to another class/program." While this "bottom line" approach ultimately might be necessary, it is not the way to begin. It prevents your gaining understanding of the specific experiences that underlie the family's position and trying to reach mutually satisfying solutions. It also cuts off the possibility that the family might become more open to diversity. An anti-bias commitment calls on us to respect others enough to open up conversations about bias and prejudiced behavior in ways that optimize the likelihood of sparking positive change.

Instead, invest some time and energy with the family. Find out what factors precipitated that family member's prejudiced stance. Listen carefully and with an open heart. Remember that none of us is free from bias. Each of us needs other people to help us sort through our experiences and identify contradictory attitudes and areas we want to change in ourselves.

Sometimes bias is based on a lack of or incorrect information. Sometimes a negative experience is overgeneralized into bias against a whole group. Sometimes a lack of validation in the person's own life contributes to a strongly held prejudice. Remember also that some people use racism, sexism, ableism, or another "ism" as an outlet for their own frustration, anger, and fear, or as an excuse for greed—and our society often allows them to do so. These factors do not make the bias okay, but recognizing them helps us to see the whole person and not just the biased behavior.

Explain to the family why you think it is so vital to children's healthy development and future life success to develop comfortable and respectful interactions with all kinds of people. Engage the family in exploring their concerns about how anti-bias education may change their child. Remember that this is a dialogue, not a monologue; make sure that family members have ample opportunity to express their views and that you are open to learning from their views, just as you are hoping they will learn from yours.

Talking with a family about their prejudiced views and discriminatory behavior may not always succeed. Some people will not want to talk; some, even after a number of conversations, will hold fast to their original stance. When this is the case, the "bottom line" approach is appropriate: "We will not allow prejudice and discrimination in our classroom.

If this is not acceptable to you, we can help you find another program for your child." Then it is up to the family to make a decision about what they want to do. If it becomes clear that a family cannot stay in the program, it is important that the director help them identify other resources in the community and handle their departure as respectfully as possible.

Connecting families with each other and with the program

Most families want their children to grow up proud of themselves and open to others, unbiased and empowered. It's something even very different kinds of families have in common, along with the desire to be the best parents possible and struggles with childrearing issues. One of the best ways we can serve the children in our programs is to help their families connect with and support one another, thus allowing them to learn about how other families deal with childrearing issues. Anti-bias work is one strong way to make those connections and provide that support.

Support families in talking together

As you become more experienced with anti-bias education, and as families get to know you as an anti-bias educator, activities such as those following become wonderful times of community building that can affect families for many years.

● Family get-togethers and potlucks—Shared meals are wonderful occasions to help families connect, as they share their own experiences with anti-bias issues and what they hope and want for their children. The same Stop & Think questions that you are invited to consider in this book make for meaty, exciting discussions between families and staff.

● Targeted discussions—Small discussion groups focused on specific topics (e.g., biracial families, nonsexist parenting) will attract families who want to learn more about these topics. Each family provides a new perspective, and their discussion builds support for anti-bias parenting. Some family members may be interested in working in the classroom more regularly on particular anti-bias topics. Communicating with families about what is happening in the classroom now and what will be happening in the future keeps family members aware of and interested in anti-bias issues.

● Group activism—Sometimes group activism is the spur that starts anti-bias education in a program. When one group of families rallied together to speak to state legislators about program cuts, it began a whole series of parent discussions about what they wanted to have happen for their children. Sometimes, after staff have been building anti-bias family partnerships, community projects or other activist efforts are the result.

Another group of families decided to meet with the various video stores in their neighborhood to present an alternative list of quality children's videos that did not support the racist, sexist, and classist stereotypes so common in children's media. In another center, families traveled by train (with their children and the teachers) to the state capitol to meet with their legislator about the importance of bilingual education for both native English speakers and English language learners. In a fourth center, families took an interest in the national campaign to limit advertising of certain products exploiting popular TV characters during children's programming.

Keep families in the center of your curriculum

When we reach out to families to include them in every aspect of our program, families feel that they are teachers' true partners. Then children receive the wonderful benefit of seeing both their home and their early childhood program as equally welcoming, safe, and enriching places.

● Create spaces in the classroom for families to place personal photos, objects, and the like—Some teachers create a family wall. Each family adds information to the wall about various aspects of their lives (e.g., birth or wedding announcements, photos of themselves at work or play, maps showing a family's place of origin). Teachers can suggest topics and encourage family members to write on the wall.

● Keep families informed about your anti-bias activities and what their child says or does—Send home children's work with an enclosed letter explaining the purpose of the activity. Let families know about their child's anti-bias learning though informal conversations, a daily class log, or newsletters. Tailor your writing to the style, vocabulary, and languages of your particular group.

● Invite families to participate in the classroom— Chapters 5 through 11 suggest ideas for many activities in specific areas of diversity. Family members can read to children in languages other than English and tell stories about special family members and family experiences related to their culture and/or movements for social justice. The box "Anti-Bias Homework for Families" explains another way to include your families in your program.

Anti-Bias Homework for Families
by Eric Hoffman

Once a month, my staff and I send home a fun, voluntary activity for children and their families to work on. We use the results to create classroom bulletin boards and table displays, circle time presentations, charts, and books. Because most of the parents in my program are college students (I work at a community college child care center), their children feel very grown up doing what they see their parents doing every night—*homework*.

While my family homework topics have covered all areas of the curriculum, we designed many of the assignments to stimulate discussion about how the children and their families are the same and how they are different. Here are some examples:

• "What are your family's three favorite foods?"—we made a recipe book from the responses

• "Bring in something red that represents your family"—we set up a color display table that changed color every week

• "Draw a family portrait"—children took home markers, then we created a bulletin board display of the portraits

• "Find a book in our lending library that your family loves to read, take it home, and do a family book report"—some families drew pictures, some took dictation from the child, and one family created a skit for circle time! We took a picture of each family holding their book and posted the pictures in the reading area along with the book reports

• "Write about a time when someone in the family saw something that was unfair and helped make it fair"—we made a very popular book from the responses

• "Ask adults in your family to share answers to the following questions: What games did you like to play when you were young? What are your earliest memories of school? Tell us about a mistake you made and how you corrected it"—we made more books from these questions!

Along the way we made a few mistakes in our assignments. When we asked for photographs of each family's front door, it brought up issues of economic competition for several parents, and it angered a family who had been homeless. An assignment about pets left out several children who didn't have any and was upsetting to a family whose child couldn't have a pet because of his sister's allergies.

However, these mistakes proved valuable, as well, because they stimulated important discussions among the adults about family differences and bias that were concrete and personal. Each time, we thanked the families who objected and told them they had opened our eyes to important issues.

Source: Adapted from L. Derman-Sparks & P. Ramsey, *What If All the Kids Are White?* (New York: Teachers College Press, 2006), 58–59. Used with permission.

The visual and material environment

The toys, materials, and equipment you put out for children; the posters, pictures, and art objects you hang on the wall; and the types of furniture and how you arrange them all influence what children learn. An environment rich in anti-bias materials invites exploration and discovery and supports children's play and conversations in both emergent and planned activities. It alerts children to which issues and people the teacher thinks are important and unimportant. What children do *not* see in the classroom teaches children as much as what they do see.

An anti-bias environment is also culturally consistent for the children and families it currently serves. In other words, anyone who enters your classroom can tell immediately who is in your program at that time (see the box "Starting with Who Is"). The look and sounds of the room reflect the family cultures and daily lives of those children. Because the physical environment begins with who children are, each early childhood classroom will have its own unique look.

(Chapter 5 provides a further discussion of making your program culturally consistent for the children and families it serves.)

In addition to seeing themselves in their learning environment, children also need materials that honor diversity both within and beyond their own identity groups. This includes learning materials that accurately and nonstereotypically reflect:

● all the children, families, and staff in your program in their daily lives

● other children and families similar to those in your program in their daily lives

● children and adults from the various racial and ethnic identity groups in your community

● families from a range of economic groups performing all types of work (e.g., working class, professionals; work in the home, work outside of the home)

● people with disabilities of various backgrounds working, playing, spending time with their family

● diverse family structures

┌───┐

Starting with Who Is

by Julie Bisson

Saturate the classroom environment with the children, families, and staff who currently make up your program. Stand in the doorway and imagine that you are each one of the children:

• Do I feel comfortable here? Does this place remind me enough of my home and my community that I feel I belong here and will be cared for and safe?

• Do I see children and adults who look like me represented in the learning materials and room decorations?

• Do any of the teachers speak my home language?

• Do I see reflections of my family structure, daily life, and neighborhood in the learning materials?

• Are there props provided that would enable me to act out a story that happened in my own home or community? Art materials in my skin tone? Many books with main characters whose lives are similar to mine?

• Do I hear any of the music that I hear at home?

• Do snacks and meals include foods I eat at home?

● images of people, past and present, who have enhanced the quality of life and worked for social justice in the children's own communities and in the larger society

In programs that serve the children whose lives are too often made invisible by the dominant culture (children of color, children from poor families, etc.), plentiful images of themselves, their families, and their communities—in all of their diversity—help to counter the harm of invisibility. A useful rule of thumb is that more than half of the materials in the environment should reflect the identities of the specific children in that classroom. In programs primarily serving White children, a culturally consistent environment also reflects the children's real lives, families, and communities.

Then, once you feel confident that all currently enrolled children and families are visible in all parts of your learning environment, the next step is to look at which other people, groups, and families from the larger society are missing and then bring in more diversity. In an all-White program, for example, be sure to go beyond traditional early childhood materials, which mainly reflect middle-class and professional, suburban, White people. However unintentional, using materials that primarily reflect this one particular group of people teaches children from the dominant culture that they are indeed the norm and implies that others are marginal or "less than,"

and makes invisible the lives of children from certain groups within the White population, such as low-income, working-class, and rural families.

To really "see" your own program, use the form "Checklist for Assessing the Visual Material Environment" provided after the epilogue. This tool will significantly help you focus on what it is you are doing now and where you want to go with your classroom setup. It would be beneficial to go over this sheet with other staff, but whether you do so alone or in a group, we encourage you to go over the list once a year.

Selecting and making learning materials

Creating and assessing your learning environment is an ongoing process. Your materials will need to change over time to reflect each new group of children and families. It is useful to make a wish list with two columns, one titled "To buy or get donated" and the other "To make or revise." Prioritize your list and work with families and other staff to get what you need. Often families will be willing to help. Grandparents sometimes can donate money or goods. Some families in your program probably work in places that have local giving plans. Often local merchants will donate (particularly toward buying books). Small donations are often easier to get than large grants, and most people in a community care about what is happening to young children and will support you to create a rich learning environment for them.

Purchasing new materials

Since the 1989 publication of *Anti-Bias Curriculum* (the first edition of the current book), many more national and some local education supplies companies now produce useful materials that reflect and support exploring diversity. Posters, children's books, skin tone art colors, diverse people figurines, puzzles, and music are all available, depending on your budget. Consider purchasing flexible, open-ended materials that you can use in many ways. For example, one of the best tools you can have for anti-bias work is a camera, which will permit you to make books, posters, classroom bulletin boards, and learning materials specific to the families and children in your program. Having access to a computer with a color printer allows you to create several types of materials designed for your specific group of families. This may be an item for which families would be willing and able to fundraise for your program.

When purchasing materials, it is necessary to use your critical-thinking lens and evaluate each object carefully. If you are not a member of the identity group for which you are selecting materials, ask someone who *is* to help you decide whether the materials are appropriate. Select materials to show the diversity that can exist *within* groups. In other words, do not choose just *one* picture, doll, object, or book to represent any particular group or way of life. Even if the item you select is excellent in itself, having only one risks teaching or reinforcing overgeneralizations and stereotypical thinking.

Here are some other general cautions to consider when purchasing new materials:

● Be sure your images counter stereotypes—don't always show boys playing outside, girls playing inside, African Americans as athletes, White people working as professionals, and so forth.

● Be sure your images reflect both similarities and differences *within* every group as well as *between* groups.

● Be sure that families who differ from the majority in your class are just as visible.

● Avoid the pitfalls of "tourist curriculum"—*tokenism, trivializing, misinforming/misrepresenting,* and *stereotyping* (discussed in the section "Curriculum Planning, Including Persona Dolls" later in this chapter).

● Do not confuse or substitute images and information about another country's culture for American culture—for example, images of a Japanese child's life and a Japanese American child's are not equivalent.

● Do not show only traditional, ritual, or historical images of a group—this happens frequently with Native Americans, for example.

● Do not show images that depict misinformation or stereotypes about a group—to avoid this, you may have to check with families from that particular group.

● Do not show images that depict people unrealistically, with exaggerated features that make them look like caricatures—when in doubt, buy something else.

Once you have a clear sense of what you are looking for, keep an eye out wherever you are. Regularly check out local toy and book stores as well as advocacy organizations in your own city for diversity and social justice materials. (Also do this elsewhere when you travel.) Check out the increasing resources available online. Several small companies with websites, as well as organizations and associations (e.g., NAEYC, National Black Child Development Institute), specialize in diversity and social justice materials appropriate in programs for young children (For these and others, see the additional resources list posted in the "Anti-Bias" section of the NAEYC website: www.naeyc.org.)

Making materials

To ensure that all children and families in a program are visible in your learning environment, you may need to supplement purchased materials by making your own. It is not always possible to find materials appropriate for a particular group of children. Besides, no commercial product has the power that photographs and images of children's own families do. With ingenuity, patience, resourcefulness, and some help from families and friends, many teachers have created their own remarkable and powerful anti-bias materials, such as the ones listed below—having a wonderful, creative time while doing so!

● Learning games, placemats, bulletin board displays, posters—Photographs of the children and families in your program and of people and places in the children's own neighborhoods make very useful raw materials. Take your own photographs, send cameras home, and ask parents for duplicates of family pictures. (Be sure you get a family's permission to photograph their child and to duplicate and use their images!)

● Books—Using images from home and school to make small, personalized books can be invaluable. Books can focus on a theme ("We All Have Families: Our Families Are Different" . . . "Babies Come in Many Colors"), can be about one family ("Meet Jamal and His Family" . . . "Maria's Abuela Comes to Visit"), or can be about events ("Día de los Muertos in Our Classroom" . . . "We All Made a Garden"). Keep the text simple. Use tag board or other sturdy paper. Cover the front of the book with contact paper. Many school districts or community colleges have resource centers where you can laminate and bind books. Find out how you can access this support.

● Puzzles—Locate someone who knows how to use a jigsaw or will teach you how to use one (e.g., family members, resource centers, small businesses). Mount enlarged (8"x10") photos or accurate pictures clipped from magazines, then cut them into puzzle pieces appropriate to the age of the children.

● Dolls—To supplement purchased dolls, ask for help from family members and friends who can make cloth dolls with different skin colors and shades, hair textures, and eye colors. You can also make dolls with different physical abilities, such as a doll with a wheelchair or leg braces, a hearing aid, or an assistance dog. Make sure each doll's features are realistic and individual, rather than being caricaturized or stereotypical. Also, make sure your dolls with disabilities reflect various racial and ethnic backgrounds.

Repurposing stereotyped materials

Many of the materials that programs and teachers already have are stereotypical or inaccurate in how they portray people. Sometimes when you more closely examine materials, you will find they are actually racist or sexist (e.g., books that portray the Mexican character as lazy, the disabled character as needing rescue). It is better to remove these stereotypical and inaccurate materials from the classroom than to reinforce misinformation. Alternatively, teachers can use the biased materials to initiate a discussion with children about what is fair and what is unfair. That is, such materials should be brought out only for specific teaching purposes, not available for daily use.

When materials teach inaccuracy or stereotypes by omission (e.g., portraying only two-parent families; not including girls in active, adventurous roles), the materials can be supplemented with those that contradict the misinformation. Remember that "Invisibility erases identity and experience. Visibility affirms reality." Be sure that you have more images that contradict stereotypes than those that omit them.

Using children's books in the anti-bias classroom

Good stories capture the heart, mind, and imagination. They entrance and engage children, and let teachers be their most lively and creative selves. They also provide a wonderful, ongoing way for children to learn about diversity and fairness.

Selecting good books

Books are one of the richest resources for helping children meet the anti-bias education goals. Because books are so influential, thoughtful and balanced book selection is essential. The majority of children's books tend to show only dominant culture representations of who people are and how they live. Even stories about animal families usually show the characters living with two parents and in isolation from other animal families!

The first step in building an anti-bias library is to ask yourself: Can all the children in my classroom find themselves in my book collection? . . . Do the books I provide support *every* child's family, racial identity, cultural identity, home language, and so on?

In response to the social justice efforts of many Americans, including early childhood teachers, publishers now pay greater attention to the social diversity of the children and families in their reading audience, and there are many wonderful books that combine fine storytelling, rich language, and beautiful artwork to depict diversity. You can find quality books through several sources. Three good sources of suggestions are www.childpeacebooks.org, www.teachingforchange.org, and the "Anti-Bias" section of NAEYC's website: www.naeyc.org. Local libraries will often help you identify books about specific types of families. Independent bookstores can usually also help you find or order the book you need.

In selecting books, look for interesting stories, a delightful use of language, and images appealing to children. Age-appropriate, lively stories capture their minds (e.g., *Susan Laughs*, by Jeanne Willis and Tony Ross, a funny, warm story about a little girl in a wheelchair). Again, as with other materials, beware of tokenizing, stereotyping, and other tourist curriculum errors. The less experience children have had with a group of people, the more important it is to offer a *variety* of stories about that group to prevent children from forming stereotypes.

Dealing with stereotypes

A *stereotype* is any depiction of a person or group of people that makes them appear less than fully human, unique, or individual or that reinforces misinformation. A book in which a Mexican character is wearing a sombrero perpetrates a stereotype if it keeps him nameless or portrays him as lazy or foolish. If the book portrays him as an interesting, complex person who is doing interesting things, his sombrero becomes merely one type of hat worn in warm climates. A book that portrays little girls in fluffy pink tutus who are focused on "looking pretty" and being giggly perpetuates a stereotype. A book that shows a tutu-wearing girl who is seriously learning ballet and loving it is not stereotyping.

Elizabeti's Doll (by Stephanie Stuve-Bodeen) portrays a young Tanzanian girl as poor, barefooted, and rural—a stereotype about African people. But the book also portrays Elizabeti and her family as loving, thoughtful, creative, and competent. The positive messages prevail, and the bare feet become a true picture of how some people in Africa live. It would be helpful to pair this book with one that shows urban African people, to broaden children's understanding, but *Elizabeti's Doll* is a rich and wonderful story on its own. A good rule of thumb is to ask yourself whether children will make generalizations about the group of people portrayed after viewing the images of the individual characters in the book.

Sometimes a book can work if you change some of the wording, such as shifting *he* to *she* or substituting more accurate terms for hurtful ones (e.g., "Jacey lives in two homes" rather than "Jacey comes from a broken home"). Some wonderful books include just one page where there is a hurtful message, and teachers can simply skip that page or remove it. For example, a charming book about a loving African American family includes a page depicting cousins as "fat and lazy." The staff may decide to glue that page down and continue to use the book.

Sometimes it is useful to keep a book with stereotypes specifically for engaging children's critical thinking. For example, one kindergarten teacher helped children to think about sexism with a book in which the little girl helps her mother cook and clean and the little boy helps his father mow a lawn. She asked the children whether they knew any fathers or brothers who cooked or cleaned and any mothers who mowed lawns. The children decided that the book "didn't really tell the truth" and ended up making their own book about all the things that boys and girls do to help at home.

Curriculum planning, including persona dolls

Curriculum is the sum of all the activities in which children engage, be they child- or teacher-initiated; formal or informal; individual, small or large group. The ideas for anti-bias education curriculum can come from children's questions, interests, and teachable moments; what adults think is important for children to learn; and significant events that occur in the children's communities and the larger world. For example, the wars in Iraq and Afghanistan might prompt a teacher to initiate learning about people who are Muslim because he hears children's comments indicating fear of Muslims ("I don't like ladies with scarves on their heads. They hurt people") or because he knows children are likely to be hearing comments and seeing negative images about Muslims at home or in the media.

Additionally, although some classroom activities are designed specifically with the intention of addressing diversity issues, *any* activity or curriculum approach carries messages about what teachers do and do not value and how they think and feel about human differences.

Making anti-bias themes a part of every curriculum every day

Our understanding of anti-bias issues shapes how we put curriculum together each day. Just about every subject area in the typical early childhood program has possibilities for anti-bias education themes and activities. In particular, themes of self-discovery,

family, and community are more effective and honest when they include explorations of gender, ability, racial identity, culture, and economic class.

Even favorite preschooler themes such as dinosaurs can include anti-bias education, as one child development center in a California community college discovered:

> During an introductory discussion uncovering children's ideas about dinosaurs, one child comments, "Dinosaurs are boys." One teacher then asks the group, "Were some dinosaurs girls?" The children decide that all the dinosaurs were boys because they were so big and strong. The teachers decide to do a unit that explores the differences and similarities among various dinosaurs, discussing how there were girl as well as boy dinosaurs, how some laid eggs and had babies, and some were vegetarian while others were meat eaters.

Every time you plan any curriculum, stop and answer the following important questions:

● What aspect(s) of diversity can be part of this topic?

● How can I use this topic to help children explore and enjoy the theme of "We are all the same; we are all different" in the many areas of diversity?

● What ideas, misconceptions, and stereotypes might children have about this topic?

● How can I use this topic to provide accurate information and counter misconceptions and stereotypes?

● How can I design activities for this topic to include all children, given their differences in culture, family structure, language, racial identity, gender, abilities, and economic class? How can I be sure no one is invisible or unnoticed?

● How can I use this topic to support and strengthen children's innate sense of justice and their capacity to change unfair situations to fair ones?

● What do I need to learn to teach this topic accurately?

Consider attaching these questions to whatever curriculum planning forms you use as a reminder.

Curricular planning approaches

Webbing is an especially useful technique for brainstorming the many possibilities for incorporating identity, diversity, and equity issues into your daily curriculum, regardless of which curricular approach you use. Like a spider web, you begin with a central point and spin connecting vertical and circular threads to create the whole. The beginning point might be a child-initiated teachable moment, a teacher-guided topic, or an event in the children's lives.

You can use webbing to help you name and select anti-bias issues in a variety of planning approaches. Remember to respect children's learning process when planning all materials and activities. Take into account their learning styles, home languages, and the teaching strategies they know from home. Find out what children know, think, and feel about a topic before you plan. Then build further curriculum from there.

Emergent curriculum

If you use an *emergent curriculum model*, planning typically begins with children's questions and teachable moments as they arise. Planning is cyclical rather than linear, as each activity opens up further possibilities. Inviting children to communicate their thoughts (questions, assumptions, opinions) on a specific topic also opens up ideas for activities.

For example, asking children what they know about "Indians" will let you in on what specific misconceptions you want to challenge through the activities you do. You begin your planning by making a webbing chart. Write down the children's various statements and questions about Native Americans in a circle in the middle of the page. Then draw lines from each item and write down possible activities that would address each question or statement. See how these activities might interconnect, and draw lines between them. Decide which activity you will use first and then follow the interconnections to the next, and so on.

Unit or theme

If you use a *unit* or *theme model,* planning involves creating a number of activities for a designated period of time (a week, a month) around a predetermined topic (as opposed to relying on children's questions to guide your choice of topics).

Common preschool and kindergarten themes typically focus on self-discovery, children's families, children's neighborhoods, community helpers, transportation, work, and harvesting food. You can then use webbing to identify possibilities for learning about differences and similarities of culture, racial identity, abilities, gender, family, and economic class within these particular themes. (Use the curriculum planning questions listed above in the section "Making Anti-Bias Themes a Part of Every Curriculum Every Day.")

Be sure to learn how children in your group think and feel about a specific topic before finalizing your activity plans. This enables you to build on the knowledge and ideas (accurate or inaccurate) that the children will bring with them to specific activities.

Skill-based

If you use a *skill-based model*—planning around specific cognitive and social objectives—anti-bias content will serve to support the development of specific skills. For example, if you are planning activities for fostering number literacy, include in your counting materials objects and pictures that depict the children's home lives and other kinds of diversity. If you are doing a unit on phonemes, you can use rhymes from various cultures or objects from various families that begin with the same sound. (See the section "Selecting and Making Learning Materials" earlier in this chapter.) If you are focusing on cooperation, make sure to create partnerships and small groups that include children across diverse identities.

Tourist curriculum is hazardous to growing children

Tourist curriculum is a teaching approach to diversity that visits "other" people's ways of life—that is, ways that differ from the dominant culture. In a tourist curriculum, instead of making diversity a normal part of the ongoing, daily curriculum, activities about "other" cultural groups occur only once in a while, to celebrate a holiday, to enjoy a special food, or to welcome a one-time guest. The daily life of these cultural groups is invisible. A teacher may even choose to create a special unit highlighting a specific cultural group, who are then not seen again as part of the curriculum until that time next year; a unit on "Indians" around Thanksgiving is a classic example. Or perhaps the achievements of women are celebrated on Mother's Day, but the daily learning environment does not encourage girls and boys to explore new activities, and teachers continue to praise girls for how they look and boys for what they achieve.

Because the "normal" curriculum reverts afterwards to a daily learning environment that relies on dominant culture images, norms, and rules of behavior, tourist curriculum thus transmits the message that the dominant culture is the "right" and "normal" way of life. Exploration of the specific ways that cultural groups are similar as well as different is absent, so the tourist approach does not help children understand everyone's common humanity, nor that there are many equally valuable ways to live that common humanity.

As you examine your teaching materials and activities, you may discover that some of them fall into tourist curriculum traps. Do not get discouraged.

Acknowledge the problem and figure out how to fix it. We all make mistakes—how we handle them makes the difference. The pitfalls of tourist curriculum to avoid are the following:

Tokenism

Tokenism happens when staff use just one teaching material or image to represent a whole group of people. Examples include putting out one dark-skinned doll amidst many White dolls, displaying just one poster or book with a picture of a child who uses a wheelchair, or providing just one book to represent "Asian people." Even if the information is accurate, not showing the diversity that exists within groups leads to children drawing overgeneralized conclusions about a group of people, which opens the door to stereotyping. Here's one example:

> Teresa had looked at *Mama Zooms* (by Jane Cowen-Fletcher), a delightful book, but the only one in the school that depicted an adult in a wheelchair. When a father in a wheelchair arrives to pick up his child, Teresa insists he couldn't be a daddy: "Wheelchair *mamas* take care of babies," she says. "Daddies have to drive the car."

Tokenism also occurs when teachers do just a short unit about a particular group of people and then put the topic away for the rest of the year; for example, teaching about African Americans only during the week of Martin Luther King Jr.'s birthday.

Trivializing

This one takes the form of reducing the rich patterns of one or even multiple cultures to one or two small pieces; for example, representing the diversity of American Indian culture by having children make fry bread, sing "Ten Little Indians," or make paper feather headdresses.

Misinforming/misrepresenting

This pitfall can happen in several ways. A teacher may use pictures and books about a group's country of origin to depict their life in the United States (e.g., using images and stories about life in Vietnam to teach about Vietnamese Americans). Or a teacher may show a group of people as they lived in the past, or only in ritual dress, rather than in their current, everyday lives. Or a teacher may misinform children by giving them inaccurate information about a cultural group, such as mixing up ways of life among cultures that are actually different (e.g., assuming that people from Central America and Mexico all practice the same traditions).

Stereotyping

In stereotyping, images and information not only treat all members of a group as the same but also dehumanize people through exaggeration, caricature, and inaccurate overgeneralizations. Common, negative examples of stereotypical portrayals might include books about Africa that treat its wide range of countries, cultural groups, and languages as being the same, or show only its animals, or only its rural life; books in which children or adults of color are always shown as "tag-alongs" to a group of White people, never as central characters; and more recently, books showing people of Arab heritage portrayed with cartoon, exaggerated features or as terrorists.

Stereotypes also can convey inaccurate, *positive* overgeneralizations, not just negative ones. Teachers may presume that all children with an Asian heritage are going to be good at math and science or that all African American children are natural dancers and athletes. What all stereotypes have in common is the mistaken assumption that if you can identify a person as a member of a particular group, then you can know essential information about that individual person.

Storytelling and problem solving with persona dolls

Many anti-bias educators use storytelling with persona dolls to introduce stories related to the children's lives, as well as to broaden their awareness of various aspects of diversity.

Build a collection of persona dolls, some reflecting the specific children and families in your classroom and others introducing new kinds of diversity. To do this, make and/or purchase a variety of dolls to express specific physical characteristics, and then assign them individual back stories, including ethnic and cultural identities, economic class status, a family configuration, and personal and family histories.

Here are a few examples of persona dolls adapted from the work of Kay Taus, an originator of the persona doll method:

> "Joe" (age 4) is Black. He lives with his mother, father, two brothers, and sister. [One year Joe was a Jehovah's Witness because I had two Black children whose families were of that faith.]

> "Joshua" (age 5) is Jewish. He is adopted. Joshua's parents are divorced. He spends one week living with his father and one week living with his mother. He has a younger brother who is 3 and is also adopted.

> "Marisela" (age 3) is from Mexico. She and her mother came to Los Angeles when she was 2. Her father and mother are divorced. Her father lives in Mexico and she doesn't see him. She has aunts and uncles in Mexico and in Los Angeles. She speaks English and Spanish.

"Jennifer" (age 5) is White and lives with her mother and her mother's partner, whom she also considers to be her mommy. She is profoundly deaf. Her primary language is American Sign Language. She is learning to read lips and to talk, but it will take time to learn really well.

"Mary" (age 6) is Navajo. She lives with her mother and father. Her grandmother and grandfather still live in Arizona on the reservation. She knows a little of the Navajo language (Diné) because she visits her grandparents.

"May" (age 5) is Chinese. Her family is from Hong Kong. She lives with her father and sister. Her mother died when she was very little. She speaks Cantonese very well because that is her first language, and she is learning English.

For any specific group of children, the teacher would develop the dolls' back stories both to reflect the backgrounds of those children and to bring in specific additional aspects of diversity not represented in the group. (See the box "About Storytelling with Persona Dolls.")

Developing persona doll stories

Inspiration for specific, anti-bias persona doll stories can come from several sources:

● Children's everyday identity issues, interactions, emotions, and family relationships—When choosing to use experiences of a particular child, ask the child first if it is all right. Children usually say yes.

● Common experiences among the children across diverse identities—Themes such as saying goodbye at drop-off in the morning, getting a new sibling, visiting grandparents, and getting sick make good beginning stories.

● Issues you want children to explore—Such issues might be helping children explore typical developmental questions about diversity (see chapters 5 through 11) and hurtful behaviors that happen to them in or outside of school. Encourage them to express their feelings and learn ways to solve their problems, and suggest new ways of acting. Stories may also introduce diversity beyond what is present in the program, once children are comfortable with the dolls and with the diversity within their class. Always individualize each doll's story so as not to stereotype or tokenize.

● Current events that appear in the news or in children's or their family's conversations—Although we might wish it otherwise, the hard issues of the real world do intrude on children's awareness and lives. They need adult help to explore their ideas and feelings, and they need adults to provide accurate, developmentally meaningful information about such events.

● Stories from social justice history—As Kay Taus relates,

> I don't expect 4- and 5-year-olds to remember all the details, but I do want to give them a sense of the many people who lived/live the spirit of justice and freedom. I use historical stories about topics such as the Montgomery Bus Boycott, Helen Keller, Jane Addams, Chief Joseph, current stories about the United Farm Workers, women in the Olympics, and families banding together to keep the libraries open. These stories are full of adventures, and children often request them. (Adapted from Derman-Sparks & the ABC Task Force 1989, 19)

Introducing and using the dolls

Get started by telling the children the doll's basic identity information: name, age, family members, and some favorite activities. Explain that this is the doll's first day, and ask the children to help make their new

---

About Storytelling with Persona Dolls
by Julie Bisson

Even as more children's books explore various kinds of diversity, you still may not find ones that reflect every aspect or family in your particular group. In addition, events in the children's daily lives can be useful springboards for anti-bias learning through storytelling and discussion. In these cases, persona doll stories can be used to introduce diversity issues from beyond the classroom as well as from within it. In helping the persona dolls deal with issues of identity, diversity, and discriminatory teasing and exclusion, children can safely explore how to handle these issues in their own lives.

Ruth Beaglehole and Kay Taus, two early childhood educators, originated the "persona dolls" method of storytelling to explore issues of identity and to help children learn problem-solving skills. Now teachers around the United States as well as in countries such as Australia, South Africa, the United Kingdom, and the Netherlands use persona doll storytelling as part of their anti-bias education (Van Keulen 2004).

Persona dolls belong to the teacher, who keeps them separate from the dolls freely available to the children. The teacher is the one who assigns each doll a unique identity, which stays constant throughout the school year as the doll's experiences unfold. Children in classrooms where persona dolls are used effectively often talk about the dolls and their adventures as if they were real, and for this reason it is helpful to develop a system for keeping co-teachers and parents up to date about the various dolls' "identities" and unfolding "lives."

A Persona Doll Storytelling Example

The setting is a 4-year-olds classroom. The teacher has told the children that "Lucia," a favorite persona doll, is very upset because "when Lucia drew a picture of her family—herself and her grandma—another child said to her, 'That can't be your family, 'cause there's no mommy and daddy in it!'"

The teacher asks the children what Lucia might be feeling, and they decide she might be "upset," "mad," and "confused."

Teacher: Why is Lucia so upset, mad, and confused?

Children: 'Cause of what that kid said. . . . He said her Gramma's not her family! . . . Did Lucia cry?

Teacher: She might have been upset enough to cry. Is her grandma her family?

Children: Yes, that's right. She told us before. . . . That's why she drew her grandma.

Teacher: It seems like that other kid wanted everybody's family to be the same. But it's not true that all families are the same, it is?

Han Eul: No. I live with just my mom and my brother.

Teacher: Yes. That is your family, Han Eul. A family is the people who love and take care of each other. There are many different ways to be a family. How would it feel if someone told you your family isn't right?

Han Eul: I'd be mad.

Children: I'd say, "That's not true!" . . . That would hurt my feelings.

Teacher: I'll bet it would! That is just how Lucia felt. Now we know that it is not right to try to tell someone she has to be the same as someone else. And we know how much that hurts, don't we?

_____

Source: Adapted from T. Whitney, *Kids Like Us: Using Persona Dolls in the Classroom* (St. Paul, MN: Redleaf, 1999), 140. Used with permission.

---

friend feel welcome. The next time, tell a story about the doll having a common preschool experience; invite the children to talk about their own similar experiences. After a few stories like this, relate a story that raises a cultural or fairness issue. Choose subjects that arise in your classroom or that are common among the children's age group (e.g., "Girls cannot play here." . . . "You are a baby because you cannot walk." . . . "Grandmas don't live with families!" . . . "Why is your skin so dark?"). Describe a specific event, the doll's feelings, and how the doll did or did not respond. (See the box "A Persona Doll Storytelling Example.")

Keep stories brief. Leave time for children's comments and problem solving. Invite the children to help the doll figure out what to do if that issue arises again. End with inviting the children to brainstorm what they might do if a similar incident happens to them. Be open to the children's ideas. They may come up with solutions that surprise you or open up additional issues of confusion and bias to be explored.

To ensure you tell *respectful* persona doll stories:

● Sort out your own feelings, attitudes, and knowledge about the specific issue you plan to explore in your story. (See chapter 3 for exercises to help you do this.)

● Make sure the information you include in the story is accurate. Check with people who identify with the area of diversity that is the subject of your story.

Two excellent books by experienced anti-bias educators offer detailed steps for creating and using persona doll stories: *Combating Discrimination: Persona Dolls in Action* (Brown 2001) and *Kids Like Us: Using Persona Dolls in the Classroom* (Whitney 1999).

Putting it all together

Relationships and interactions with children and families, the visual and material environment, and the daily curriculum all come together to create the anti-bias learning community. This does not happen overnight—it takes time and hard work—but every step we take counts. Acknowledge and celebrate each small change! Together they add up to creating a learning community that truly nurtures and supports all children, and that makes our efforts worthwhile and exciting.

Anti-Bias Education in a Family Child Care Home

by Bj Richards

As a family child care provider, I have a tremendous influence on children's developing views of the "bigger world." Throughout my many years as an early childhood professional, I've worked to unlearn and overcome the stereotypes and biases I've held, while instilling anti-bias values in the children I teach. I believe that our world will be a better place if all children grow up in anti-bias homes and child care settings.

Children must feel safe, loved, and nurtured to develop the basic trust they need for healthy development. My goals are for children to develop a strong and positive self-concept and empathy for others through healthy intellectual, physical, social, emotional, and moral development. I hope that my experiences may serve as examples for other caregivers as well.

Provide diverse, anti-bias materials

All child care environments, including family child care homes, can provide excellent anti-bias materials. I find my materials through a variety of sources, such as catalogs, the internet, yard sales, and bookstores. Here are the types of materials I rely on:

Books: These crucial anti-bias tools introduce children to the love of reading as well as to human differences and similarities. Even if a book does not meet my anti-bias criteria, it may still be useful for helping children become critical thinkers.

Music: A diverse selection of CDs and homemade tapes incorporates and reflects children's home cultures and languages as well as the larger community, country, and world.

DVDs: These portray quality children's stories featuring diversity of peoples, cultures, and languages.

Dolls, figurines, and block people: A wide range of authentic people toys (including appropriate homemade dolls) featuring diversity of age, race, gender, and body types, including people with physical challenges.

Dramatic play props: A variety of clothes and toys for both genders reflects the children's backgrounds. Cooking tools and empty food containers from the children's families are included, as well as plastic foods from various cultures.

Puzzles: These feature a range of diverse people in many roles. I also make homemade puzzles using magazine photos or pictures of children and families.

Drawing materials: These include paints, markers, and crayons in a range of skin tones. I routinely offer black and brown; if a child thinks those colors are "yucky" I use them and say I think the colors are beautiful.

Blocks and Legos: These must be separated from their packaging, which often portrays stereotypes. A multicultural set of Lego people is also useful.

Wall hangings: Posters, paintings, fabrics, and other art reflect the children's home cultures.

Strategies

Much of the anti-bias education I do revolves around daily interactions and activities. I also pay attention to my language; for example, I'm aware of how negative/bad things tend to be called "black" or "dark," and try to avoid this. I also use gender-neutral terms such as "firefighter" instead of "fireman."

● **Support discussion and activities about people's attributes.**

I create an environment where the children know they may talk about the differences they observe. For example, 3-year-old Elijah, who is White, observed, "Claire has beige skin like me. Rahsaan has dark brown skin; Nya, Shane, and Remi are light brown; and Isabel is medium brown." I responded, "Elijah, good for you. You are paying attention to the many ways your friends look." I answer all of the children's questions about differences as accurately and matter-of-factly as I can. I regularly open up conversations about children's various attributes (e.g., skin color, eye shape, gender anatomy, ability aids). Persona dolls that use a wheelchair, hearing aid, and glasses create opportunities for stories and conversations about people with physical challenges. I also use stories with our diverse set of block people to help children understand different perspectives. Hair is another big topic—we make a hair chart featuring a snippet of each child's hair (with their family's permission) glued to a piece of cardboard, and we discuss the differences. We also read books about hair.

● Encourage children to express their emotions and work out conflicts.

We read many books about feelings and play games making faces to portray different emotions. I often give them words for their feelings, such as *frustration*; sooner or later you will hear a 3-year-old shout, "I am so frustrated!" instead of throwing a tantrum. I encourage both girls and boys to acknowledge their anger and express it appropriately. When there are conflicts, I use dolls to role play. I ask the children how we could solve problems, and we talk about ideas to try. When children can express their opinions, they learn from each other. We learn to agree and disagree; both are okay.

● Never allow personal attributes to be a reason for exclusion or limiting children.

I always intervene whenever children are excluded because of their identity—for example, if a game is "just for girls." If I confirm the children are excluding another child because he is a boy, then I ask the girls to think of a role for him so everyone can play. I make clear that a person's identity is never a reason for exclusion. Since I do try to respect the children's choice of playmates, I also help them learn langauge such as "This time, we want to play by ourselves. We will play with you another time."

● Help children to try *all* activities.

I strongly encourage all the children to play with dolls, blocks, dress-up clothes, and vehicle toys, although they may have differing styles of play. I want them to experience a rich range of materials and activities. If I play with blocks, the girls will join me and become more familiar with them. The same happens with trains and the vehicles. I also play a game where both boys and girls choose a doll and we create all kinds of families and act out different situations.

● Teach children to recognize stereotypes.

Each year, as Halloween and Thanksgiving approach, I raise the topic of "Indians." I introduce the term "Native Americans," and explain that they are people living in this country who have been here longer than anyone else. I explain that it hurts their feelings to see non-Native people dressing up in stereotyped "Indian" costumes pretending to be them. Only Native Americans can be Native Americans; but anyone can dress up to be a doctor, an animal, or many other costumes.

● Handle toileting and diapering routines without shame.

I always have children in diapers or who are beginning toilet learning, so the topic of who has a vagina and who has a penis comes up regularly. The children make observations, ask questions, and I provide simple, honest responses, providing matter-of-fact discussions of body parts and functions.

● Use holiday traditions and celebrations.

I celebrate holidays throughout the year, in a way that honors and explores diversity. On International Women's Day, I display a photo collage featuring women in nontraditional roles and significant women in the lives of the children I've cared for over the years. On Martin Luther King Jr. Day, my program remains open, and I host a celebration for current and alumni children and families. We make a chain of cutout hands using skin tone paper. We reenact his speech with dolls and toys, bake a cake, and sing a special song:

> We baked a cake, we blew it out,
>
> "Happy Birthday, Martin Luther King," we shout.
>
> "I have a dream," he said: "People hand in hand,"
>
> Working and singing throughout the land.

● Incorporate children's family traditions.

I invite families into my home to share their holiday celebrations. One grandfather, born in Belfast, Ireland, visits every St. Patrick's Day with Irish soda bread, stories, and a song or two. We have also celebrated the Chinese New Year, whenever children adopted from China are in the program or children's family members were born there. People enjoyed this so much that we established an annual tradition: Current and alumni families meet at a restaurant in Chinatown on a Sunday morning in February to eat and then explore the neighborhood afterward. Everyone looks forward to this event each year.

● Customize December holidays.

I incorporate my family's Christmas traditions into our program's December holiday curriculum. One highlight for me is displaying my Black Santa collection, which has expanded to include Santas from all over the world. We read books about all of the winter holidays, and I display a menorah for Chanukah and a kinara for Kwanzaa. We discuss how different families do and do not celebrate different holidays.

Partnering with families

I'm often asked if I have difficulty with parents who do not share my ideas about anti-bias education. However, I am fortunate that most of my families choose to come to my home *because* of my anti-bias program. I learned long ago to describe my philosophy in detail in my parent handbook, which I ask every prospective family to read before interviewing. If they are still interested in having their children join my program, we set up an evening meeting. I answer their questions, and ask questions as well. If it's a good match, we set up a visit for the families to see the program in action. When families enroll, they sign a contract that includes a statement that they have read the parent handbook.

Family child care becomes like a second home to the children, which in turn fosters community among families. I strongly encourage parents to interact and share their child care experiences with each other. I organize events throughout the year, including potlucks, local children's concerts, and an outdoor art day, as well as some holiday get-togethers.

I also email the families daily. I write a group message describing our day, including anecdotes about the children and information about our curriculum. It is worth the time and effort. Families feel more included in their children's lives and can use the information to engage with their children at home. I usually do my writing during naptime, and I try to include photos to brighten parents' time at work. Families look forward to these daily updates, and many print them for their child to read someday. In addition to daily group emails, every few weeks I try to write each family about their individual child's development. Child care providers without computers and internet connections can write about each child's day in a private section of a three-ring binder, which parents read at pickup. This kind of ongoing communication helps encourage families to create an anti-bias environment in their own homes.

Take it slow

Implementing an anti-bias curriculum in your child care setting can feel overwhelming at first. I suggest you take it one step at a time; the more experience you have with anti-bias work, the easier it will become. You will make mistakes—we all do. Remember, you will always have another chance to talk to children or change your reaction. The important thing is to let the children know through your actions that diversity and acceptance of others are good, and prejudice is not. When children in my program move on to kindergarten, I feel confident they are comfortable with themselves and with others.

Sample group email to families

Dear Families:

Today I read the book *The Colors of Us* (by Karen Katz), which is about all the different shades of skin color, including "peachy tan." We put our hands together and noticed differences, yet all the hands were a shade of brown. We will do more with this next week with other activities. I hope you will have time to take note of the books in the bookshelf for this week and next week regarding peace, Martin Luther King Jr., fairness, and skin color. You are always welcome to come read our books when you have time in the morning or at pickup. The children love it when you do and it is great for you to become familiar with our reading. You will have a better feel for what they discuss during the day and can be familiar with the books I mention in my daily emails.

—Bj

Learning About Culture, Language, & Fairness

5

Four-year-old Beth brings in a CD of country music for her teachers to play for her Head Start class. When her mom comes to pick her up, one of Beth's teachers returns the CD to Beth. Her mother looks a little embarrassed, explaining that she hadn't realized Beth had taken the CD to school. "But, Mom," says Beth, "that's my Culture Share!" The teacher chuckles and explains that she encourages children to bring things from home that reflect their daily life: "We call it Culture Share," she says, "and we all enjoyed listening to the music that Beth loves."

The word *culture* refers to how particular groups of people live. It is the way we eat, sleep, talk, play, care for the sick, relate to one another, think about work, arrange our kitchens, and remember our dead. It includes the language we speak, the religion or spirituality we practice (or do not), and the clothing, housing, food, and rituals/holidays with which we feel most comfortable.

Every day, in every action, we express our particular group culture and our individual relationship to our culture. Nothing is more important within a culture than how its children are raised. In everything they do, families communicate their culture's values, beliefs, rules, and expectations to their children. What is acceptable in one culture may not be acceptable in another.

Most of the time, people do not even notice their culture, just as we do not notice that we live in a sea of air. We only notice when something changes or makes us uncomfortable (e.g., when we travel to a higher altitude or smog makes it hard to breathe). When we are in familiar surroundings among members of our own culture—and thus when everyone around us is acting in accordance with that culture, it just seems like "the way things are," or the way it's

"supposed" to be. But when we find ourselves in the midst of another culture, or when we must interact with someone from a different culture, we discover that the way we do things is not the only way. How we respond to that experience will either limit or expand our understanding (and acceptance) of the idea that there are *many* ways to be human.

In a society as diverse as ours, maneuvering through its multiple cultures can be complex and confusing, as well as rich and delightful. Those of us who work with other people's children are continually juggling our own culture, the culture of our early childhood education program, and the cultures of the families in our program. As we become sensitive to the similarities and differences in our own, the program's, and the families' cultures—and if we are flexible and open to the many ways children can thrive—the work we do with them can be powerful and meaningful.

Learning about culture and fairness involves two dimensions: children's development of a positive cultural identity, and their comfortable, respectful interaction with the cultures of others. Anti-bias education supports both dimensions.

A word about culture

The world in which you were born is just one model of reality. Other cultures are not failed attempts at being you: They are unique manifestations of the human spirit.

—Wade Davis, anthropologist

All too often, when early childhood educators think about culture, they think about the surface things that are easy to see, taste, and define. Costumes, holidays, foods, and the objects that people use in everyday life frequently become the focus of their teaching. But culture is much deeper and more significant than those things, as shown on the diagram below. All the items listed there are elements of culture.

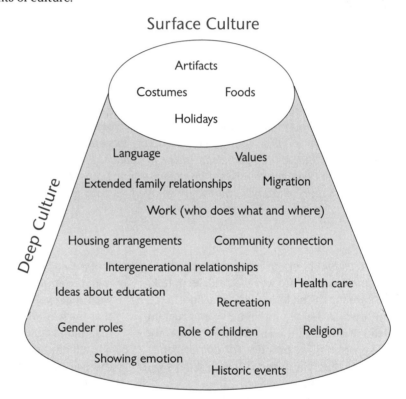

A person's *cultural group* is related strongly to his or her ethnicity, which reflects the place of origin and cultural background of the person's ancestors—whether parents, grandparents, or relatives who lived hundreds of years ago. Within an ethnic group, its members both share some cultural patterns and also reflect cultural differences resulting from generational, economic class, urban/rural, and other influences. A person may be a member of a particular ethnicity without practicing or believing *all* of its aspects. And many people in the United States have multiple ethnic heritages (e.g., Navajo and Irish, Mexican/Filipino and French). For all these reasons, knowing a person's or family's ethnicity does not tell you much about how that culture might actually be reflected in their daily life.

In addition to having a cultural group, each person also has a *cultural identity*, which has three dimensions. The first dimension is how the cultural group(s) to which we belong tries to shape the way we live (a process called *cultural socialization*). The second dimension is about how we learn to name, describe, and feel about our particular ethnic/cultural group membership. A third dimension, which comes into play as we mature and establish an adult life and family, is the decisions we make about what specific elements of our cultural socialization we choose to continue, to modify, or to reject.

Goals for Children

• Children will feel pride in and will have the language to express their family's cultural identity, traditions, and heritage. (ABE Goal 1)

• Children will use their home culture knowledge in the group setting, as they also learn to thrive in the culture of the school and larger society. (ABE Goal 1)

• Children will continue to develop in their home language, while also learning to be bilingual. (ABE Goals 1 & 2)

• Children will demonstrate curiosity, enjoyment, ease, and empathy with cultural differences and similarities. (ABE Goal 2)

• Children will identify disrespectful interactions and learn to interact respectfully regarding cultural differences. (ABE Goals 3 & 4)

Our cultural identity also influences how we live our other social identities (e.g., our economic class, gender and sexual orientation, racial identity). Conversely, our other social identities influence—but do not determine—our cultural identity. Finally, a person may identify with a specific cultural group without embracing *all* of its aspects. For example, a person can identify as Mexican American and not like all Mexican food. A person can identify as White American without believing in its cultural norm that "getting ahead is really important."

For all these reasons, it is essential to learn how each person defines her or his cultural identity, rather than make assumptions based on generalized or stereotypical ideas about a cultural group's way of life, how a person looks, or a person's family name.

The comments of some early childhood education teachers in one of Julie's anti-bias courses show the complexity of cultural identity, as they tried to define their *culture, ethnicity,* and *race*:

Luz S: Culturally I'm Mexican American, and probably a Westerner. And definitely Catholic. My ethnicity is Mexican, but also Mixotecan. I'm only beginning to learn about the Mixotecan part of my history. I have dual citizenship in the United States and Mexico. Here in the United States, I'm a woman of color.

Jennifer E: Culturally I identify as working class, Californian. I guess I'm also White. My ethnicity is a mystery to me. I'm a true Heinz 57 flavor. My family has been here forever. I am a U.S. citizen.

Peggy D: I'm Black, and that's both my racial identity and my heritage. My culture is Black, rural Arkansas, with more and more California city girl thrown in.

Mario V: I'm Italian American, but I mainly live my day-to-day culture as a gay man. On my mother's side we're pretty much Choctaw and Cherokee—and I love learning about those lives. But I haven't lived my life as an Indian, so I guess it's my heritage, not my culture.

Leroy B: People always think I'm Black. I guess I am, because my grandfather was Black. But I think of myself as Louisiana Creole. That's the part of my heritage that is alive for me. I guess my culture would be Creole, Californian, and Christian. My citizenship is American.

Leslie C: My parents are from China. I am Chinese American. If you have to put me into a larger group, say "Asian American," but don't ever call me "Oriental." Oriental is a rug, not a human being.

What is dominant culture?

Most modern, complex societies have a "dominant" culture and multiple subcultures of people who live within the dominant culture. Thus, the term *dominant culture* does not necessarily or always mean the culture of the majority. Rather, it is the culture of the people who hold the social, political, and economic power in the society.

Stop & Think: Understanding your own family culture

■ What is the history of your first name? your family name?

■ What do you know about your family's history in the United States? If they immigrated, where did they come from? Why? How? How were they treated when they first arrived?

■ When you were growing up, what was most important to your family about your behavior at home and in the community? What did they believe mattered about your behavior as a girl or a boy?

■ What were your family's beliefs/expectations/rules for adult-child relationships? teacher-child relationships?

■ What did your family expect of you as an adult? To what degree do you still hold to your family's values and beliefs?

■ What did your family teach you about money? about being on time? about speaking up in a group?

■ What do you want other people to know about your culture from your childhood family? from your current family? How do you want the people you work with to learn about your family culture?

■ What are things you do not like people to say about members of your cultural group? How would you like to address people who behave in hurtful, misinformed, or disrespectful ways?

■ How do both your childhood and your current cultural contexts influence your work as an educator?

The characteristics of a dominant culture are closely connected to the history of the particular country. In the United States, the roots of our current dominant culture were planted by the English immigrants of the 17th century, especially by those with the power—that is, White, English-speaking, male landowners, political leaders, and Christian religious leaders. The culture they established was very different from the many cultures of the indigenous peoples, who were, to begin with, more numerous than the colonists. The Europeans generally considered the Native cultures "barbarian" and inferior, and there were many attempts to destroy all aspects of them.

As new waves of immigrant groups arrive in the United States, they bring with them their heritage home cultures, which vary more or less significantly from the established, dominant one. In order to survive, and to become part of a common nation, newcomers have been expected to learn and assimilate to the dominant culture. At the same time, some maintain aspects of their original heritage cultures.

The degree to which a particular group, family, or person incorporates aspects of the dominant culture and maintains a heritage culture varies considerably. Some of this variation is related to the number of generations a group has lived in the United States—but not always. Many factors (economic class, racial identity, religion, political beliefs) influence the balance between heritage culture and dominant culture as expressed in the way a group and its members live. And as culture is always changing, so is the dynamic tension among family/heritage cultures, shifting economic and political times, and the elements included in the dominant culture.

Today, the dominant culture ideal in the United States is easiest to see by watching the advertisements on commercial television. The image is English speaking; well dressed (slim for women); private, neat, well furnished and equipped suburban home; married couple with one or two biological children, each of whom has his or her own bedroom; private, well maintained yard; professional employment; celebrators of Christian holidays. The image conveys the covert message that this is *the* ordinary and desirable way to live.

Many people use the term "mainstream" to describe this cultural image. But *mainstream* implies that most people (the "main" stream) in the society actually live like this, and more importantly, that it is the correct way to live. This "mainstream" image becomes a standard by which people, families, or groups are judged, and the degree to which they differ from it becomes the basis for prejudice against them.

We use the term "dominant" instead, as we believe it more accurately describes the relationship between the idealized image and the far more complex and rich reality of how people live in the United States. The anti-bias approach embraces and respects this diverse richness, as well as fostering the skills for our living and working together in the same larger society.

Children's early experiences and understandings of culture

The formation of a child's cultural identity begins at birth. Infants and toddlers absorb the ways their family's culture touches (and doesn't); the tones of voice used to express pleasure or displeasure; how close to or far away from one another people stand; who eats with whom; the "right" way to sleep, to dress, to go to the bathroom, to bathe. Long before very young children are aware of or have words for what they are doing, they internalize a profound sense of "rightness" and familiarity with the particular way the people in their culture behave. This sense lies at the core of the child's evolving cultural identity.

During the preschool years, children begin to sort out which variables are flexible (e.g., it's okay to ask for candy in one grandma's house but not in the other's) and which ones are absolutes (e.g., it's never okay to spit at someone). These messages about what is and isn't acceptable are rarely simple, nor is cultural identity itself simple in a diverse society such as the United States.

What's more, unless adults actively guide them, children can develop negative reactions from encounters with people who behave in unfamiliar ways. Without help, children may come to feel—though often at a subconscious level—that the way their family does things is "natural" and "ordinary" and "right," and that any other way is at least strange and worrisome, and perhaps even "bad." Such feelings may turn into prejudice. On the other hand, unless the larger society values and includes a child's home culture, children as young as ages 3 and 4 may internalize a sense of not belonging and of themselves and their family as somehow being "wrong."

● **Children become aware of society's attitudes toward their family's cultural way of being.**

All young children first develop their self-concept within their family, getting their initial sense of place in the world from who their family is and where they fit inside it. By preschool age, they begin also developing group cultural identities and other social identities. Messages from the society's dominant culture (from media, peers, teachers, religious leaders) are also critical. Children growing up in families that closely match the dominant culture ideal are more likely to feel societal support for their family's way of life; children growing up in families whose ways of life differ from the dominant culture are more likely to feel devalued and excluded.

Early childhood programs and teachers often are the first representatives of the larger society to regularly interact with children, so they bear an important responsibility to recognize and honor children's home cultures. Missteps such as continually mispronouncing some children's names will chip away at those children's sense of belonging. (A mistake like this looms big for children, even if it seems small to the teacher.) Likewise, the invisibility of children's home culture in their program's visual and material environment undercuts their evolving self- and social identities. When children do not see families like their own portrayed in books and play materials and elsewhere in the program, and when their home language is not supported, they can internalize a message that the program thinks there is something unimportant or wrong about their family and therefore about them.

Remember, invisibility erases identity and experience; visibility affirms reality.

Children growing up in families with the culture of the dominant group, while much more likely to encounter positive support for their evolving cultural identity, still face risks to their positive development as they move outside of their home culture. Two possible sources of risk are the social dynamics of racial identity and of economic class, which are both addressed in later chapters.

● Children struggle with cultural continuity and discontinuity.

The way a child's family does things feels natural and normal, and all young children bring that feeling with them when they enter care. When an early childhood program's ways of eating, talking, disciplining, nurturing, and playing are similar to his or her family's way, the child experiences *cultural continuity.* Continuity consists of many little things: If you burp at the end of a meal, is that rude, or a compliment to the cook? Do you shake hands firmly and look a person in the eye when you meet them, or are those behaviors disrespectful, even intrusive? Do babies sleep in cribs, in hammocks, in cradles, alone next to their parents, alone in their own rooms, with their grandmother, with their older siblings? To the degree that those and other practices differ between the home and the program, children experience *cultural discontinuity*, especially if the program considers its way "right" and others' "wrong."

While all children experience some degree of cultural discontinuity between their home culture and the culture of the group setting, for some of them the gap is huge. Children whose homes reflect the dominant culture are most likely to find a high degree of home-to-school continuity, and thus to feel most "at home," because the curriculum, materials, and teacher interactions in most early childhood programs reflect dominant culture norms. This continuity supports their positive feelings about their home culture, and therefore, about themselves.

At the other end of the continuum are children who experience so much discontinuity that their early childhood setting feels unsafe, which may cause them to feel discomfort or shame about their home culture. In response to such discontinuity, some children feel compelled to take on the dominant culture's ways of being, rejecting their home culture and becoming outsiders in their own family. Other children may hold on to their home culture but feel continually ill at ease, disrespected, or even inferior when in the dominant culture. It takes thoughtful, sensitive support to help children live with comfort and respect in dual worlds.

We cannot know all the consequences of sharp cultural discontinuity for young children's development. We do know that children thrive when an early childhood program respects and integrates their home languages and cultures into all of its aspects. In such programs, children can learn and develop because they feel "supported, nurtured, and connected not only to their home communities and families but also to teachers and the educational setting" (NAEYC 1995, 2).

● Children start forming attitudes about other cultural ways of living.

By preschool age, children begin to absorb stereotypes and attitudes about other ethnic/cultural groups from their family and the larger society. These biases are easily absorbed because very young children lack accurate information about the lives of other people, including classmates and teachers. Supplying accurate information is one necessary strategy. For example:

Jane's mother, Ann, tells the teacher that Jane has said she doesn't like Erlinda (a Salvadoran assistant teacher) because Erlinda "talks funny and is too dark." Ann reports that she explained that Erlinda is from another country where people have darker skin and that Erlinda is learning English. And that she told Jane, "I like all of your teachers, and I want you to like all your teachers, too." Jane had listened, but still insisted that she didn't like Erlinda. Ann tells the teacher, "I don't know what else to do!"

The teacher suspects that Jane is uncomfortable because Erlinda is very different from anyone else the child knows. She talks with Ann about how to help Jane learn more about Erlinda, both at home and at school. That night, Ann talks to Jane about El Salvador and shows her some picture books about the country; Jane seems interested.

In school, at the teacher's suggestion, Erlinda talks to Jane's snack group a number of times about her life, showing them photos and objects from her daily life. Ann follows up by inviting Erlinda to their home for a meal. This plan works. Neither her mother nor teacher sees any repetition of Jane's discomfort.

Current events, and the societal issues that result, can also negatively affect young children's evolving feelings about people from particular ethnic/cultural groups. For example:

Margaret, a 4-year-old, refuses to play with Mariam, who wears a traditional Muslim headscarf. "Go away, you no-good Arab," she yells. Mariam backs off, looking first surprised and then near tears.

Their teacher immediately intervenes. She puts her arm around Mariam and hugs her, then firmly says to Margaret, "This is a hurtful and unfair thing to say to Mariam." Before the teacher gets any further, Margaret insists, "My dad told me not to play with her. He says Arabs are no-good." The teacher puts her arm around Margaret, too, and says, "Margaret, in our classroom everyone plays together. I have a different rule than your father. I don't think the same thing he does about Arabs." Margaret looks uncertain and the teacher adds, "I'm going to talk with your father about our different ideas and rules. Right now, Mariam is feeling very sad about your words, and I'm going to read a book to her. You can come with us if you want." Margaret looks confused and turns her back on the teacher.

The teacher quietly asks another teacher to check in with Margaret and then takes Mariam by the hand. "Mariam, I am so sorry that Margaret said such an unfair, untrue thing to you. I'll remind her again that in our classroom we take care of each other and do not leave anyone out."

In this situation, the teacher chose to support Mariam immediately, because she was concerned about the effect of Margaret's behavior on Mariam. The teacher also knew from previous conversations with Margaret's parents that they had strong prejudices against people of Arab heritage. While she tries to support all of the children and their families, she felt it was essential to teach the children that they must not attack each other's identities. After school, the teacher phoned Margaret's parents, related what had happened, and described how she handled the incident. She set up a time for a conference with them to increase her own understanding of what was behind the family's bias and to discuss the principles and practices she saw as vital to the program.

The teacher also spoke with Mariam's family, explaining what had happened and how she responded, and asked them to let her know if Mariam showed any further distress. In addition, the teacher shared her plans to do educational activities with all the children to provide them with accurate information about Arab and Arab American people, and thus enable them to resist stereotyping. She assured the family that she would not put the spotlight on Mariam but rather would use children's books and persona doll stories to accomplish her objectives. The teacher also made clear that she would monitor any further incidents and continue to support Mariam.

● **Children begin to use cultural/ethnic terms and try to sort out what they mean.**

"Are we Jewish? Josh says we can't be 'cuz we have a Christmas tree." . . . "I am not Black. My skin is brown!" . . . "Is this my Black blood or my Japanese blood?" asks Jamón, who is biracial, as he stares at his skinned knee. . . . "He doesn't speak anything!" exclaims Leah after she tries out the few Spanish words she knows on Ramesh, who has just arrived from India.

Young children pick up words that name their own and others' ethnic and cultural groups, but often with little understanding of what they mean. They do not yet understand which characteristics determine membership in one group or another. The different kinds of ethnic/cultural group names baffle them ("Why is Carmen 'Latina' but Lupe is 'Mexican'?"). The relationship between physical and cultural characteristics also often confuses them. For example,

The teacher notices Priscilla pulling her eyes up at the corners several times during the morning. When she asks why, Priscilla replies, "I want to speak like Seon Jung." Seon Jung, whose family recently arrived from Korea, is her favorite playmate at school.

Stop & Think: Remembering belonging and being an outsider

- What are your earliest memories of realizing that the way your family believed or did things differed from other families? Who, if anyone, helped you think about this?

- In what situations, if any, did you feel that your family "belonged"? In what situations, if any, did you feel that your family was odd, strange, not as it was "supposed" to be?

- As you were growing up, did you have words for the things that set you apart or connected you to the majority of people in the community? to the dominant culture of your country?

- In raising children of your own, what values, behaviors, and attitudes from your family of origin would be most important to you to pass on? to put a stop to?

Create a culturally consistent and respectful program

When young children enter any early childhood setting, their circle of experience widens beyond the cultural rules and practices of their own family. At home, they may sit on Grandma's lap to eat, while at school they must sit on their own small chair. At home, they may play with older siblings and cousins, while at school they play only with children close to their own age. At home, they may nap on the couch snuggled with their cousin, with the television on and busy family life all around them, while at school they must nap alone on a cot in a darkened, quiet room. Perhaps most significantly, at home they may speak a language that at school no one even knows. Teachers who create learning environments that incorporate and build upon children's home cultures promote healthy social, emotional, and cognitive development and academic achievement.

A culturally consistent learning environment requires teachers to learn about the rules, traditions, and expectations of the families in the program. Gaining this knowledge is a process that progresses in steps, building as it goes. In order to learn about the families, teachers must develop relationships with them. In order to build those relationships beyond superficial interactions, teachers need to understand something of each family's culture. When this happens, families are able to help teachers create environments and approaches that are culturally consistent with children's experiences outside the program. Equally important, teachers can help families to learn the skills of advocating for and supporting their children's school success and to practice the skills of negotiating differences between their ethnic/cultural group and other cultural groups.

As Carol Brunson Day reminds us, *our* way is not the only way:

> We can learn principles for creating culturally consistent programs. However, there is no recipe for being there. The *there* is built by you with families and staff. It is always a dynamic process and depends on the people who are together in a program at any given time. It calls on everyone to be willing to negotiate and compromise if necessary. If you stay open to the fact that your way is not the only right way, trust in the ability of people to figure out differences, and really work on it, you can get to where you want your classroom to be. When everyone has access to deciding on a solution that works for them, then there is real equality.

Most cultural differences between the family and the early childhood program can be resolved. Both teachers and families want children to be secure, happy, and able to learn. Both want children to succeed in their school lives and beyond. Teachers and families should work toward developing mutual respect—with families recognizing that teachers may well know more about children in groups and children's development in general, and with teachers recognizing that families know more about their child in particular. Both types of knowledge are necessary for children to flourish.

Attend to differences between the early childhood and home cultures

The field of early care and education has its own set of rules, values, and acceptable behaviors. Some of the field's beliefs about what children need to develop and grow do not necessarily match what's considered acceptable or "normal" across all ethnic/cultural lines. Much of the child development research and writing about early childhood education are based on premises and children from the priviledged group—that is, White, affluent, suburban. As with any research-based practice, the more children's backgrounds match the research sample group's, the more applicable are its conclusions—and the reverse is also true. As teachers learn about each child's home culture, they will find that some practices must be adapted or rethought for children and families from some cultural backgrounds.

Unthinkingly accepting all early childhood practices as universally applicable can be damaging to children's cognitive, social, and emotional development. NAEYC (2009) recognizes this fact in specifying that for any practice to be developmentally appropriate, it must take into account not only a child's age group and individual characteristics but also the social and cultural contexts in which the child lives. Once early childhood staff begin to discuss these factors openly with one another, it becomes possible to figure out how to adapt our teaching to *all* children, whatever their home and community cultures. Here are examples of practices commonly found in early childhood programs in the United States that conflict with the practices of some cultures. Think about whether they match *all* of the home cultures of the children in your program:

● **Early childhood practice has tended to promote children's independence, autonomy, and initiative.**

All families want their child to become competent and confident. However, in many cultures (e.g., some Native American, some Southeast Asian), it is important for the adult to first model how to perform a task or how to use materials before children are allowed to put their own ideas into action. This is seen as teaching respect for the materials as well as for adult knowledge.

● **Many early childhood teachers make a practice of acknowledging individual children for their efforts and achievements as a motivation technique.**

However, some cultures emphasize the importance of *inter*dependence among peers and do not agree with singling out one child for praise as if that child's activities existed outside of the group. In this case, families want their child to learn and achieve—in order to contribute to the group's well-being as well as his or her own.

● **Early childhood practice tends to focus on individual "rights."**

For example, if one child is using a toy and a classmate also wants to play with it, early childhood teachers usually set up a schedule of turns. However, some cultures feel strongly that learning to share with others is far more important than a child getting his own way—and may ask teachers to have the two children play together right away, instead of waiting to take individual turns.

- **Early childhood teachers typically expect that a child will speak directly to them, look them in the eye, ask questions freely, and freely express thoughts or desires.**

However, some cultures consider such behavior disrespectful; children are expected to wait for the adult to acknowledge them before speaking and to be thoughtful about what they say. These families want their child to feel safe and assured around adults—but to be respectful at the same time.

Use what you learn to individualize your curriculum

A fundamental principle of developmentally appropriate practice is to individualize curriculum in all areas—physical, emotional, social, and cognitive—to meet the learning and developmental requirements of each child. For young children, individualizing and adapting your curriculum according to each child's home culture is as essential to healthy development as substituting cream cheese for peanut butter is for the child who is allergic to peanuts. Moreover, explaining your adaptations to children as "each of us has different needs" is what we already do in developmentally appropriate approaches.

Individualizing according to each child's home culture always requires striking a balance. In this example, staff devised a plan that was both responsive to the family and consistent with the principles of developmentally appropriate practice:

> Two sisters, recently arrived from Mexico, join a program that, like many centers, organizes children by age. Day after day, the older child keeps coming into the younger child's classroom, and the teacher keeps sending her back to her own. The problem, their aunt explains, is that the older sister has always watched over the younger one, and neither girl feels safe separated. After brainstorming together, staff in both rooms agree that the older child may join the younger one at specific, reliable times during the day and whenever the younger sister asks for her.

By using information about these children's home culture to individualize its age-based policy, this program went a long way toward reassuring the family—who were leaving their children with strangers for the first time, and in a new country. The decision also significantly helped the girls adjust to their new setting.

Create a third space between school and home

The concept of *third space* means that when two parties do things two different ways, neither party simply gives up its ideas; instead, both parties seek a new way, a compromise that incorporates what is important to everyone. The notion of finding a third space in the early childhood context means creating a learning community that accommodates the ideas and approaches of both the staff and each family. Such a learning community is the result of ongoing discussion between them. It evolves and changes as the composition of the program (children, families, and staff) changes and as the two groups learn more from each other. Thus, no class or center looks like a "universal" or "model" program; nor does it replicate any child's home culture. It is a new way—hence a *third* space.

Here is one example that center director Antonia Lopez often shares (e.g., in Bredekamp & Copple 1997, 47):

> Families are giving gifts to center staff to show their appreciation and respect for all that the teachers are doing. However, gifts violate state regulations. Moreover, the individual gifts are creating competition among the teachers (and some of the families), which runs counter to the kind of center the staff want to provide. Still, the teachers do not want to disrespect the families and their generosity, which is an integral part of the families' ethnic/cultural tradition.
>
> To prompt a solution, the center's director tells the teachers: "Here are my two rules: You cannot refuse the gifts, and you cannot accept them. Find another way." After their initial surprise and laughter, the teachers figure out a workable, respectful solution: They explain to the families that they appreciate and accept the gifts in the name of the whole center. Everyone shares food gifts. But gifts of jewelry and art objects they put on display, along with short written, bilingual explanations of that family's history in regards to their gift. Thus, the objects become tools for the children, staff, and families to learn about one another.

Carol Brunson Day shares another example of creating a third space, in an infant/toddler program:

> Licensing rules [and NAEYC's Accreditation Criteria] require that children nap in their own cribs. However, some of the babies served by the center sleep in hammocks at home, and they will not go to sleep in the cribs. So the staff get creative. They tie hammocks diagonally from the crib posts. The result: The infants sleep and licensing requirements are satisfied, because the infants are still "in the cribs."

This program's third space solution worked for everyone because the teachers were able to make a change while meeting the licensing requirement. Each baby was indeed in his or her own crib. And the licensing agency could see the advantage of allowing the babies to sleep in a way consistent with their families' practices that was still healthy and safe. (For more on integrating children's home and community cultures with early childhood principles, see *Culture and Child Development in Early Childhood Programs*, by Carollee Howes.)

When no resolution can be found...

Sometimes it is not possible for a program and a family to reach agreement on a matter. This may happen for a variety of reasons. It can be because of regulations (e.g., licensing requires children to be vaccinated, but the family does not believe in inoculations). It might be because of the program's basic health and safety policies (e.g., the family wants care when their child is feverish and sick, but the program cannot risk other children being infected). Or it can be because of issues tied to caring for children in groups (e.g., the family wants their 3-year-old to be fed by an adult, but the program has eight children at a table and cannot hand feed each child).

Usually, if staff have made clear how much they care for the child and respect the family, creating a mutually acceptable solution is possible. But sometimes, despite everyone's best efforts to find a third space, the discussion between program and family may reach one party's nonnegotiable "bottom line." In some cases, the issue may be tied to anti-bias principles. An anti-bias educator cannot, for example, agree to abide by a family's desire to prevent their White child from playing with a child of color or with dark-skinned dolls. Perhaps the family insists that their son should not have to do any type of cleanup tasks, or that *all* the children should pray before each meal as their child does.

Whatever the issue, when it becomes clear a family cannot stay in the program, it is important that the director help the family identify other options in the community, and handle the departure as respectfully as possible.

Stop & Think: How does your individual culture affect your teaching?

■ What beliefs from your own cultural background about working with children are most important to you?

■ Which principles and beliefs in early childhood education are most important to you?

■ Are there any practices from your home culture that you think could be adapted or rethought? Any from early childhood education?

■ Which practices are "bottom line" for you—that is, principle-based practices you are unwilling to adapt?

■ What kind of balance do you have between practices you are willing to adapt and ones you consider "bottom line"?

Respecting all children's home languages and developing bilingualism

The United States has always been a nation of many languages. Now, in the 21st century, new waves of immigration, as well as migration within the country, mean that early childhood programs are serving increasing numbers of children whose home language is not English. All children need English in order to thrive in their new country. They also need support in maintaining their home language in order to stay deeply connected to their families, as well as for the many advantages of being bilingual.

An anti-bias approach includes finding ways to support children's home language as an essential component of respecting and integrating home cultures into early childhood programs. It also assumes that the development of bilingualism is important for *all* children, who are growing up in an increasingly multilingual world.

It is beyond the scope of this chapter to describe the specific techniques of how to teach English language learners or how to help all children acquire a second language, although effective approaches for doing so are vital (see the box "Additional Resources about Culture and Language"). Instead, this section focuses on the attitudes and beliefs that support a welcoming, affirming environment that respects and makes visible all languages and supports bilingualism as an important aspect of cognitive development.

Learning English and continuing development in the home language

> For young children, the language of the home is . . . the language they use to make and establish meaningful communicative relationships, and the language they use to begin to construct their knowledge and test their learning. . . . For the optimal development and learning of all children, educators must accept the legitimacy of children's home language, respect (hold in high regard) and value (esteem, appreciate) the home culture. (NAEYC 1995, 1–2)

Early childhood programs serve as a two-way bridge between the dominant culture and the child's home culture. When the programs support children's home language while also helping them learn the language of the larger society, teachers convey the important message that the child's home language matters as part of cognitive, social, emotional, and bilingual language development. When this principle is not honored, we run the risk of undermining children's positive identity and connections with their families. Consider the following story told by a student in an early childhood education class at East Los Angeles

College about her experience in the preschool where she was student teaching:

> I taught the children a song in Chinese. One child, who is Chinese himself, covered his ears and said, "I don't like Chinese songs. I like English songs only." I asked him if he heard Chinese songs at home. He replied, "My grandma always listens, but I don't like to listen to that." I know that the child was in another pre-school last year where he wasn't allowed to speak any Chinese. I wonder if that is why he now says he doesn't like it.

Of the 40 students in this college class, one quarter of them then related that they had similar experiences with children in their preschools.

English-only schools and programs, however well meaning, immerse children in a world they do not understand. In these programs, children are at risk of absorbing the message that the language of home is of lesser value because it has no presence in their school. Disrupting preschool children's continued development of their home language can also lead to the rejection or loss of their "mother tongues." This loss risks cutting the children off from their family and community, often ending close relationships with elders and making them outsiders in their home cultures (Wong-Fillmore 1991).

Furthermore, while young children in English immersion programs may initially perform well in some aspects of English, there is evidence that shifting from their first language to a new, unfamiliar language too early may actually have a negative effect on English fluency, comprehension of text, and academic achievement from preK to third grade and beyond (Espinosa 2008). Such children develop "playground" English but cannot use English effectively for academic learning (Garcia 2006).

Numerous studies confirm the benefits of early childhood programs that nurture children's home language while also fostering English learning. Most focus on Spanish-English language learners, but these studies still offer educational implications for all children whose home language is not English.

The Society for Research in Child Development has found that encouraging prekindergarten attendance in dual-language programs rather than English-only programs improves learning opportunities for English language learners and increases their chances of success (SRCD 2009). Furthermore, helping children continue to develop in their home language while beginning to learn English has been shown to foster earlier development of academic skills, lead to more proficient English (Crawford 1991), and support children's ability to communicate with their families (Wong-Fillmore 1991; Hakuta, Goto Butler, & Witt 2000).

One study that collected data on more than 700,000 language-minority students from 1982 to 1996 in schools that were using different kinds of well implemented bilingual programs found that children who remained for the longest time in programs that supported their home language and provided strong, content-based English as a second language instruction showed the most academic success. It is significant to note that students who received English-only instruction without any home language instruction in the early years of schooling fared the worst academically (Collier & Thomas 1997).

Bilingualism for children whose home language is English

In the United States, most conversations about bilingualism focus on children who need to learn English, yet there is ample evidence that integrating other home languages into early childhood programs benefits English-speaking children in several ways. It teaches them respect for other languages, while also helping them to feel comfortable learning a new language. They gain the skill of learning a second language in this global economy and increasingly multilingual society. In most industrialized countries other than the United States, children become at least bilingual, and many speak three or four languages. There is no reason why children in the United States shouldn't have this same advantage.

Families and teachers sometimes worry that if a classroom includes languages other than English, the children who are native English speakers won't get the support they need for their continuing language and cognitive development. Research by the National

---

Additional Resources about Culture and Language

Baker, C. 2007. *A parent's and teacher's guide to bilingualism.* 2d ed. Buffalo, NY: Multilingual Matters Ltd.

Chang, H.N-L. 1993. *Affirming children's roots: Cultural and linguistic diversity in early care and education.* Oakland, CA: California Tomorrow.

Chang, H. N-L. 2006. *Getting ready for quality: The critical importance of developing and supporting a skilled, ethnically, and linguistically diverse early childhood workforce.* Oakland, CA: California Tomorrow.

Howes, C. 2009. *Culture and child development in early childhood programs: Practices for quality education and care.* New York: Teachers College Press.

Tabors, P.O. 2008. *One child, two languages: A guide for early childhood educators of children learning English as a second language.* 2d. ed. Baltimore, MD: Paul H. Brookes.

Association for Bilingual Education (NABE) showed that in two-way language programs in which English-speaking children learn Spanish and English language learners learn English, *both* groups show stronger achievement in language fluency and academic progress compared with children in monolingual programs.

Home language support—Challenges and concerns

NABE (n.d.) has found that sentiment against supporting a home language often stems from the mistaken belief that "bilingualism threatens to sap our sense of national identity and divide us along ethnic lines [. . . or] encourage immigrants that they can live in the [United States] without learning English." However, this belief reflects a serious misunderstanding of bilingual education, which in fact has learning English as its primary goal. It is also a misconception that people whose home language is not English do not want their children to learn English. Most families look to early childhood programs as a place for their children to begin to learn the language they need to succeed in school and the larger society.

Stop & Think: Uncovering your ideas and experiences about second language learning

- What languages did your ancestors speak? Are these languages still part of your life? What is that like for you? When and why did those languages disappear from your family, if they did?

- Have you had any experience being in a setting where people did not speak your language? How did you feel? What do you think that is like for a small child?

- If you have experience in learning to speak a second language, what has that been like? What was it like to make yourself understood? How did it feel?

- What connections do you make between fluent English speaking and intelligence? Between people who speak English with an "accent" or a dialect different from your own? How might your beliefs/feelings affect your work with families?

- What are the challenges for you to implement strategies that support children's home languages while also fostering English learning? What will support you? What new knowledge and skills do you think you need?

In fact, some families may challenge programs that support home languages at school because they think such programs may undermine their child's English learning. This is yet another misconception that reflects a lack of awareness of the dangers posed

for children when early childhood programs ignore home languages. Once families understand the dangers inherent in English-only programs and recognize that young children can learn English while also continuing their home language, they generally come to value bilingual education.

Valuing the whole family across lines of language

In spite of considerable evidence pointing to its benefits, supporting a home language in school can be a daunting challenge for many early childhood teachers. Many teachers feel overwhelmed by how to actually do this, especially if multiple different home languages are represented in their program.

Fostering children's home language begins in our relationships with families. We must demonstrate that we value and respect the languages they speak and that we are eager to communicate with them to share information and make decisions about matters affecting their children.

This means teachers have to find ways to speak and write to families in their home language—which requires us to make connections with others who speak the home languages of the children we care for. It requires us to focus on the family member (rather than the translator) during a conversation that is being translated and to address our comments directly to him or her. We show our respect by presuming that parents are intelligent and loving, even when we do not have words we can share, and by never making the mistake of assuming that those who don't speak fluent English are ignorant or incapable or uncaring. (See the box "Why Don't They Learn English?")

Supporting children from different linguistic backgrounds

Each early childhood program will have a unique mix of language learners. Do the majority of children come from families speaking the same home language? Are several different languages spoken? Do only one or two children speak a language other than English? Do you have any staff who speak the children's home languages? Do you have access to people who can help you with the children's home languages? What available resources can you use, and what further resources do you need?

There is no "one size fits all" learning environment to support the English learners and the native English speakers on their important path to bilingualism. Whatever combination of strategies you choose

"Why Don't They Learn English?"
by Luis Hernandez

This is a frequently heard question from teachers and families who speak only English. They forget that learning a new language is extremely difficult for almost all adults and that it takes years to develop fluency, even when the learner is given support and approval for trying instead of scorn for "not doing it right." As anti-bias educators, we should:

• Respect each family's steps in learning and using English.

• Keep in mind that parents may not be literate (i.e., able to read and/or write) in their first language.

• Consider each family's amount of exposure to and opportunities to study and practice the new language during a typical day, and find out the levels of English use and proficiency at home among family members.

• Provide encouragement, praise, and modeling. It takes courage for language learners to use a new language with people who may be judgmental. Show your own spirit of adventure by learning and using basic words in the families' home languages.

• Remember, speaking English loudly will not make you easier to understand!

to use in your program, the commitment to address this issue is one of the central principles of effective anti-bias education. Here are a few ideas for supporting children's home languages (SRCD 2009):

● Hang welcoming signs in all languages, label classroom materials, and display pictures labeled in each child's home language for each curriculum area and for food, water, and the bathroom.

● Provide home language books, stories, and songs on tape (which families and other community members can help make).

● Learn key words and phrases (greetings, requests for help, terms of comfort and encouragement, etc.) in each child's home language. If many home languages are represented in the class, different staff members can learn key words for different languages.

● Regularly invite family members (nuclear and extended) who speak the child's home language to your classroom.

● Make sure you intentionally promote the inclusion of children who are English language learners in all activities. (Some children may stay on the sidelines unless they receive encouragement to participate.)

● Plan part of each day when English language learners are supported in their home language. If you have sufficient staff (or volunteers), you can plan snack time or a special story time in home language groups.

● If you do not yet have bilingual teachers for each classroom, but you have one or two staff members who are bilingual, consider having at least one of them serve as a "rover" in all the classes to help monolingual teachers. Group English language learners together in fewer classes so they have support from other children who speak their home language and also have more time with the bilingual staff. Invite community volunteers who speak the children's home languages to come regularly to your class.

● Organize a group of people to help you translate your program's handbook, forms, newsletters, or other ongoing written communications into children's home languages. Use photographs of all the activities and daily procedures, labeled in the home languages to communicate what is happening in your program. (Family members and community volunteers can help with this.)

● Encourage families to continue to develop their child's home language, including by reading to their child in that language. Create a lending library of children's books, and invite families and friends to help you create some books in languages that are not currently available commercially.

● Especially when many families share a language—Spanish, for example—give priority when feasible to hiring staff who speak this language and to finding ways to enable other staff to learn the language.

Finally, two very creative and integrated multilingual approaches come from child care programs in Sydney, Australia, that serve working-class families in a culturally diverse district. They show what can be done when there is the will.

> In a center serving 3- to 5-year-olds, and with four main home languages as well as English, several staff members are fluently bilingual. Major learning centers (e.g., blocks and manipulatives, dramatic play, music, art) are located in different rooms of the center, are supervised by these staff on a rotating basis, and are available to all children for a large portion of the day. This way, as children choose activity centers, they are also able to choose to be with a teacher who speaks their home language as well as English and still spend time in all the various activities. Family members, delighted with the program, also volunteer to help each day.

> In another center, where two home languages are spoken in addition to English, the staff have organized a multilingual literacy curriculum. Children meet in lan-

guage family groups with a bilingual staff member for a designated period of time every day. They also sometimes, at their choice, visit another group. Children's early writing, visible on the walls, reflects their literacy development in their home language and in English. An additional benefit is the significantly increased participation of the children's family members, including grandparents, because they see their home language respected in the classrooms.

Planning for how your program will include staff who speak the home languages of the families in your community calls for commitment and strategic thinking. Our profession needs to find ways to enable teachers to become fluent in languages other than English and to recruit more people who speak languages other than English to become early childhood teachers. Continued research to determine the most effective methods for implementing bilingual or multilingual approaches in varying settings will also help us support children's home languages in all of our programs.

Make cultural sameness and difference real

No matter how homogeneous your program appears to be, it is essential to explore the many cultural differences and similarities represented among its families and staff. Remember that all children have a home culture and each family has its own style of daily living. Even when all or most of the children come from the same racial group (e.g., White) or ethnic group (e.g., Mexican American), differences exist in how each family lives. When early childhood programs foster comfort and respect with regard to differences, they create a foundation for children's ability to thrive in our culturally complex world.

One approach to supporting children's understanding of human diversity is to develop the theme "We are all the same; we are all different." Given young children's difficulties in understanding abstract ideas about things they cannot touch, taste, or experience, it is important to ground your teaching about culture in everyday issues. The same/different theme can be built into the ongoing curriculum throughout the year, with a tone of delight, interest, respect: "All people eat, but they eat different foods." . . . "All babies are carried, but they are carried in different ways." . . . "All people sleep, but they sleep on many objects." . . . "We all have words, but we have different words, different languages (even so, we all say *Mama*!)." At the center of this theme is *family* as the basic unit: "In some families Big Sister cooks dinner, and in some families Daddy cooks dinner, and in some families everyone cooks dinner together."

Conversations about human sameness and difference can take place during many teachable moments throughout the day. For example, "All the children are painting, but you each made different pictures." . . . "Everyone at the table wanted a drink with snack, but some of you liked the orange juice and some of you wanted water."

Principles for planning activities

There are many activities that work for exploring cultural diversity and similarities as long as those activities adhere to a few basic principles. We will discuss those principles here and get into more specific ideas for activities in the next sections. Following these principles will facilitate your helping children to feel proud of their own culture and learn respect for others (see chapters 1 and 4). The principles will also help you to avoid the traps of a tourist curriculum (described in chapter 4). Remember to address any and all signs of misinformation, discomfort, fear, or rejection of cultural differences. Use both immediate and long-term interventions and teaching strategies (see the sections "Positive Interactions with Children" and "Curriculum Planning, Including Persona Dolls" in chapter 4).

● **Connect cultural activities to concrete, daily life experiences.**

Culture is not an abstraction to young children. It is lived and learned every day through the way family members interact: through language, patterns of communication, family stories, family routines, religious practices, music, household customs, and the responsibilities of family members. Talk about these family interactions with children to develop the theme of "We are all the same; we are all different" (e.g., "Yes, in your house children watch a video before bed, and in Micah's house children listen to a storybook"). Talk about the similarities and differences among children's everyday experiences (e.g., "Saresh's mom isn't wearing a costume. We call her dress a *sari*. It's a different kind of dress than the one your mama wears." . . . "You went to the St. Patrick's Day parade with your family this weekend. Mickey and his family spent Sunday at a church picnic. And I was at home making playdough! We all do such interesting things on the weekend").

● **Be intentional about including the cultural life of all families in your activities.**

Remember that every child has a home culture and every family in some ways is both different from and the same as every other family. Do not make the mistake of focusing on only the culture of children from so-called "ethnic minority" groups. Children from White ethnic/cultural backgrounds, including those children whose families have lived in the United States for many generations, are cultural beings, too.

● **Explore the similarities that exist among people across all their differences.**

Everyone laughs, cries, eats, works, and plays because we are all human beings. Yet people do all these activities in different ways. No group's way of doing things is superior to others, nor is one culture's behavior the standard and all others simply variations from that norm. For example, sleeping in a bed together with siblings is just as "normal" as sleeping in your own room is. Likewise, speaking languages other than English is equally effective for communication (e.g., "Tomás asked for *leche*, and Tommy asked for *milk*. You both wanted the same thing!"). In our culturally diverse world, there are many ways to meet the common human needs that all peoples share.

● **Avoid the editorial "we" when talking with children about cultural practices.**

"We do such and such" makes assumptions about homogeneity that may not be true. Say, "This is what I do," or "This is what we do in our classroom; you do it differently at home. Both ways are okay."

● **Avoid singling out one child or only a few children in your program whose cultural backgrounds differ from the rest.**

Remember that children in the cultural minority in your program are in a vulnerable position. They may not want to be different from the other children and will need teacher support to be comfortable with who they are as they find ways to connect with their peers. Make learning about these children's families part of learning about every child's family. Help the children learn that there are many other people like their classmates. Before beginning activities that address the culture of a child who is in the program's minority, talk with the child and family about what you plan to do. Tell the child, for example, "I want the other children to know more about people who are Vietnamese like you, so I'm going to read some books, tell a story about our doll Trang, and invite some friends of mine to school."

● **Always begin by exploring the cultural similarities and differences among the children, families, and staff in your program. Then expand to cultural groups beyond your classroom.**

This principle is vital to building children's understanding that differences and similarities are part of and enrich all of our lives. This is the bridge to respectfully learning about cultural ways of life with which the children do not have direct experience.

Activities to get you started

Now that we've explored basic principles for planning activities, here are a variety of activity suggestions to get you started exploring the diversity among the families in your program. We'll look at how to engage children in learning about several specific areas of a family's daily life. Additional areas of cultural life are discussed in chapters 6 through 11. In particular, the many ways family members work are explored in chapter 8, and how families celebrate holidays is explored in chapter 11.

As you read our activity suggestions below and create ones of your own, remember that cultural diversity exists even when families are all members of the same racial and ethnic/cultural group. If you look for diversity, you will find it!

The many people in our families

This is a good starting place to explore similarities and differences. While the structure of families both within and across cultural groups varies greatly, all families carry out many similar tasks.

● Borrow and take photographs of all the people who live with each child and any others seen by the child as part of the family. Make a bulletin board of "The People in Our Families." Label each photo with the person's name and relationship to the child. Talk with children about the similarities and differences among their families in terms of who lives in each household.

● Make a class book about "Our Families" for children to take home to share. Make a page for each child and each teacher about who lives with them and what work their family members do in and outside of the home. For the children's pages, get information from family members and from the child. For example, Maurice's page might say:

> "This is Maurice's family. He lives with his dad and his grandma. His aunt and uncle sometimes take care of him, too. Maurice's dad goes to college to learn to be a teacher, and he cooks dinner for Maurice and puts him to bed. Maurice's grandma brings him to school and works as a secretary. A dog named Gruffy lives with Maurice and his family."

Focus on what the child's family members *do* on any given day, not on where they are employed. Be aware that some children's family members may be temporarily or chronically unemployed. And some children may have a family member who is incarcerated (see the box "When a Child Has a Parent in Jail" in chapter

9 for suggestions on how to support children in this situation).

● Create a family shelf for families to take turns displaying objects they use in daily life and on special days. Or ask families to bring in an object that fits a specific theme, such as "Things we use to make our homes pretty." Intervene if a child makes fun of any object. Explain that it is hurtful to make fun of an object another child's family uses, even if he has not seen it before. Ask the child if he wants to learn about how his friend uses the object, and invite the friend to show him how it is used.

● Read children's books about families that are reflective of the ethnic/cultural groups in your class. Always use more than just one book about a particular group—no matter how accurate and respectful that book is. Talk about the differences and similarities between the children's lives in the books and the lives of the children in your program (e.g., "Is this how you make dinner in your family?"). Eventually, expand your selection of books by reading about cultural groups that are not represented in your classroom but that are present in your larger community or visible in the media.

● Tell persona doll stories. Have the dolls' stories reinforce specific families' ways of living, introduce new variations on a group's cultural patterns, and provide opportunities for the children to explore similarities and differences within and among families (e.g., "How is Luisa's family like yours? How is her family different? Isn't that interesting?").

The many ways our families speak

Learning about the many languages spoken by children's families is one part of exploring cultural similarities and differences. (This curriculum area, learning about language diversity, is not the same as supporting home language development and bilingualism discussed earlier in this chapter.) Even if all the children in your program speak English as their home language, people speak English in different ways. In addition, English-speaking children need to become comfortable with the reality that people in the larger community outside their classroom speak other languages.

None of the activity suggestions that follow requires you to know another language well—although it does help, and learning a second language as an adult will give you a wonderful way of connecting with families who themselves are learning English. If you choose to learn another language, however, plenty of resources are available, including friends, dictionaries, CDs, and college and community college faculty. You can even learn along with the children in your classroom.

The following activity ideas suggest possibilities for both multilingual and monolingual groups.

● If your group is multilingual, you will already be incorporating their home languages into your program through writing as well as speaking. You likely already have labels, children's books, signs, and so on, in their languages. All children can learn the words for common objects, numbers, days of the week, and so on, in the languages represented in your program. The families and children are resources to help staff do this. At snack time, refer to food in more than one language. Make a poster and a book about "The Ways We Speak" featuring four or five words children commonly use: names of family members and pets, *thank you, water, play,* and the like.

● If your group speaks only English, then use some of the methods just described to introduce a language that the children are likely to hear in their community. Display different writing systems (e.g., Chinese, Hebrew, Braille) to broaden their understanding that there are many ways to write the same words.

Respecting the English Language Learner

I used to go in early to the center to pick up my daughter, Amanda-Faye, so I could stay to observe. One day I decided to stay for story time. Mohammed, one of the teachers, was reading a book and mispronounced some of the words. When the preschool-age children started giggling, he put the book down gently and said, "I want to tell you that I come from a country called Iran, and we speak Farsi there. English is my second language, and many of the words are difficult for me. When I make a mistake and people laugh at me, it hurts my feelings. It's okay if you will help me say them right."

He was so gentle in his delivery. From the look on the children's faces, I could see that they understood. From then on, when I would hear Mohammed reading and making a mistake, I would also hear the children say, "Mohammed, that's not the right way. This is how you say it." Then he would thank them for their help.

I realized that it didn't matter that I still mispronounced words. I decided to try Mohammed's technique with adults and children and found that it really generated respect and understanding.

Source: Adapted from L.I. Jiménez, "Finding a Voice," in C. Alvarado, et al., *In Our Own Way: How Anti-Bias Work Shapes Our Lives* (St. Paul, MN: Redleaf, 1999), 32–34.

Consider introducing American Sign Language if you know it or know someone who does.

● Ask friends or staff who speak other languages to teach you how to sing a simple song in those languages. Luz Cardona, a preschool teacher, had parents help her learn to sing "Where, oh where, is our friend [child's name]; way down yonder in the paw paw patch" (a favorite song game) in English, Spanish, Croatian, Russian, and Japanese. The children would call out the language they wanted her to sing and would then sing with her, adding their names in the appropriate place.

Teach all children respectful ways to interact with people who speak a different language or speak English differently than they do (see the box "Respecting the English Language Learner"). Never let children tease or make fun of someone about how he or she speaks.

The many religious beliefs and practices of our families

As children learn about one another's families, they may note differences in religious practices. Families worship in various places—in churches, synagogues, temples, mosques, perhaps outdoors. Some families do not worship at all. Accept children's talk about their religious ideas as part of their family's way of life. Explain that each family has its own ideas about what and who God is (or isn't), and that all deserve respect in the classroom.

Religion often comes up when children are trying to understand issues of life and death. One 3-year-old asked her teacher if she could visit her grandfather in heaven. The teacher asked her what her mother said about that. The child replied she hadn't asked. "Let's ask her together when she gets here," her teacher said. This conversation inspired another child to announce that if they all said a prayer before eating, they would go to heaven. The teacher replied, "Some families say prayers before eating, and some families don't. Here at school you can say a prayer if you want, or you don't have to."

Religious beliefs are a central part of many families' home cultures and can provide direction, focus, and comfort for family members. Although public programs cannot teach a particular religious perspective or utilize religious icons, children often bring those objects into a classroom. For example,

> Stefania and Betina arrive at the center from a homeless shelter, where the sisters and their mother had taken refuge after an earthquake, shaken both emotionally and literally. Each child comes with a white satin Bible and instructions from their mother to keep it with them at all times. The staff aren't sure at first how to respond, but it is clear the Bibles are a source of comfort and reassurance. The teachers help the girls find clean places to put the Bibles during art and snack. Over the weeks, as the family recovers, the Bibles are left in the girls' cubbies for more of the day and eventually at home.

Children may make biased comments about religious beliefs. Handle such incidents as you would any other attack on a child's identity. In an anti-bias curriculum, every family has the absolute right to believe as they wish. At the same time, no one has the right to insist that one belief is better than another or to reject someone because of his or her family's religion. For example:

Five-year-old Andrew casually announces at circle time, "All you kids are going to hell." His teacher asks, "Why do you say that?" Andrew replies, "Because they didn't go to my church like I told them to." The teacher calmly answers, "Everyone does not go to the same church, and this is okay. You cannot tell others which church to go to. It hurts their feelings when you tell them they will go to hell."

In a religious school, where a particular belief system is part of the curriculum, anti-bias activities would include teaching respect for people who do not practice that religion.

The many ways our families eat

Activities involving food should be part of a larger exploration of the many ways children's families are the same and different. Whenever possible, provide what children normally eat at home for snacks and lunch. Include foods eaten by every child's family.

● Cooking and food preparation activities provide one way to build pre-literacy and pre-math skills, to encourage healthy eating, and to infuse anti-bias education into the program on a regular basis. Ask families to help with recipes and ideas for places to get ingredients. Choose easy-to-prepare foods that are appealing to young children and healthy such as salsa dip and vegetables, bean curd sticks, and *dolmas* (rice in grape leaves). Check out local farmer's markets for sources of interesting foods that reflect the cultural diversity in your community.

● Do not stereotype. For example, if you cook black-eyed peas, emphasize, "This is one of the things that Selena eats at home with her family. I like them, too." Do not say, "This is what African American people eat." If other children from the same cultural group eat different things, point that out.

● Do not mix up specific cultures. Families from Guatemala do not eat the same food as families from Mexico. Families recently from Mexico may not eat the same foods as third-generation Mexican Americans.

● Teach children ways to decline food without disparaging it. Invite, but do not force children to try new foods. Help them understand that "sometimes we like new things and sometimes we do not." Intervene immediately if children make fun of the food or call it "yucky," explaining that it is hurtful to make fun of the food another child likes. Teach them to respond considerately by saying things such as, "I've never tried that before; what does it taste like?" or "It tastes different to me." Teach them to say, "No, thank you. I don't want any today," when they really do not want to try a food.

The many ways our families sing, dance, and make music

Regularly play music from the children's home cultures and from the cultures in your community at movement and dance times, for relaxing at rest and nap times, and as background music at eating times. Also have this music available in the listening area. Use songs from all the cultural groups in your community that people from those groups really sing and listen to, not songs made up by a person from outside the group. Ask family members for suggestions. Choose songs that reflect concrete aspects of life that interest young children: work, lullabies, adventures, funny stories. Gather a collection of rhythm instruments used by those groups. Sharing one another's music not only helps children enjoy other cultures but it also contributes to building a sense of community among the whole class.

The many important people in our communities

Children thrive on stories about heroes—female and male, past and present—who have made important contributions to society. These heroes can include people in the larger society that children hear about, but it is important to begin with those people closest to the children's lives and families. Children often see especially beloved family members as heroes, as well as people in their neighborhoods who help their families with various tasks or who tell wonderful stories. Some children know people who work with others to improve their community. For example, Louise's mother worked with people in the housing project where Louise grew up to get a new school for the neighborhood.

When discussing well known people, be very concrete and tie their contributions to children's interests and everyday life. For example:

"Stevie Wonder is a composer and singer who has made many people happy with his music. He is also blind. He wrote a special birthday song for Dr. Martin Luther King Jr., now sung by many Black families on the birthdays of their own children."

"Dolores Huerta helped farm workers and their children have better homes, food, toys, and education."

"Maria Montessori was a doctor and a teacher, and it was her very good idea to have chairs and tables that are just the right size for you to use!"

Be sure to include the heroes of every child in your class.

Introducing diversity beyond the classroom

Once you have established a classroom culture that honors the diversity *within* your group, then you can begin to add learning opportunities about cultural groups beyond your program. Choose people from cultural groups with whom the children are most likely to interact in the broader community and when they go on to elementary school. Learning about people of even one new ethnic/cultural group helps children to think more broadly about human differences and sameness. You are also modeling respectful ways to learn about people with whom the children are not yet familiar.

● Get to know people—Invite in members of ethnic/cultural groups you want to introduce to the children. Choose people who are able to participate regularly in your program so the children can get to know them. Guests can tell the children stories about their families and their work, show and explain household and art objects, and teach songs and new words (if they speak a language other than English). They can also join in the children's activities. You may want to include people who are artists, as well as people who are especially respected for their contributions to their communities.

● Read children's books—Put together and use a selection of accurate books about children and families from the cultural group you plan to introduce. Most of the books should focus on current life in the United States (unless the group is transnational and travels back and forth between the United States and their home country on a regular basis; then you want books that show both lifestyles). Look for books that discuss themes that are common in the children's

lives. (For ideas on where to get books, see the "Anti-Bias" section of the NAEYC website: www.naeyc.org.)

● Create your own materials—Give one or two persona dolls the cultural identity of the cultural group you are introducing. Tell stories about the dolls' lives that relate to the lives of the children in your group. Interview people from that cultural community and make a poster or Big Book with photographs about them.

● Use folktales appropriately—Folktales (fairy tales, fables) are stories that come from the oral tradition, and every culture tells some. However, folktales do not teach children about the current, daily lives of people. Because the illustrations in most folktale books depict past times, using them to introduce new cultures can reinforce young children's misconceptions. Would you use *Cinderella* or *Sleeping Beauty* to teach children about current European or American life? Then don't, for example, use an African folktale to teach children about people's lives in today's Africa. Instead of misusing folktales in that way, use the many beautifully written and illustrated folktale books as a way to help children explore the many moral dilemmas these stories portray. Ask children, "How would you solve this problem?"

*   *   *

Fostering children's development of a positive cultural identity and their comfortable, respectful interaction with the cultures of others is the foundation of all anti-bias education work. In the following chapters, we look at several additional areas of identity and fairness—race, gender, economic class, family structure, abilities, and holidays.

As you move from one chapter to another, think of a kaleidoscope. Like the glass at the kaleidoscope's center, the core elements of anti-bias education are unchanging. Yet each turn of the kaleidoscope—like the diverse perspectives we hope to support as anti-bias educators—shifts those unchanging elements to create a new pattern. The values of anti-bias education will never change, but the perspectives on it are endless.

Remember to do culture and language activities that cultivate all four anti-bias education goals

Supporting New Immigrant Families and Children

by Luis A. Hernandez and Lisa Lee

People entering our country today follow in the footsteps of a long American history of ethnic and national groups seeking a better life for their children with the hope of economic betterment, religious tolerance, political freedom, and educational and individual opportunity. Increasingly, early childhood programs in communities all over the United States now include children from immigrant families. These "new American families" reflect the economic and political changes taking place in our country and in the world. How we act in the face of these changes helps to either open or close the door to the better futures families seek for their children

The 21st century immigrants to the United States are from a diverse range of populations and bring many different types of experiences with them to this country. Some immigrants are refugees from war, political persecution, and violence and may come into the country with nothing but the clothes they are wearing. Others come from professional and middle-class families and bring high levels of skills and education. Some come from farming communities and are prepared to work in the fields and factories that produce our food. Each immigrant family faces specific challenges and has distinct hopes for their children. For almost all of them, the experience of leaving their precious children in the care of strangers is a new and uneasy idea.

Stop & Think: Considering immigrant experiences

- What do you know about the experiences of new immigrant families in your community?

- What are your beliefs and feelings regarding immigrants?

- How have population changes in your community affected your life? How has your early childhood program been affected by immigration? What has that been like for you?

- Have anti-immigrant sentiments affected families and children in your community and state? your early childhood program?

- What is difficult for you in working with immigrant families? What gives you pleasure?

Misinformation about immigrants is everywhere. One prevailing and false assumption is that people who come from the island of Puerto Rico to the mainland are immigrants. They are not—Puerto Rico is part of the United States. However, their home language and cultural norms are usually not the same as the dominant U.S. culture, so they face some of the same struggles as immigrant families. A second common misconception is that all immigrant families from the same continent (e.g., South America, Asia, or Africa) share the same language, religion, customs, and nationality. They don't. A third mistake is confusing the culture of American-born people whose ancestors were immigrants from those continents with the culture of new immigrants from there.

Immigrant families from Latin America and their children

by Luis A. Hernandez

Families from Spanish-speaking countries were part of the American experience long before the English settlements at Jamestown. Across the nation, some of these families can trace back their histories 16 generations. More recently, immigrants from many parts of Latin America are changing the demographic picture of communities throughout the United States.

Like most immigrants, Latino families have had difficult decisions and choices to make in determining to come to this country. The most compelling reason lies in the stark contrast between our rich nation and the poverty faced by the immigrants in their homelands (to which U.S. multinational corporations sometimes contribute). People come through a variety of routes. Some U.S. companies directly recruit or encourage "word of mouth" incentives for already settled immigrants to bring other family members and neighbors to come work. The passage for these families can be difficult and dangerous, be it through legal routes or illegal crossings.

The Latino immigration pattern typically starts with men as the first arrivals, working along with other men from their home village or town, sharing housing and transportation. Initially, they send money back to their families, and eventually wives and children may join them. Many women, too, make the trek on their own, working as house cleaners or nannies and sending their earnings to sustain their children back home, sometimes not seeing or visiting them for years at a time. Once families have moved to a community in the United States, they slowly settle and assimilate, becoming our neighbors and sending their children to our schools and early childhood programs.

Whether they are urban professionals, rural farm workers, or any of a host of other possibilities, each family has a highly complex and dynamic, individual immigration story. A political and conflict-ridden debate exists around issues of legality, language use, and cultural adaptation at every level of community, state, and national life. New Latino immigrants experience a variety of culture shocks: adjusting to a different climate, enduring separation from loved ones, learning a new language, and a navigating a new dominant culture.

While Latinos have a common root in Spanish language and history (except in Brazil, where the language is Portuguese), each Latin American country has its own identity and cultural norms. Language use (amount, type of discourse, and even word choices and slang) by a person from Mexico is different from that of someone from Chile or Honduras. Families may speak Spanish or one of the many indigenous languages that existed in their native region before the Europeans arrived. External forms of culture—objects, art, music—differ widely. Immigrant families also are diverse according to their educational history and preparation, economic circumstances, urban or rural background, religious values and beliefs, and race or ethnicity.

Recognizing the many variations and nuances in immigrants' backgrounds and cultures, early childhood staff will understand the importance of learning from families about their history, hopes and dreams, goals for their children, and expectations regarding the program and teachers.

Caution: *Hispanic* or *Latino*?
Although the original federal policy term *Hispanic* was meant to refer to all Spanish-speaking groups, the term *Latino* is more current and embraces people from all across Latin America. Some people may prefer a "hyphenated" term such as *Mexican American* or *Cuban American*. It is always best to ask the person how he or she prefers to be described; we may be surprised by the range of answers reflecting the rainbow of immigrants.

Learning from my work with Asian immigrant families

by Lisa Lee

As Luis wrote about Latino immigrants, many Americans also erroneously believe that Asian immigrants are a homogeneous group. Asia is a huge continent containing many nations with different languages, religions, histories, and belief systems. In fact, depending on the socioeconomic, political, and historical circumstances in their nation of origin, the values, traditions, and religious and parenting practices of one family differ markedly from another as well as from mainstream American culture. In my work in San Francisco's Chinatown, I met many parents with professional backgrounds who now work in sewing factories and restaurants, as well as families who carried their economic wealth with them to the United States. And there are some families who came with hopes of survival, fleeing from war or political strife. At any given time, I heard multiple languages and dialects spoken in our small Asian community, and there are myriad stories behind why a family came to be in America.

Some immigrant families also are culturally quite different from American families whose ancestors came from the same country of origin in the past. One of my first teachers about this was a 4-year-old girl, the daughter of Chinese immigrants, who wisely declared, "Lisa, you're not Chinese!" I was the newly hired director of a program serving 99 percent Asian immigrants, the granddaughter of immigrants from China, with 100 percent Chinese heritage, so the child's comment stopped me in my tracks. Asking what made her think this, she reasoned, "You don't talk Chinese. You do not act Chinese. You are not Chinese!"

Even as I was focusing on how we were alike, this child was demonstrating awareness of the cultural, linguistic, and generational differences between us. I might *look* Chinese, but she clearly knew that I did not act or speak like her mother, who had grown up in China. Even in our seemingly homogeneous Asian community, she was able to see the complex diversity that existed within our ethnic group and between my assimilated customs and those of her own immigrant family.

For most families who choose to immigrate to America, life is not easy. Confronting bias and even virulent anti-immigrant sentiment, you cannot always be certain that you or your voice will be welcome. When there is much to learn, when you must navigate unfamiliar systems in an unfamiliar language, it is easy to feel "less than." When bias is woven into the fabric of society, it daily touches the lives of children and their family members.

Experiences with bias can be devastating. However, at the heart of anti-bias work, these experiences can be opportunities for positive action. I recall an incident of bias when the children and families in our program went on their annual fruit picking field trip. Despite previous arrangements, when our two busloads of families pulled into the farm parking lot after a two-hour ride, the owner refused to let the buses unload. "You people just pick and never pay for the fruit," he said. Despite the limited English speaking abilities of the adults in the group, they clearly understood his insult. The children watched as their parents grew silent and frustrated as the owner refused to serve them. He would have continued his refusal but for a lone, second-generation, American-born mother who accused him of discrimination in perfect English and threatened legal action.

Word of the fruit picking incident spread quickly during the following week with the result that the children and families in the entire center felt victimized. Witnessing their distress helped me to understand that when someone in power makes disparaging remarks about immigrants, such as "Go back where you came from," the entire community may feel frightened and unsafe. We responded as a community—parents, board members, and children. Teachers talked with the children. We wrote letters and sent complaints to the local business authorities and newspapers. Equally important, we sent a message to the children about standing up together.

However, it's important to know that engaging in action for social change is a cultural practice that can raise hidden fears as well as build unity. While nearly 90 percent of children of immigrants under age 6 are U.S. citizens, most live in mixed-status families with one or more non-citizen parents (Dinan 2006). I remember working in a school that served high numbers of immigrants and lamenting to a coworker about how hard it was to get some families involved, particularly in events that so obviously (to me) were beneficial to both children and parents. He helped me understand the difficulties that some immigrant families face with public institutions and other aspects of American life by asking me to think about the current anti-immigrant sentiment in our society. He then asked, "Would you choose to come to a parent meeting when you knew that by coming you might bring unwanted attention to your family? If you thought that when you left the safety of your home you might not get to go home to your children afterward, would you come? Would you march in a public protest with television cameras if you thought that your eligibility for citizenship or someone you loved might be impacted?"

Faced with this reality, a family's cautious interaction with institutions made perfect sense. Though I had good intentions, I had given little thought to the issues faced by many families of mixed legal status. My own privilege as a third-generation American clouded my appreciation and understanding of the context in which new immigrant children and their families find themselves.

Issues for children in immigrant families

As Lisa observes, "Every immigrant family I have met shared that they came to America with the hope that the lives of their children would be better than their own. Like my parents and grandparents wanted for me, they wanted their children to be successful in America." However, this desire does not mean that it is easy for either the children or their families.

Placing their children in the care of "foreign strangers" is a deep emotional experience for most immigrant families. It is far removed from the traditional child care practices in many of their home countries; it may even cause conflict within the family. Yet, they trust us with their children. Teachers who do not understand or sensitively address this reality will not provide quality care and education to these immigrant children. Conversely, the more teachers pay attention to the challenges immigrant families face and the strengths they bring, the better the children's education will be. For example, be prepared to give families as much time as they need to separate from their preschool child. If possible, ask another immigrant family who has been comfortable with having their child in the program to act as a temporary support.

From the stability and security of their homes, immigrant children and their families enter a world full of possibility, questions, misinformation, missing information, and contradictions. Early childhood educators introduce new ways of behaving and thinking to the children. The children of immigrant families must learn how to code switch (a cross-cultural jump between two or more languages and/or value systems, based on the context of a given situation) many times a day across home, school, community, and play. At the same time, many activities may set up cultural conflicts between school and home. For example, activities that encourage independence, such as self-toileting, taking turns, and promoting self-help skills, and which seem routine to teachers, may cause conflicts and confusion for young children who live in homes where *inter*dependence is highly valued. Families want their children to learn how to live successfully in the larger, dominant culture society, but they do not want the children to disconnect from their heritage. As children get older, this dilemma becomes more challenging for both children and families, often culminating in adolescence.

They also begin to become aware that certain differences are related to power and privilege, while others result in disrespectful treatment of people. Too often, children observe negative treatment toward their non-English-speaking family members and see the challenges they face in accessing supports and services. Combined with the growing emphasis from families and teachers to learn English quickly, some children stop speaking their home language at school and at home. Some begin to internalize the biases they are exposed to, subordinating aspects of their identity and home language at an early age.

The goals of anti-bias education easily adapt to the needs of children from immigrant families, provided that, as with other children, you respectfully partner with their families, incorporate the children's home cultures, promote their home languages and bilingual development (see chapter 5), and pay attention to each child's specific developmental issues. In addition, build awareness and sensitivity to your families' immigration experiences and to the conditions of their life in the United States. Network with community organizations that serve immigrant families to access local resources and services.

Learning About Racial Identity & Fairness

6

"You got eyes like Mei Ling," Anders says with interest to his Vietnamese teacher. . . . "How do people get their color?" asks 3½-year-old Heather. . . . Abby (age 4) asks her teacher matter-of-factly, "If I'm Black and White, and Tiffany is Black and White, why is her skin darker?" . . . Christopher, a White 4½-year-old returning from a vacation at the ocean, worriedly asks his teacher, "Am I still White if my arms are brownish?"

As these comments illustrate, young children are aware, curious, and have feelings about those physical features that connect to what our society calls "race." Eye shape, skin color, and hair fascinate children and are the first aspects of racial identity that they notice at the beginning of their long racial socialization journey that starts in early childhood and lasts through adulthood. Let's begin by looking at what we mean by race, and the societal realities within which American children grow up.

The system of race and racism we have inherited

The concept of *race* is a socially defined construct used as a way to fraudulently divide people into groups ranked as superior and inferior. The scientific consensus is that *race* in this sense has no biological basis—we are all one race, the human race. What the system of race *does* have is a long history in the world as a tool to justify one group's mistreatment, economic exploitation, and annihilation of other groups.

Throughout this history, racial groupings have been based variously on tribal affiliation, geography, culture and language, religion, and/or physical attributes. In the United States, skin color and other phys-

ical characteristics have been, and continue to be, the major grouping markers in a system of racism that has ensured economic and other societal advantage to Whites as a group. The earliest definitions of racial groups in colonial times focused on dehumanizing two groups, "Indians" and "Africans" for the purpose of stealing of the land from the indigenous people and creating the "White/Black" divide to justify slavery. When first written, the U.S. Constitution counted enslaved Africans as only three-fifths of a person and didn't count Native Americans (unless taxed) at all.

Arising from the work and struggles of millions of people over many years, and continuing today in the ongoing work by people of every racial group to end all forms of racism, we have seen some major, positive changes both in social attitudes and in the law. Among these are passage of the 13th and 14th Amendments to the Constitution, the 1964 and 1968 Civil Rights Acts, and perhaps most dramatically, the 2008 election of the first African American President.

Yet, the impact of race and racism continues to powerfully influence the life prospects of America's children. In every aspect of society, White children are more likely to have access to resources that support healthy development and future success, such as safe neighborhoods and good schools. Children of color are still disproportionately living in poverty.

Goals for Children

• Children will have accurate information about and feel comfortable with their physical characteristics linked to racial identity. (ABE Goal 1)

• Children will feel positive, but not superior, about their racial identity. (ABE Goal 1)

• Children will have accurate information about, and respect for, each other's individual physical characteristics; and they will appreciate their shared human physical characteristics. (ABE Goal 2)

• Children will demonstrate appropriate skills for identifying and challenging misinformation and stereotypical ideas about "race." (ABE Goal 3)

• Children will develop nonbiased responses to racial differences and will demonstrate beginning skills for interrupting biased behaviors and for creating a fair classroom environment. (ABE Goal 4)

Children of color are more likely to be members of low-income families who cannot afford health insurance or primary doctors. They are more likely to live in environments where they are exposed to toxic conditions, and their families have less access to healthy food at the lower prices for similar food available to higher-income families (Annie E. Casey Foundation 2009).

As Tarah Fleming, director of a multiethnic education program, explains,

While race is indeed a societal, made-up system, racism continues. It is therefore premature to decide not to talk about "race." Not talking about it does not end a hurtful system still very much in place. Instead of denying the term, we can understand its history and the way race works in accordance with access and power. Then we can begin to move toward new ways of talking about our ancestry.

Racial identity is shaped from the outside and constructed from the inside

In the United States, *racial identity* is a central social identity (along with gender, culture, and others). As such, it has reality and power in each of our lives. From our birth, we receive a racial identity based on the racial identities of our biological parents and on how the society in which we live defines racial groupings. Since the social-political constructs of race and racial identity are systemic realities, we cannot opt in and out of them. Regardless of whether or how we want to be identified by race, each of us continues to be subject to an externally defined and imposed racial identity—and to receive either the societal advantages or disadvantages connected to our racial identity.

However, as adults, we do have choices about how we understand and feel about our racial group membership—and the degree to which we identify with our racial group. (In some cases, such as some people of multiracial or mixed heritage, their sense of racial identity may not match how others perceive them.) We also have choices about *how we act* on our racial identity. Members of the White racial group can choose to believe in the myths of superiority that justify advantages and privileges to their group and intentionally help to continue the system of racism. Or they can reject and work against its myths and institutional dynamics in order to end the system of racism. Members of groups targeted by racism (*people of color*) can live as if the myths of inferiority are true descriptions of themselves. Or they can reject those damaging notions and work against the ideas and societal structures that create racial disadvantage for them.

People of one racial group can choose to incorporate cultural aspects from a different racial or ethnic group; for example, a White person can become fluent in Spanish and choose to live in a neighborhood where Latino people are in the majority. But he cannot choose to not be assigned a White racial identity by the larger society or to not have available the advantages accorded to Whites by the society. Conversely, a Black person may choose to live in a neighborhood where White people are in the majority and to take up their lifestyle, but the larger society still will define her as Black and she probably will experience racial discrimination

Racial identity, then, is about how we are treated by the society's institutions and by other people *and* about how we come to understand, feel, and live our racial group membership. It is both what other people say about us and what we say about ourselves.

Children gradually construct an internalized racial identity as they grapple with making sense of the relationship between their external experiences and their internal responses. Four interacting factors affect each child's racial identity journey—the larger society in which they live; their families and other significant people; their individual life experiences; and their stage of cognitive development. The messages and treatment children receive from people outside of their family (e.g., a teacher, a police officer, a pastor); from media (e.g., the kind and degree of visibility of one's racial group); and from personal interactions (e.g., rejection by a classmate because of their skin color) all interact with the lessons children learn within their families. Skills they learn for recognizing and negotiating racism dynamics also matter. All these factors deeply influence how children make sense of and feel about their racial identity.

The language of racial identity

People tend to think of race, ethnicity, and culture as being interchangeable aspects of identity. They are not the same, although they interact and overlap. Members of one racial identity group may have come from quite distinct ethnic/cultural groups, speaking different languages and having different religions. For example, African Americans originally came from many different tribal groups, with different languages and beliefs. Today in the United States, there are also Black people from Ethiopia, Belize, Cuba, and other countries. And many ethnic/cultural groups include members of different racial identities. For example, people from Mexico have skin colors that vary from very light to very dark; they might be considered Black or Indian or White.

How a society defines racial groups is determined by its dominant group using their own economic, historical, and social-political lenses. In his or her country of origin, a person may "look like" those in power and be identified as simply a citizen of that country. Yet, when immigrating or traveling to another country, that person may be considered and treated as "a person of color." For example, in the United States, an American citizen of Latino background may be incorrectly assumed to be an "illegal alien" because he is dark-skinned and speaks Spanish and may even be arrested during sweeps by the government.

The terms for racial identity vary over time *within* a society, as historical realities, legal definitions, economic and political relationships, and social consciousness change. Until recently, for example, the U.S. Census specified only a few racial categories. However, reflecting the greater recognition of diversity in the population, as well as political demands by specific groups, the 2010 Census will offer a more complex set of choices for answering the question about one's race. (Confusingly, some of the terms to choose from are based on "race constructs," while others are based on ethnicity.) The 2010 question-

naire offers many choices: *White; Black, African Am., or Negro; American Indian or Alaska Native (print name of enrolled or principal tribe); Asian Indian; Chinese; Filipino; Japanese; Korean; Vietnamese; Other Asian (print race); Native Hawaiian; Guamanian or Chamorro; Samoan; Other Pacific Islander;* and *Some other race (print race).* An additional question asks about "Hispanic, Latino, or Spanish origin"—that is, requesting that one answer both a question about Hispanic origin and the question about race.

Children grow up surrounded by misinformation about racial identity, confusing racial categories and terms, and contradictions between what people say and do. These factors make it challenging for young children to make sense of the world around them and to figure out who they are within it. Understanding this calls on teachers to pay attention to the larger societal contexts as well as the individual family and life experiences that influence the racial identity and attitude development of each child we serve.

When we understand that a children's racial identity is shaped from the outside *and* constructed from the inside, teachers can play a critical role in helping children make sense of the confusing and often emotionally charged messages they receive about who they are racially and how the world feels about who they are. Early childhood educators can foster children's accurate knowledge and positive feelings about their racial identity and about anti-bias relationships with others.

Stop & Think: Your earliest lessons about racial identity

- What is your earliest memory of noticing that people have different skin colors, eye shapes, hair texture and color? Did any adults help you think about racial differences?

- What messages did you get either directly or indirectly from your family, school, faith-based setting, media?

- As a child, what did you learn about talking about those differences? How do you feel talking about them today?

- When did you first begin to think about yourself as having a racial identity? What name did you put to it? How did you feel about your racial identity then? If you did not think about this as a child, why do you suppose that was?

- What is an early memory of realizing that some people receive hurtful treatment because of their racial identity? How did you feel about this? Did you have any information about people doing something to change the bad treatment?

Children's early experiences and understandings of racial identity

Children grow up impacted by many political and economic realities, as well as the contradictions connected to race and racial identity. Each child gradually constructs an internalized racial identity—based on how he is defined, valued, and treated by others as well as how the child himself thinks and feels about who he is. This requires teachers to pay attention to larger societal contexts as well as the individual family and life experiences of each child they serve. Pretending racial identity doesn't exist or doesn't matter leaves children to find their own way within a system of misinformation, confusion, and injury.

If we want children to thrive in a diverse world and to chose to stand up for themselves and others to create a more just place for all, then we must be proactive in helping children to construct a healthy, positive racial identity and respectful attitudes toward people of differing racial identities.

Children's comments, questions, and behaviors illustrate how they try to make sense of the society's teachings about racial groups and begin to construct their internal racial identity and attitudes toward others. For example:

> "What color blood do we all have?" the teacher casually asks a group of 3-year-olds in a child care center after having read a story to them about a child who hurt himself. "I have light red," says Michelle, who is White, "but I think Janine [who is Black] has dark red." As the children have certainly seen each other's blood from the times they have scraped or cut themselves, their surprised teacher asks if anyone else thinks, like Michelle, that people with different skin colors have different color blood. Some say yes, others no. She then explains, "I can see why some of you might think that if people have different skin color, their blood might also be a different color. But everyone has the same color blood, no matter what the color of their skin."

Children's ideas and feelings also reveal a beginning awareness of the power dynamics tied to the idea of race. For example:

> In one child care center in a California college town, a group of 4-year-olds is making books "About Me." Their teacher asks them to describe their skin color. The African American and Latino children respond with "black" . . . "brown" . . . "tan-ish." Several of the White children respond, "My skin is regular." . . . "Ordinary." . . . "You know, it's *skin* color."

Many people want to believe that children do not notice skin color, or they think that talking about the differences children see all around them will cause problems. But when adults are silent, children's lim-ited experiences and ability to make sense of what they see and feel may become the first step in developing prejudice or undermining their self-concept. Adult silence may also lead young children to conclude that the topic of racial identity is somehow dangerous. By providing language and information, we help prevent racism from harming children's evolving self-concept or influencing them to reject or fear others.

● **Infants and toddlers show awareness of skin color.**

When shown a series of photographs of faces, infants below age 1 were less and less interested as similar faces appeared. However, when a photograph showed a face with a different skin color, the infants' interest picked up, indicating that they were aware of the color difference. Infant/toddler caregivers can also vouch for the fact that children notice differences in skin color and facial features at a very young age. For example:

> When an Asian visitor enters the 1-year-olds room, an 18-month-old child takes her hand and leads her to one of the two Japanese American children playing on the floor. The child has clearly noticed a similarity and is "matching" child and adult. The teacher observing this says, "This is our visitor, Mrs. Chang. Are you introducing her to Lisa? Do you think she looks a little like Lisa's mommy?"

● **Preschoolers talk about their own and others' racial characteristics.**

Many adults spend considerable time teaching young children the names of colors and describing things based on their color and yet are surprised when these same children indicate awareness of skin color. Regardless, young children are frequently interested in the color of people's skin, as well as hair color, hair texture, and eye shapes, as these examples show:

> During story time, Hector (age 4) leans over and touches Jamal's hair. Jamal pushes his hand away. The teacher asks Hector if he has ever touched hair like Jamal's before. Hector shakes his head no. Jamal interjects, "He didn't ask me if it's okay." "Would it be all right if Hector asked first?" the teacher asks. "Yes," Jamal answers, turning to Hector. "Ask me and then you can touch it. Then I want to touch your hair." Because Jamal has given his permission, the teacher says, "Yes, it's fun to touch and learn about each other's hair as long as we ask first. Did Jamal's hair feel the same as or different from your hair?" (If Jamal had said it was not all right for Hector to touch his hair, then the teacher might have said, "We have to respect what Jamal says. There are other ways to learn about each other's hair.")

"Craig's eyes go like this," says 4-year-old Ruth, pulling her eyes up. The teacher replies, "Craig's eyes are a different shape than your eyes. Both your eyes do the same thing—they let you see!"

Sometimes children's comments about their physical characteristics also give us signals about how they feel about their skin color, eye shape, or hair texture. For example:

Two 4-year-old friends, one Black and one White, are chatting.

Mike: I'm going to get new pants.

Doug: What color?

Mike: Blue.

Doug: What about brown?

Mike: I don't like brown.

Doug: Oh, then you don't like me.

Mike (looking surprised): Yes, I do.

Teacher: There's something important I want to help the two of you figure out. Doug, why do you think Mike doesn't like you?

Doug: I'm brown; he said he didn't like brown.

Teacher: Mike, Doug thought when you said you didn't like brown you meant you didn't like his brown skin either. Is that how you feel?

Mike: No, I don't like brown pants; I like brown Doug.

Teacher: Doug, is that okay? (Doug nods his head yes and the two go off together.)

Immediately responding to children's questions and comments, as well as initiating activities for all the children to explore their observations and curiosity about skin color, hair, and eyes, supports healthy identity development. Ignoring, diverting, or reprimanding young children's curiosity about physical features connected to race (e.g., "Oh, it doesn't matter what color you are; we are all people." . . . "We don't talk about that. It isn't nice") conveys the message that these aspects of themselves and others are at best embarrassing, and at worst bad.

● **Preschoolers want to know why physical characteristics differ and will create their own explanations.**

Preschoolers' questions reveal their powers of observation, their curiosity, and their efforts to make sense of what they see. In the process, they create their own unique explanations about the physical characteristics of racial identity based on their experiences and according to the cognitive tools they possess at their stage of development.

"How do people get their color?" asks 3½-year-old Sandra. "What are some of your ideas?" her teacher responds. Sandra explains, "Well, I was wondering

about pens." (Sandra likes to use felt pens to color her hands and arms with different colors.) "I'm glad you are trying to figure things out," her teacher tells her, "but that's not how people get their skin color. It is a little hard to understand how it happens. We get our skin color from our birth mommies and daddies."

With children 4 years old and up, teachers can read simple books that explain about skin color.

Nick (age 4) likes to play with Miyoko, a child recently arrived from Japan. His teacher notices him pulling on his eyes, trying to make them the same shape as Miyoko's. When the teacher asks Nick about what he is doing, Nick says, "I want to make my eyes like Miyoko's. If I learn to speak Japanese, will I have eyes like hers?" His teacher tries to clear up Nick's confusion by explaining, "Each of you gets your eye shape from your family, not from the language you speak."

If the child is adopted, explain that eye shape comes from the child's birth family, using whatever term the family uses.

Four-year-old Rudy tells his teacher, "I want my skin to be as dark as Paolo's. He's my best friend." His teacher responds, "It's great that you and Paolo are best friends. I know you have a lot of fun playing together at school and at home. You don't have to be just the same to be best friends."

As these examples illustrate, children can be very inventive. It is important to take the time to ask them for *their* ideas before jumping in with your own explanations about skin color and other physical characteristics. Provide accurate information in ways they can developmentally grasp. They can begin to hear—in simple terms—about the scientific reasons for physical differences, but they will not fully grasp these concepts. For example, preschoolers will not fully understand the idea of melanin, but introducing the concept lets children know that there *is* a reason for skin color differences.

Young children are curious about a whole range of their own and other's physical characteristics, not just those linked to racial identity. Effective early childhood education helps children learn about all aspects of themselves. (See chapters 7 and 10 about differences based on gender and on disability.)

● **Preschoolers try to understand the names of and criteria for racial categories.**

Young children find the connections between racial group names and the actual color of a person's skin confusing. They wonder why two people with different skin tones are in the same group. Using their preschooler logic, they try to make sense of what are truly nonsensical socially/politically invented racial groupings.

"Why am I called Black? My skin is brown." . . . "I'm not yellow; I'm tan." . . . "My skin isn't white; it's pink." . . . "I'm not Black; I'm African American."

Preschoolers also express puzzlement about the relationships between "color" terms and the names of different ethnic groups.

Carmela asks, "Is Mexican my color?" Her teacher replies, "No. 'Mexican' is not a color. It is the name of a big group of people to which your family belongs."

"Am I red?" Leroy, a 4½-year-old Navajo child, asks in a puzzled tone. "Tate (a 4½-year-old White child) said I'm a 'Red Indian,' but I don't see any red on me." His teacher responds, "You're right, Leroy, there is no such thing as a 'Red Indian.' You are Navajo, and your skin is brown, not red. Let's go talk with Tate and explain to him so he won't make the same mistake again."

"You're not Black, you're White," 4½-year-old Leticia, an African American child with dark brown skin, tells 4½-year-old Carol, a light-skinned African American child. Carol looks confused. The teacher intervenes, saying, "Leticia, Carol is African American just like you even though the shades of your skin are different. You are both Black because you are part of a big family called Black people or African Americans. At group time I will read everyone a book, called *Shades of Black* (by Sandra L. Pinkney), about the different skin shades of African Americans."

At preschool age, children usually do not yet understand the politics and history of racial group terms. Nor will they yet grasp the distinction between race and ethnicity. However, they do need adult help sorting out their ideas and getting some accurate information. For example, adults can help children learn that the racial names grown-ups use for a large family of people is not the same as our actual skin color. Exploring these topics with children conveys the message that it is okay to want to understand.

● **Biracial or multiracial children and children in transracial adoptive families have additional questions.**

Children in these families often struggle with which categories of racial identity to apply to themselves. They also have to deal with their peers' confusion.

"Which part of me is Black and which is White?" asks a 3-year-old biracial child. He shows his hand to his mother and says, "This part (the top) is Black, and this part (the palm) is White." His mom replies, "All of you is both Black and White."

"Who's your real momma?" asks Mateo when Pilar's White mother brings her darker skinned daughter of Salvadoran heritage to school. "This is my momma!"

Pilar indignantly proclaims. "She don't look like your momma," Mateo insists. Their teacher steps up and, smiling at Pilar's mother, says, "Mateo, are you noticing that Pilar and her momma have different color skin? That's true. But Mrs. Carter *is* Pilar's momma. Pilar's skin is a mix of her daddy's color of skin and her momma's color of skin. Isn't that wonderful?"

Kim Lee keeps insisting that his black hair is "yellow" and that his brown skin is pink like his mother's. In his artwork, he always colors his mother and himself with the same hair and skin colors. The teacher decides to talk with Kim Lee's family about ways they can help Kim Lee eventually understand that his mom is his mom even though they don't look the same and that she and his father love him just as he is.

Teachers need to listen for and be responsive to the questions of children whose parents differ from each other in racial/ethnic identity, or children who differ from the rest of their family. Adults must help children sort out their ideas and feelings in ways that work at their developmental level. It helps to find out what term(s) each family uses with their child to describe the child's identity (e.g., *interracial, biracial, multiracial, multiethnic, mixed*). Some will prefer the name of the racial group of color (e.g., "Maya is Black, not biracial"). Some parents will need support for sorting out their ideas and feelings about how to name and teach their child about his or her racial identity. When possible, use the same terminology in the classroom as the family uses at home.

Tamara's kindergarten teacher asks the children to raise their hands if their families are Japanese American. Tamara raises her hand high. Then the teacher asks the children to raise their hands if their families are Mexican American. Again, Tamara raises her hand up high. "Oh," said the teacher, "you must be half-and-half." "I am not!" Tamara says indignantly, "I'm all Tamara!"

Preschoolers in transracial adoptive families can find it difficult to understand how they got their physical characteristics. It helps when children get clear messages about the distinction between *birth* families (whom they may not know at all) and their *adoptive* families (who are their real, everyday love and identity connection). Once they are developmentally capable of understanding the concepts of *birth parents* and *adoptive parents*, children's questions become very similar to those of children in biracial or multiracial families.

Similarly, ask the family how they have described adoption to their child and what words the family members use to describe racial physical differences. Use children's books about transracial adoption and persona doll stories to help children articulate their confusion and get clarification. (See chapter 9 for more about adoptive families.)

● **Preschoolers need help resisting harmful messages about their racial identity.**

Hearing and absorbing disparaging messages about any aspect of their physical appearance and racial identity is toxic to young children's evolving self-concept and confidence. The old adage "Sticks and stones may break my bones, but names will never hurt me" would be more accurate changed to "but names will break my heart." Teachers need both immediate and follow-up strategies for interrupting and handling harmful messages about all aspects of a child's identity.

> "I'm going to make my eyes straight and blue," 4-year-old Cindy tells her teacher. "Why do you want to change your lovely eyes?" Danica, her teacher, wonders. "It's prettier," Cindy says. Danica replies thoughtfully, "Cindy, I don't think straight eyes are prettier than yours are. Your mommy, grandma, and grandpa don't think so either. We like you just the way you are, with your beautiful, dark brown eyes shaped just as they are. Why do you think straight and blue eyes are prettier?" Cindy answers, "Sarah said I had ugly eyes. She likes Julia's better." Danica tells Cindy that Sarah was wrong to say that, adding, "It is not true, and it is unfair. Let's tell her about it."

It is also important to nurture a positive racial identity in White children that does not include ideas of superiority. For example:

> A 4-year-old White child, noticing that her skin is darker than her two White friends', asks worriedly, "Does that mean that I'm not White anymore?" and repeatedly asks for reassurance that she is still White. The teacher reassures her, "You are still White. White people have different skin colors. All skin colors are good." The teacher decides that he will plan several activities to explore skin differences and to build children's awareness of how people of color and White people contribute to our daily lives.

● **Pay attention to covert as well as overt messages that children hear.**

Take seriously all of children's expressions or behaviors that reflect negative messages about their racial identity or feelings of inferiority or superiority. Remember that what may seem like "a little thing" by itself to *you* can add up with other little things to cause serious harm—so don't ignore it. Be alert for indicators of discomfort or potential bias (e.g., anxiety, teasing, name calling, or exclusion) and be sure to learn more about possible underlying causes as you plan further action.

Frequently children pick up negative messages about skin color from subtle cues in the world around them. For example:

> After being taken to see a popular children's film, 3-year-old Alice says soberly, "I don't like all those dark people." At first, her grandmother is puzzled, as all the animated characters in the film were animals. But then she realizes that all the "good" animals were golden, and all the "evil" ones were dark. While her grandmother struggles to think of what to say, Alice adds, with relief in her voice, "I'm not as dark as Audra (her older sister)."

If you can't think what to say, are uncomfortable responding directly and matter-of-factly to an incident, or later feel you mishandled it, talk to someone you trust to explore your feelings and possible responses. *Always* go back to the child with your new response. (See "Positive Interactions with Children" in chapter 4 for guidelines for addressing these matters.)

Stop & Think: Talking about racial identity

■ What is it like for you when a child raises an issue about race? How comfortable are you talking about this topic with children? What makes you uncomfortable? What would help you to respond appropriately?

■ In what kinds of situations in your life today do issues of racial difference come up? What is that like? Are there things you wished you understood better so you could speak more clearly about them?

■ What, if anything, do you do when you see or hear racial prejudice, including a racist joke? What would you feel and do if someone told you that you spoke or behaved in a prejudiced way?

Strategies for learning about physical differences and similarities

Creating a rich anti-bias learning environment sets the stage for discussion and activities about racial and other physical differences and similarities. The richer the environment, the more likely children will ask questions, even in classrooms where the staff and children come from similar racial backgrounds.

In all activities, highlight that physical diversity among people is desirable, and that all colors, shades, and shapes of people are beautiful. Talk about differences in a tone of delight and interest. Create a vocabulary that encourages children to look at themselves and others and admire their sameness *and* their uniqueness. Just as we do not wait until a child asks questions about how to read before planning how to provide a range of literacy learning opportunities, anti-bias education is the teacher's responsibility, not the child's, to initiate.

As you decide on activities to do with children, you may want to review the Goals for Children at the beginning of this chapter and the ideas in the section "Curriculum, Including Persona Dolls" in chapter 4. As you adapt activities and invent your own, you will want to tailor them to the specific cultural and developmental needs of the children with whom you work.

Caution—Never single out one specific child when you do activities about the physical characteristics linked to racial identity. Every activity should be about *all* of the children, as everyone has a racial identity. Moreover, doing activities about all children reinforces that differences and similarities can be found within each racial identity group as well as across groups.

Exploring skin color, hair, and eyes

Children are active observers of physical characteristics. As they become familiar with some of their own features and those of their classmates, help them to have vocabulary and ideas to understand sameness and difference.

● Ask children for their ideas about what skin does for us. Talk about how all skin does the same work for people, regardless of its color. Do the same for hair and eyes.

● Make a life-size cutout of each child from butcher paper, and use mirrors to help each child observe his or her skin, eyes, and hair color and then select the crayons and paints that most closely match those colors. Alternatively, provide a range of skin-tone drawing paper and mirrors and invite children to draw portraits of themselves. Older children can work with partners, deciding together which colors to use. Invite children to tell about their cutout figures or portraits at circle time. Mount them around the room. Comment on the beauty of each child's color choices.

● Make a wall chart of children and staff handprints using skin-tone paints or photos. This can also be a class book with each child's name written under his or her handprints.

● Take two photographs of each child—one of the back of the child's head and one of the child's face. Mount all of the photographs on stiff paper, and make a matching card game called "Can You Find Whose Hair Goes with Which Child?" Include pictures of staff in your game. Similarly, make cards with photographs of only the children's eyes and let children match to their full facial photos. You can also use photographs of children's faces to make a book or chart about different skin colors and eye shapes/colors (Wolpert 1999).

● Read books about the beauty of different kinds of hair and skin color—for example, *Hairs/Pelitos* (by Sandra Cisneros) and *All the Colors We Are/Todos los colores de nuestra piel* (by Katie Kissinger), both of which have simple language and beautiful images.

Focus on children's confusion about their own skin color

If, when you invite the children to make self-portraits, a child chooses colors that do not correspond to his actual skin, eye, or hair coloring . . .

● Consider gently encouraging the child to choose the color closest to his skin color.

● If the child objects, it may be better not to pursue the subject immediately, but rather to observe whether this continues to happen at other times, such as when the child is drawing herself spontaneously.

● If the coloring is playful (some children paint themselves with rainbow colors, or bright green), and the child is relaxed and comfortable, then you don't need to take further action.

● If you judge that the child is showing signs of rejecting how he looks (perhaps thinking that physical characteristics closer to those of White people are more desirable), make a plan for what you can do to strengthen the child's identity. This may include speaking with the child's family about what they want their child to know about his racial identity and coming up with a shared plan.

Exploring how we are alike and different

There are many ways to involve children in discovering similarities and differences among themselves, their teachers, and their families.

● Make a book about the physical characteristics of every child and staff member. Take color photos of each person, paste each on its own page, and ask children to describe themselves, writing what they say under the photo. Include skin, hair, and eye color among the characteristics. Be sure to have sufficient lighting when photographing darker skin tones so that facial features show up clearly. When the book is complete, read it to the children at circle time.

● Make a bulletin board of color photographs of each child and the members of each child's immediate and extended family. You can take photographs of family members yourself, and/or invite them to provide their own. Talk about ways in which each child looks and does not look like her or his family members. Focus on the fact that we get our looks from our birth parents, but we never look exactly the same as them. Place the bulletin board at the children's viewing height.

● More fully explore the range of physical differences among individuals *within* a racial group and the physical similarities among individuals of *different* racial groups (e.g., eye and hair color, skin color, height). Even in a classroom of all White children, differences in skin color and features will exist (e.g., freckles, skin tone, eye and hair color). You may also extend your exploration to include similarities and differences other than physical features (e.g., wearing glasses, choice of hairstyle, food preferences, favorite games). Integrate math concepts by helping children graph the range of skin, eye, and hair colors and hair textures represented in the classroom.

● Talk about how children who look different from one another still often like to do the same things. Take photographs of the children doing various activities, and use them to make a Big Book featuring children who look different doing the same activity (e.g., "Adeel and Adam like to play with blocks" . . . "Maria and Amanda like to play ball"). Be careful never to make sweeping generalizations about a group of people (e.g., "White people like to eat . . .").

● In kindergarten and beyond, introduce children to very basic scientific explanations for variations in skin color, hair texture, and eye shape. Talk about the advantages that certain physical attributes give people in certain environmental conditions: Darker skin provides more protection from the hot sun than lighter skin; the "epicanthic fold," which determines the eye shape of people with Asian origins, provides protection against the glare of snow or from flying dust. Blue eyes and "white" skin are predominant among peoples who originated in Northern Europe where the sun is less strong. Be sure to explain that these changes took *thousands* of years and that traveling to another part of the world won't change their characteristics.

Expanding awareness of racial similarities and differences

After helping children become aware that the people within their family are alike and different, it is important to expand their knowledge and awareness to groups of people beyond those in the classroom and neighborhood. As children grow, they move into ever wider and more diverse settings, and we want them to be open to and respectful of all kinds of people they may encounter.

As we have discussed, teachers need to be very careful in their efforts to acquaint children with other groups in ways that do not make the groups seem exotic or strange ("tourist curriculum"). For example, if the only Asian people children see are in pictures and wearing kimonos, they can come to believe that all Asian people wear kimonos—and that they wear them all the time!

Following these strategies will help children extend their awareness of the similarities and differences of racial groups outside of their family or neighborhood.

● Make sure you know the people who make up the children's larger community. Remember that the people they see on television are part of their wider awareness.

● Find out children's ideas about people whose racial identity is not present in your classroom. Show accurate pictures and ask: "What do you know about a person who looks like this?" . . . "What do you think this person eats? Where do you think this person

lives? Where does this person sleep?" . . . "Does this person have a family?" . . . "Does the girl/boy have the same or different color skin, hair, and eyes as you do? How do you think she/he got that skin color?" . . . "Do you know people who look like the person in the photo?" Once you have this information, you can then plan a series of activities to counter children's specific mistaken ideas and to teach them accurate information.

● Tell persona doll stories that introduce children to diversity in racial identity. (This activity will overlap with persona doll stories about different cultural ways of living.) Make sure that stories address similarities shared with the children in your group, including diverse family ways of life.

● Read authentic books about children from different racial backgrounds who are doing activities familiar to children in your program (e.g., going to a birthday party, visiting the doctor, welcoming a new sibling). Help children identify similarities and differences between the child in the story and themselves. Ask them: "What did you like about the story?" . . . "What is he/she doing that you like to do? What is different from what you do?" . . . "How is her/his family, home, etc., the same or different from yours?" . . . "Does the girl/boy have the same color skin, hair, and eyes as you do?" This is another place where "We are all the same; we are all different" makes a lot of sense to children.

Fostering critical thinking and respectful relationships

Positive and accurate learning experiences about human differences and similarities help to give children a foundation for resisting incorrect and harmful messages about themselves and others. Preschoolers are ready to begin thinking critically about the accuracy and fairness of the information and images they encounter. They also have the capacity to use their developing empathy to understand that unfair behavior hurts people and can learn respectful ways of interacting with others. Teachers can use the following strategies to promote young children's development of these understandings and competencies.

● Cultivate children's empathy and ways to deal with the hurt of stereotyping. Read books that depict children experiencing unfair treatment based on their racial identity. For example, *Amazing Grace* (by Mary Hoffman) shows a spunky little girl whose classmates tell her she can't be Peter Pan in a play because she is a girl and because she is Black. Children quickly

understand that something hurtful and unfair has happened and love to read about Grace's eventual success at playing Peter Pan. Talking about the prejudice and hurtful messages as well as Grace's resistance gives children language to put to their feelings and reactions.

● Another way to cultivate empathy is to tell persona doll stories about a discriminatory incident between dolls (e.g., one doll saying to another doll that her skin is "dirty" because it is dark), engaging children's empathy and problem-solving skills. Or have a persona doll present specific images that children see regularly (e.g., stereotypical images of Native Americans in greeting cards or a children's book); ask children, "How do you think the doll might feel when she sees the untrue picture?" . . . "How do you think you would feel if it happened to you?" Encourage children to think of various things the dolls could do to deal with the hurtful image.

● Intentionally plan activities to counter potential overgeneralizations or existing stereotypes in the children's general environment.

> A harvest curriculum is being planned for late October. Living in California, the staff worries that some of the children might believe that only people with brown skin harvest food and that only White people sell food. They have already decided to invite some farm workers to school, but now they make sure that it is a multiracial group. They read books such as *Gathering the Sun* (by Alma Flor Ada), which celebrates Mexican farm workers, and *Apple Picking Time* (by Michele Benoit Slawson), which shows a family of pickers who are White.

● It is also important to support children as they demonstrate awareness of stereotyping.

> Benjamin is playing with his Lego toys, one of his favorites. Suddenly, he looks at his teacher and announces, "You know, all of the people in this set are White!" His teacher responds, "Hey, you're right. There should be Black and Asian and Hispanic figures, too. I'm proud of you for noticing because it is important to notice when things are unfair like that."

● Engage children in group action. It is empowering when we help children take action to turn something "unfair" into something "fair." Sometimes this involves addressing personal conflict, helping a child speak up to another child, for example. But it is particularly powerful when children act together. The following examples illustrate ways that early childhood teachers in different settings have worked with children to respond to specific issues of racial bias in their programs.

Nancy Spangler's class of 3- and 4-year-olds was a multiracial group, and she had worked hard to see that her classroom reflected every child. One day she grabbed from the storage room a box of game cards that matched people in work outfits with the tools they used. The cards were wonderfully gender neutral, but Nancy noticed that all the people were White.

Nancy called the children together and asked, "Do the people on these cards look like all the people you know?" The children said no, identifying skin color, age, and even pregnancy status as "missing." "Is it fair to have cards that exclude so many people?" The children agreed it was not. With Nancy's help, the children wrote a letter to the manufacturer explaining what was wrong. Then she got out the skin-tone pens, and the children re-colored the cards so they would "look real." They also colored in the dogs in the pictures!

Sometimes families get involved in classroom activism, as well:

Bj Richards, a preschool teacher working in a setting with African American, Latino, and White preschoolers, wanted to diversify her doll collection of five White dolls and one Black doll, but she had only a tiny budget for new materials. She decided to raise the problem with the children. She showed them a collage they had made with their photos and then their doll collection. "Are there dolls that look like you? How many look like you? Do you think that is fair to everyone?" Most children agreed it wasn't fair. "Do you think we need more dolls to be fair?" Again, most children thought they did.

Bj then suggested the children, the staff, and their family members help make cloth dolls. The children dictated a letter to their families explaining the problem and inviting them to a doll-making workshop. Bj showed the children an example of a cloth doll, and the children made a list with her of materials they would need: cotton fabric in sand, beige, and several shades of brown, plus a variety of materials for hair of different colors and textures.

Knowing that one child's grandmother was a skilled seamstress who had experience making dolls for the family, Bj asked for her help in making patterns and sewing the dolls. After the parent-staff workshop, some family members offered to finish any uncompleted work. The children dictated a thank you note and drew cards for the participating families.

Other times children become activists in their neighborhoods:

Molly Scudder and her predominantly White kindergarten class regularly walked to a play area a block from their school. One afternoon she saw that someone had written racial slurs on a nearby wall. She stopped the children: "Do you know what is written on this wall? It makes me very angry." She read the words, and the group talked about what the words meant, how they are very hurtful to people, and what the children could do about them. They decided to paint over the words. She also decided to follow up with classroom activities, including reading the children a few books about prejudice and developing a wall chart about what to do if a friend says something hurtful about how another person looks or who she or he is.

* * *

If we want children to thrive in a diverse world and choose to stand up for themselves and others, then we must choose to help young children make sense out of the confusing and often emotionally charged messages they receive about themselves and others. The commitment to support each child to develop pride and self-confidence and deep connections with others calls on us to foster *all* children's healthy racial identity. When we give children language to discuss their identities in an atmosphere of interest and delight, and the tools for addressing the unfairness they will inevitably encounter, then we know we have helped children construct a strong foundation for the next phases of their lives.

Remember to do activities about racial identity that cultivate all four anti-bias education goals

Supporting Multiracial, Multiethnic, and Mixed Heritage Children and Their Families

by Tarah Fleming

Multiracial and multiethnic children are a fast-growing population in the United States. Families are interracial or multiethnic by marriage or partnership or transracial adoption. They negotiate daily the color and culture lines of American society, and, by preschool age, so do their children.

About multiracial, multiethnic, and mixed heritage families

The terms "multiracial," "multiethnic," and "mixed heritage" cover a wide range of racial identity and ethnic combinations—including parents who racially or ethnically identify differently from each other (e.g., an African American mother and Mexican father); or one or more parents who themselves identify as mixed heritage (e.g., a Navajo-Arab-Japanese father and Pilipino-Indian mother); and parents of the same racial identity who adopt a child of a different racial identity (e.g., a White couple and an Asian baby). People may use any one of these three terms depending on the context, as well as other terms as their own. Always ask what terms a family uses to describe its identity as well as their child's.

It is also important to understand the distinction between a White multiethnic ancestry and a multiracial or multiethnic ancestry of people of color. Having a mix of European ethnicities in your family history (e.g., Polish, Russian, English) has a very different impact on a child's identity development than does being in a family in which members come from both the White (dominant) cultural group and racial/cultural groups of color. Having parents who look very different from each other or very different from you makes the reality of "difference" very present in the family early on.

In addition, every multiracial or mixed heritage family experiences racism. However, each family feels the impact of racism differently, depending on their particular backgrounds, identities, and strategies and skills learned for coping with stereotypes, bias, and racism. In addition to the various forms of racism experienced by people of color generally, such as invisibility and fear, multiracial and mixed heritage families often experience special bias because they don't "fit" the social stereotypes created by racism. One unique source of injury is the institutional pressure on official forms to choose one racial group or else be "other." Stereotypical assumptions made by others are another source of injury.

Stop & Think: Having a mixed racial identity

- Do you have a multiracial, multiethnic, or mixed ancestry? If so, what are its various elements? How much do you know about the various aspects of your identity? What do they mean to you?

- How did your family talk about your racial and/or ethnic identities? Did your family keep secret or simply not talk about any aspects of your identity when you were a child? If they did, why?

- When you meet someone who is multiracial, multiethnic, or of mixed heritage, what guesses or assumptions do you make about how they self-identify? About their family structure or physical appearance?

Issues facing multiracial, multiethnic, and mixed heritage children

It is impossible to decipher the individual makeup of multiracial or multiethnic children because they can come in almost any color, shade, or hue. Their hair can also be any texture, regardless of heritage. Because how young children feel about their appearance directly influences their feelings about identity, it is important to beware making assumptions from appearance or making mixed heritage children "exotic" (by redundantly pointing out their beauty or unique physicality). Families and educators must consciously help multiracial and multiethnic children embrace how they and others look. Within their families and communities, children's observations about differences in skin color (and other outward characteristics) will start as early as age 2 and continue throughout their lifetimes.

Knowing who they are—and having a name for their identity—is essential for children's positive identity development. Like everything else in a young child's life, this begins within the family. Multiracial and mixed heritage families tend to take one of four positions about the identity of their child: (1) the child's identity is that of the parent of color, when the other parent is White; (2) the child is "mixed heritage" or "multiracial," and each parent's heritage is considered equally important; (3) racial/ethnic identity is "not important" for the child; or (4) the family feel confused about how to deal with their child's racial/ethnic identity.

To serve families effectively, it is essential that we first find out which position they take. With that information we can help their child begin to embrace a full understanding of his or her identity. For example, many families have transracially adopted children who were old enough to have begun forming their identity. Their families and teachers need to support them to develop within the framework of *both* cultures.

Issues for children in families that are multiracial or multiethnic by marriage or partnership and those by transracial adoption are similar in many ways, but not all. For example, a child of color adopted by White parents faces the additional challenge that the parents have not personally experienced racism and are therefore not as comfortable with or skilled at preparing their child for negotiating a race-conscious society. Parents who actively connect with resources and community can, however, gain the necessary understanding.

What would you do?

A high-quality early childhood program plays a critical role in supporting families and their children across all these issues.

Pamela, 4 years old, is in foster care. Her file says her birth mother was African American and her birth father was Latino. However, it identifies her only as "Black/African American" and she looks African American. She has never known her birth parents. Pamela's friends in preschool are Latino, and she tells them that she is, too, and pretends to speak Spanish. Her foster parents are African American. They want to support her in the best way possible but are not sure how to. They want to talk with Pamela about this issue, which has come up a number of times at home and at school. They ask you to give them ideas on how to handle this important issue.

What would you tell Pamela's foster parents?

Max and Tina, a White couple, adopted a 2½-year-old girl from China, whom they named Jean. One day Jean is still finishing snack when her parents come to pick her up. You have a few minutes to chat with them. You mention that they now have a "multiracial" family. They are quick to respond: "There aren't any differences—she's American now, like us." . . . "Jean doesn't see race; and we see everyone as equals, so we're not making it an issue."

Do you agree with Max and Tina's views? Why or why not? How would you respond?

Jilly and Sam are playing on the outdoor climbing structure. Jilly says, "Sammy, who is your mommy?" Sam looks upset because he has been asked this question many times before. He says, "You know my mommy, she brought the cupcakes yesterday." Jilly replies, "She can't be your mommy; she's white, and you're brown." Sam starts to cry. One of the teachers overhears the conversation and comes quickly over. She squats down at Sam's eye level, puts her arm around him, and pats him a couple of times. He stops crying. "Look," she says enthusiastically, "Miss Diane is setting up a new activity in the yard. Let's all go try it out."

Would you have handled this situation between Jilly and Sam differently? Why or why not?

Strategy Tips for Welcoming Multiracial, Multiethnic, and Mixed Heritage Families

In addition to the usual strategies for creating a welcoming environment for all families:

• In your philosophy statements and admittance forms, be sure to include sentences that specifically name and support multiracial and mixed heritage families.

• Find out what terms each family prefers you to use for their child's racial/ethnic identity. Do not assume.

• Include information about all kinds of families in staff training. Be sure to seek out resources and information to be up to date on all the possible racial/ethnic configurations.

• Provide opportunities for families if they want to think through their child's identity issues with you or with other families in the program.

• Include in a welcome package for all families positive images, materials, and children's literature that depict multiracial and multiethnic families.

Learning About Gender Identity & Fairness

7

Annie is one of the most rambunctious 4-year-olds in the classroom. She loves gross motor play, speaks in a loud voice, and rarely sits still on her own. While we are talking about a book we have just read together and the gender stereotypes in it, Annie says, "But Julie, I don't like girls." I am surprised, as one of her two best friends is a girl. "Why not, Annie?" "'Cuz girls can't run and shout and have a good time," she says sadly. "But Annie, you're a girl. And you love to run and shout and have a good time," "No," she replies, "I'm a pretend girl." I am stunned. How could it be that a 4-year-old has to deny her gender in order to be who she really is? That is when I decide I have to engage in an effective anti-bias curriculum around gender.

Gender is the first core identity that gets young children's attention. It develops very early: By age 2, children begin to notice physical differences and begin to describe themselves as boys or girls, although they are not yet sure what that means (Sprung 2007). By age 3, children have ideas about behaviors, activities, and toys that go with gender: "Boys don't cry." . . . "Girls can't play with a hammer." . . . "He can't have a doll, he's a boy!" . . . "Toby is a boy's name; she can't be a Toby." Three- and 4-year-olds tend to define gender by behavior and appearance rather than by anatomy. By age 4, children are often rigid in their insistence on limited and stereotypical gender role behaviors. By 5, most children have deeply incorporated a gender identity reflecting the gender expectations of their family and the larger society (Klein et al. 2007).

Gender identity includes both gender anatomy and gender role. The physical (anatomical) characteristics that will define us as being male or female are a product of our biology. Then our environment (family, culture, peers, society) teaches us about male and female gender expectations; that is, how

someone with that anatomy is "supposed" to behave. Individual experience and disposition also influence how we understand and carry out those gender roles, but gender role expectations and limitations are still among the strongest messages children receive.

Typically, a person's gender anatomy and gender role align. Sometimes, however, a child is born with anatomy that is not unambiguously that of one gender or the other or has features of both genders (*intersex*). Sometimes a child's anatomical make-up does not match the gender role he or she identifies with (*transgender*). These children and their families will need support for a more complex developmental journey.

While gender anatomy is universal, the behaviors and attitudes considered to be typical and acceptable for each gender differ from culture to culture. And just as cultures are always changing, so are gender role definitions.

Supporting all children to develop their fullest range of abilities and skills is one of the key principles of the early childhood education field. Learning environments and activities that are gender-equitable put this principle into practice. However, when children absorb messages that limit their exploration and play, neither boys nor girls are able to prepare fully for the intellectual and emotional realities and demands of life (Klein et al. 2007).

For example, limits on boys learning how to express and manage feelings (e.g., "A big boy like you doesn't cry") may curtail their development of emotional literacy, which risks leaving boys with only physical methods for dealing with their own strong emotions or else poor communication and problem-solving skills. The connection of being "manly" with boisterous, gross motor activity can undermine boys' willingness to engage in quieter, less physical activities that are important for cognitive development (e.g., reading books, doing puzzles). Messages that girls are not strong and must be very careful not to get hurt can inhibit (or eliminate) their active play and spirit of adventure; these messages may also result in poor spatial and mathematical cognitive development. Many adults still praise girls for their looks rather than for their achievements—a message that devalues girls fully developing their intellects.

Effective teaching strategies for meeting the goals of this chapter (as for all anti-bias education goals) take into account families' cultural views, as well as children's individual development. Gender role expectations vary from family to family within a culture and from cultural group to cultural group. Building strong partnerships with families is essential to finding ways to create gender-equitable learning environments that are also culturally sensitive. The ideas and guidelines discussed in chapter 5 on culture and language will help you understand better how to do this.

Children's experiences and understandings of gender identity

Young children struggle with many issues as they attempt to understand what being a girl or boy means. The support they do or do not get in their preschool years lays the foundation for the rest of their gender identity formation.

● **Many preschoolers are not yet clear about what actually makes them a boy or a girl.**

Rather than their gender anatomy, young children typically focus on the external and cultural aspects of their gender identity—that is, they believe that how they dress (appearance) or what they like to do (behavior) is what makes them a girl or boy.

> Three-year-old Logan says to Marcus, "You're not a boy. You have long hair." Marcus looks confused.

> Caitlyn puts on a hard hat and goes to play at the woodworking table. "Look at me," she announces. "Now I am a boy. Later I will be a girl again."

These ideas may come from children's observations of people in their home and community life or on television, from what they hear adults say, or from a combination of sources.

Young children also often believe that they can switch their gender from male to female or from female to male by shifting their behavior. Coming to understand *gender constancy*—that how they behave does not change their being a girl or a boy—is a significant developmental task that early childhood teachers can help children figure out.

> John's mom has just given birth to his sister. At the child care center, he puts a pillow under his shirt and asks his teacher, "Can I be a mom and have a baby when I grow up?" "You can be a daddy," she replies, "and right now you can pretend to be anything you like."

Goals for Children

• Children, regardless of gender, will participate in a wide range of activities necessary for their full cognitive and social-emotional development. (ABE Goal 1)

• Children will demonstrate positive feelings about their gender identity and develop clarity about the relationship between their anatomy and their gender role. (ABE Goal 1)

• Children will talk about and show respect for the great diversity in appearance, emotional expressiveness, behavior, and gender roles for both boys and girls. (ABE Goal 2)

• Children will recognize unfair or untrue messages (including invisibility) about gender roles. (ABE Goal 3)

• Children will practice skills for supporting gender role diversity in their interactions with peers. (ABE Goals 3 & 4)

"Sara says I'm not a girl because I don't like dresses," teary-eyed Kalia complains to her teacher. "Do you think you are still a girl?" her teacher asks. Kalia shrugs her shoulders. "Well, you are still a girl," her teacher answers. "You are a girl no matter what you like to wear. Your body makes you a girl, not your clothes. How you dress is fine. Let's explain this to Sara."

● **Children may not have words for gender anatomy.**

By preschool, many children have already learned discomfort or embarrassment with the anatomy that makes them a girl or a boy.

"How do you know if you are a girl or a boy?" a teacher asks his group of preschoolers. Everyone has an idea: "Boys wear pants." . . . "Girls have long hair." . . . "Boys play with trucks, girls play with dolls." . . . "Boys like to run around, girls like to sit." When their teacher asks, "What's the difference in our bodies?" some of the children giggle.

As early as preschool, learned social embarrassment about gender anatomy begins to show up as giggling and teasing about bodies. Adult anxiety surrounding talking about gender anatomy both teaches and reinforces such behaviors and can be an obstacle to helping children sort out their confusions.

● **Children are influenced by others' attitudes about gender behavior.**

By age 3 or 4, children's comments and interactions reveal the influence of family and societal attitudes about gender behavior, coupled with children's own developing attempts at understanding the world (Klein et al. 2007). These ideas about what is and isn't "normal" for a particular gender are powerful. Under their influence, young children often impose narrow or stereotypical definitions of how females and males are supposed to look or dress on their classmates or on their own choices.

Alfonso, a teacher in the 4-year-olds room, wears an earring. At snack time, the children at his table ask him whether he is a man or a woman. They cannot agree—some insist he must be a woman because "only women wear earrings."

In a discussion of favorite activities, Pete declares, "Only girls play with playdough," even though playing with dough is one of his favorite activities. "But you were making wonderful things with your dough this morning," his teacher observes, "and other boys were at the table with you, right?" Pete names one; his teacher helps him recall two others. "I like to play with playdough, too," José chimes in. "My dad plays with it at home," adds Kimi. "So, is it true that only girls play with playdough?" the teacher asks. Everyone says no, and Pete looks relieved.

Even when their own firsthand experiences contra-

dict gender stereotypes, young children still may proclaim the stereotype as the truth.

Four-year-old Rashad and the teacher are looking at a picture book in which characters engage in highly gender-stereotypical activities. When they reach the page "Cars and Trucks," the teacher stops: "Rashad, this book is making me mad because all the drivers are men, and that is not true. Women drive cars and trucks, too." But Rashad shakes his head, "Uh-unh, ladies don't drive trucks," he declares. "But Rashad, how did you get to school today?" asks the teacher. "My momma brought me," he replies. "In what?" asks the teacher, already knowing the answer. "In our red pickup truck," says Rashad. "And your momma is a lady, isn't she?" asks the teacher. There is a long pause, then Rashad replies, "Yeah—but the truck really belongs to my *uncle*."

Don't get discouraged when stereotypical gender preferences and remarks continue despite a rich gender-equitable curriculum. The key is to provide many opportunities for new ways of thinking and acting. Over time, children's ideas about gender behavior may become more flexible and broader as their understanding of gender and gender roles develops.

● **Children may experience emotional conflict about acting differently from societal norms.**

Annie, in the opening anecdote of this chapter, finds it necessary to create a "pretend girl" category to reconcile her love of active play with her gender as she understands its definition. She is also already unsure she even likes girls or wants to be a girl, perhaps because of her impressions of the social limits on what that gender can do.

Even when a child's family or the preschool environment supports children's divergent choices, children may struggle with differences between what they like to do and what societal stereotypes or their peers say about what they are "supposed" to do. Ignoring such conflicted feelings can result in children developing a negative self-concept about their gender identity. For example,

Rosalie, an active 4-year-old, asks her teacher, "How do you think I look today?" Her teacher responds, "I think you look fine. Why?" Rosalie replies, "Sometimes I think I look ugly." Her teacher pursues this: "But why?" Rosalie considers her answer. "I don't know, I just do. . . . I look like a boy," she says. "Do you think you look ugly because you look like a boy?" Rosalie says she does.

"Why do you think you look like a boy, Rosalie?" her teacher probes. "Because boys wear jeans and shirts [her favorite clothes]," Rosalie replies. "Do you think you have to wear a dress to look pretty?" Rosalie nods. "You know," says her teacher, "you also look wonderful in jeans and a T-shirt, and sometimes it's easier to play in them because they don't tear as easily. You don't look like a boy. You look like Rosalie, no matter what you wear."

When children seem to be feeling such a conflict, it is important that adults encourage them to talk about their feelings about going beyond stereotypical rules of gender behavior.

Some of the favorite costumes in the center are made from women's skirts. Small slits cut just under the waistbands for the children's arms let the skirts become superhero capes, princess gowns, doctor's uniforms—anything the children want them to be. One morning the teacher puts out some of the costume skirts. Brad puts on the red one, but Victor hesitates. He reaches for the bright turquoise, satiny one. "Is this a boy's costume?" he asks. "Are you a boy?" the teacher responds. "Yes," he replies soberly. "Then if you wear it, it's a boy's costume," she says. Victor's face brightens, and he puts it on and with arms outstretched swirls around with delight.

A few minutes later, Giovanna comes over and stares at Victor. "That's a *girl* dress," she says emphatically. Victor's face clouds. His arms come down. He pulls the skirt off and kicks it, saying, "You're ugly," and leaves it on the ground. That is the last time he wears one of the bright and shiny costumes.

It also may be very useful to initiate activities that enable the whole group to explore feelings of conflict when what they like to do differs from the prevailing gender norms, or what a child thinks is the norm.

Victor's teacher hadn't seen his interaction with Giovanna, but she does notice that Victor has stopped wearing the shiny costumes he had seemed to enjoy so much. She casually asks him why, and he sadly tells her what Giovanna said. Knowing that other children sometimes struggle with the conflict between what they like to do and what their peers think they are "supposed" to do, the teacher plans to open up the issue with the class.

At the next circle time, she tells them all a persona doll story about a boy and a girl doll that are also told they can't do a favorite activity because it is "only for boys" or "only for girls." She explores the dolls' feelings with the children and then asks them what the dolls' classmates could do. After the children share their ideas, she adds some ideas of her own. A few days later, she notices several boys playing comfortably with the costumes. But Victor never goes back to wearing them.

● **Acknowledging children's nonsexist behavior provides further support for their choices.**

Often, providing this support simply requires a brief comment. For example:

Sofia is playing firefighter wearing the hat and jacket. Samuel wants them for himself. "Girls can't be firemen," he tells Sofia, trying to take off her hat. "Yes, they can," Sofia insists, pushing his hand away from her hat and continuing to play. Samuel walks off. Their teacher, overseeing their interaction, comments to Sofia, "I'm glad you spoke up for yourself when Samuel said girls can't fight fires. They can."

But again, it may also be useful to initiate follow-up activities with the whole group, as this teacher did:

Cody loves playing with the dolls in the dramatic play center. In his family, his dad takes care of him and his siblings while his mom is at the factory. One day his teacher sees Derek playing with blocks next to the dramatic play center. She overhears Derek tell Cody, "Boys don't play with dolls." "Yes they do," insists Cody. Their teacher decides to step in, "Derek, many boys play with dolls. Do you know that men take care of children, like Cody's dad takes care of him, his brother, and his sister?" Derek looks dubious and goes back to his play with blocks. The teacher also decides to do an activity with all the children during large group time about men who take care of young children as daddies, uncles, and teachers.

● **When teachers model a range of roles and interests that transcend traditional gender stereotypes, they encourage and support children in exploring a wide range of cognitive, social, and emotional learning experiences.**

Be sure that responsibilities for tasks around the program are not divided along narrow gender roles. Female teachers can fix broken toys, participate in active outdoor games, use tools, and do science activities. Male teachers can participate in dramatic play, comfort upset children, and serve and clean up snack. It makes a big difference when male and female staff rotate through all the tasks so children see nonsexist roles modeled in every part of the program.

Of course, it is much easier to demonstrate that women and men can and do carry out a wide range of roles and activities when your program has both males and females on the staff—and when they play a variety of roles. If your program staff are all female, as is frequently the case, then invite family members, staff friends, or community members to come tell children about the range of jobs done by men and women.

● **Teachers can unintentionally convey messages of stereotypical gender behavior in their interactions with children.**

Sometimes teachers' responses to children reflect long-learned expectations of gender roles that reinforce narrow or stereotypical ideas. We may not even still believe in these messages or realize what we are conveying.

> When I (Julie) was working at a university preschool, we had the idea of videotaping ourselves so the student teachers could see what good practice looked like. My video showed me greeting children as they arrived—down at their eye level, speaking to each child individually, like the good master teacher I was.
>
> Suddenly, I had a shocking moment of self-realization: I greeted every little girl with a patter about her clothing: "Hello Laurie! What a pretty blue blouse you're wearing today." . . . "Hi, Karla. You have new jeans and new tennies, I see!" And I greeted every little boy with a comment about action: "Hey there, Tou. I put the blocks out for you." . . . "Good morning, Josue! Your friend Devon is here already, waiting to play with you." On the tape, one little boy stood in front of me, stamping his feet. The power of unconscious stereotyping was evident, as not until he stuck his foot in my face did I notice what he was saying: "Look, Teacher! I got new boots!"

It is often hard to actually see what we are doing until someone calls it to our attention. Teachers can help each other pay attention to unconscious and unintended behaviors that convey messages about gender roles we do not want to teach. It helps if we ask someone who works with us to observe for a few days and note what we do. (See chapter 3 for more information on collaborating with colleagues this way.)

Stop & Think: Learning about being a boy or a girl

- What were your earliest lessons about there being different expectations for boys and for girls? Where did you learn these lessons (home, school, religious setting, friends, media)? How did you feel as a child about those lessons?

- As a child, what did you like about being the gender you are? Did you ever want to be a different gender? If you did, why? Did you feel any conflict between what you liked to do and what you thought you were supposed to do?

- How did the adults in your family divide work and responsibilities by gender? Have you followed or changed those roles as an adult?

- How old were you when you figured out that boys and girls had different kinds of bodies? Who, if anyone, helped you figure this out? Do you remember your reaction to this discovery?

- What words, if any, did you learn in your childhood to describe male and female anatomy? Are you comfortable now using the anatomical terms with children? If not, why?

- What do you remember learning about how important physical appearance was to your family, friends, and life success? How did you feel about yourself in relation to these messages?

- What is your current thinking about gender roles and appearance? In what ways is your thinking the same or different from what you learned as a child? How do your views influence how you work with children?

Strategies for helping children understand gender anatomy and identity

The purpose of the activities that follow is to help preschoolers understand that their being a girl or boy depends on how their bodies are made, not on how they dress or what they like to do. Exploring this distinction between anatomy and identity is one part of forming a healthy gender identity that early childhood teachers can support children in doing.

Talk with children about gender anatomy

Be prepared for giggling; handle it by being matter-of-fact and clear. Here are two examples of conversations with 4-year-olds, led by an experienced anti-bias educator:

> During circle time, Malcolm announces he has a new baby at home and that the baby "drinks milk from my momma's titty." Some of the children giggle and all of them look to the teacher to see what she will say. "That's right, Malcolm. A mother's breasts make milk to feed her baby. Some families call them 'titties,' some call them 'chi chi,' and some families don't like to say any word for breasts at all." "That's dumb," says Mei scornfully. "No," the teacher replies, "different families have different ways of talking about bodies. And that's okay."
>
> "Can men feed babies?" There was a chorus of yeses and nos. "Boys don't have titties," Malcolm insists. "Right again," says the teacher, "but there are other ways to feed babies, too." The children eagerly begin to talk about daddies and bottles and about their own experiences feeding babies.

That story and one below illustrate the dual task of being truthful with young children *and* being sensitive to family differences in talk about gender-related anatomical terms.

> As the children are getting ready to go outside for a rain walk, Malcolm pulls on a pair of flower pattern rain boots he got from his sister. "Oooh," says Antonio, "Malcolm's a girl! Malcolm's a girl." "Am not," growls Malcolm. "Are too!" shouts Antonio. The teacher intervenes. "Changing clothes doesn't change being a boy or a girl. Our bodies are what make us a boy or a girl." "I bet Malcolm's got a

girl body," teases Antonio. "No," the teacher replies, "Malcolm has a boy body. He was born with a boy body, and no matter what clothes he wears, he still has a boy body."

The teacher also writes herself a note to talk to both boys' families about this conversation, discuss how they explain to their child what makes a boy body different from a girl body, and suggest they initiate such a conversation at home.

Help children distinguish between anatomy and identity

Be proactive and responsive to children's questions. Look for opportunities to initiate interactions that offer children accurate information and let them try out their ideas about the differences between being male or female and acting like a boy or a girl.

● Encourage children to show respect for their bodies. As part of forming a healthy gender identity, all children need some language for talking about how the bodies of boys and girls differ. Using standard anatomical terms such as *vagina*, *vulva*, *penis*, and *testicles* creates a common educational language. Some families (and teachers) are comfortable with such terms, and many children know and use the terms. Other families (and teachers) use colloquial terms such as *yoni*, *'gina*, or *peepee*. What terms you use in your program is not as important as is using them in a matter-of-fact way that conveys to children there is nothing shameful about the parts of their body that make them a girl or a boy. Interrupt giggling or teasing about body parts or terms for them, anatomical and otherwise. A teacher could explain:

> "These are parts of our body that tell us if we are a girl or a boy. They are part of who we are. We need these parts just as we need eyes or arms. So, let's not make fun of them or the words we use for them."

● Read books about the body to familiarize children with all aspects of it. This will also enable you to address discomfits with talking about the body in general. Unfortunately, although there are a few good books for young children about the body (e.g., *The Human Body,* by Sylvaine Peyrols and Gallimard Jeunesse; *Human Body Encyclopedia,* from DK Publishing), they leave out gender anatomy. This transmits the message that gender anatomy is not to be spoken about. Try to find the few children's books that do show gender anatomy, such as *The Bare Naked Book* (by Heather Stinson); *Bodies* (by Barbara Brenner), which has excellent photographs of children; and *What Is a Girl? What Is a Boy?* (by Stephanie Waxman), which is out of print but may be available at a public library.

● Many programs use anatomically correct dolls. Some put the dolls out for children to play with freely; others use them in persona doll stories to help children explore issues of gender identity. These stories also provide teachers with opportunities to use anatomical terms in a matter-of-fact way. Sometimes, a family may object to your using anatomical dolls with their child. If this is an issue in your program, having respectful conversations with the family can lead to finding a third space solution (as described in chapter 4).

Work sensitively with families

Some families are not comfortable with anatomical terms for gender anatomy, others with any terms for it; some may disagree with teachers doing activities that challenge gender role stereotypes at all. Many times, this discomfort comes from a family's mistaken ideas that such activities teach sexuality rather than help children form healthy gender identities. Here are some strategies for working with families on these topics:

● Find out what the family specifically objects to and why. Ask how they explain the differences between male and female anatomy and what terms they use. Listen respectfully, and be sure to check that you have heard them accurately.

● Be clear in your own mind about the gender identity developmental tasks that young children face and the rationale for gender-equitable education.

● Be sure that you understand healthy sexual development in the preschool years. Also be sure you understand that sexual orientation (e.g., heterosexuality, homosexuality, transgender) does not develop from the activities children do, it is based in a child's particular biology. No play activities *cause* homosexuality—or stop it. (A good resource on this is *Healthy Sexuality Development* [Chrisman & Couchenour 2002].)

● Engage the family in dialogue about why you do activities that provide accurate information and terms about gender anatomy and its relationship to gender identity. Explore which activities the family can accept.

● If you notice their child saying or doing something that makes you think the child is struggling to understand gender differences, ask the family whether you can suggest to their child that he (or she) ask them, "What makes a boy (girl) body different from a girl (boy) body?" This way, families can be prepared for the question when it comes.

• Actively search for third space solutions. For example, if a family will not send their daughter to school in pants, perhaps you can all agree to keep a pair of pants at school for her to wear during specific activities, such as outdoor play. If a family believes that boys do not clean up, explain why this is important for all children to do at school and see if you can agree on an explanation that preserves the family's values at home (e.g., "Clean-up tasks at school are part of the job of learning").

• Know your bottom line. For example, regardless of a family's views, never permit the teasing of a peer based on the child's clothing, hairstyle, choice of activities, and so on. All families need to know that your first responsibility is to keep all children safe and supported. While you strive to meet every family's need, you also strive to stay true to your profes-sional responsibilities. Most of the time you can do both, by honestly searching for common ground with the absolute conviction that families love and care for their children—and so do you.

Expanding children's gender behavior and attitudes

If we just leave children alone, they naturally gravitate toward whatever activity or idea sparks their interest—without regard to gender—right? Unfortunately, the reality is that "free play" is not very free, as even young children may already hold restricting, gender-based ideas about what kind of play is right for boys and what kind is right for girls. There are many ways to help children engage in a broader array of learning activities than they may choose on their own.

The Sexualization of Childhood

by Diane Levin

Today's children are growing up in a highly sexualized environment that is marked by gender stereotyping of both girls and boys in media and marketing, violent content linked to products targeting boys, and use of sexual content and imagery to sell products to girls. A large part of the blame for this situation can be placed on the doorsteps of marketers who use sex and violence to capture children's attention and get them to buy products, in part made possible by the deregulation of children's television by the Federal Communications Commission in the mid-1980s.

The problem is not that children are learning about sex when they are young. The problem is the particular lessons they are learning in today's environment. Children's ideas about what it means to be a boy and girl and about the nature of sex and sexuality develop gradually and are greatly influenced by the information provided by their environment. Today's media and commercial culture bombard children with graphic sexual images and information that they cannot possibly understand and that can even frighten them. Children learn narrow definitions of gender and sexuality that focus primarily on appearance. Girls learn that their value is determined by how "sexy" they look, rather than by who they are or what they achieve. Boys learn to judge girls by these shallow standards and to judge themselves and each other by how strong and independent they seem—and how ready they are to fight.

When children are young, they should be having positive, age-appropriate experiences that lay the foundation for healthy sexual relationships in the future. Today, both girls and boys are learning to treat themselves and others as objects. This objectification can promote precocious sexual behavior—absent caring relationships, and long before children can understand the deeper meaning and implications of such behavior.

Caring adults can do a great deal to help children develop to their full potential as boys and girls and help lay the foundation children need to develop caring sexual relationships of their own when they grow up. For instance, we can:

• Protect children, as much and as long as possible, from popular culture's sexual onslaught.

• Counter the belief that consuming more and more products is the road to happiness.

• Help children develop a wide range of behaviors that get beyond the stereotypes.

• Stop blaming children for the sexualized behavior they have learned from the sexualized environment.

• Help children feel safe talking to us, so we can help them process what they see, answer their questions, clear up confusions, and influence what they learn.

• Provide models of caring and affectionate intimate relationships in our own families.

• Encourage parents and schools to work together to support each other's efforts to help children deal with issues of early sexualization.

• Work at all levels to create a society that supports the healthy sexual development of children and that limits the ability of corporations to use sex to sell to them.

For further reading

Levin, D.E., & J. Kilbourne. 2008. *So sexy so soon: The new sexualized childhood and what parents can do to protect their kids*. New York: Ballantine.

Moreover, how teachers organize the learning environment also influences children's choices.

Help children try out new learning centers

Observe children's play during open choice time over the course of a week. Note in what ways their choices divide along gender lines. Do girls mostly play in the housekeeping area and use "quiet" materials (e.g., puzzles, books, drawing supplies)? Do boys rarely use these quiet materials? Do boys, but not girls, most frequently play in the blocks area and use "action" materials (e.g., cars and trucks, tools, balls, climbing structures)? During dramatic play, are the boys mostly doctors, superheroes, or firefighters; are the girls mostly nurses, babies, or waitresses? Do only girls join in on dancing? Do children tell classmates that they cannot play in a specific area because they are a particular gender?

The purpose of your observations is to help children find a balance between being able to engage in their activities of choice and *also* in activities not typically chosen that are valuable for their cognitive, social, emotional, and physical development. Remember that while we want to support choice, children's choices are not completely "free," as they are influenced by both overt and covert expectations.

Based on your observations, plan how to resupply and reorganize areas of the classroom environment to encourage choices that are more diverse and less stereotypical. Changing the environment encourages most children to try new activities, although some children will need extra support. For example, join in yourself until children feel comfortable using new or unfamiliar materials. Make a point of inviting reluctant children to try new materials and activities with you until they seem comfortable initiating such activities themselves. Watch for gender stereotyping in the dramatic play area. Add new ideas to expand interest across gender-limited behaviors. For example:

> Miss Zela places stuffed animals in the dramatic play area after a field trip to the zoo, and the girls play with them day after day. The teacher talks with them about what kind of places the different animals need to play and sleep in and asks, "Do you think you could build the pandas something like that?" The girls consider the question, than go get blocks and boxes and begin constructing cages and trees.

● Expand the dramatic play area beyond housekeeping equipment and props. Add tool belts and tools for making "home repairs"; put writing and reading materials (e.g., paper, pencils, computer keyboards, newspapers) in the "study" or "home office."

● Consider putting the block area next to the dramatic play area, without a shelf or boundary between them, to encourage children to build their own additions to their dramatic play (e.g., a car or bus, a gas station).

● If you notice that the boys avoid dancing and rapidly turn any dance into loud jumping, invite a male dancer in to dance with the children. Follow up with reading a book that shows male dancers, such as the photo book *Dance* (by Bill T. Jones and Susan Kuklin).

● Have an "Everybody Plays with Blocks Day" or an "Everybody Does Art Day" once a week for a month or until many girls and boys are comfortable choosing block play and art at free choice time. (This method requires extra blocks: Team with another teacher, using her blocks on your block day, and vice versa.) Work with individual girls or boys who need extra support.

● If you've noticed that girls still tend to stay away from the block center and the boys are dominating it, have several "girls only" block times: Explain to the children that this is necessary because you have noticed that very few girls are playing with the blocks, while most of the boys are. "It is important for girls to play with blocks, too, to learn how to build things." Work with the girls during this block time, explaining, "We are going to learn lots of ways to use blocks." When they have developed confidence in their block-playing skills, have them work on their own in groups of two or three. After the girls gain experience with blocks, form boy-girl teams to play there together and help them to work together. In the meantime, boys who usually choose blocks can choose other centers—especially ones they usually avoid.

● Use the same approach of a "boys only" time every few weeks for art activities, dramatic play, and small manipulative materials to expand their repertoire of activities. These "girls only" and "boys only" days are usually very successful and can make big differences in a short time. Children mostly seem relieved and excited when supported to play beyond stereotypes.

Establish nonsexist routines and experiences

Children observe carefully and learn a great deal from how adults organize their lives. The covert messages children acquire ("When Mommy and Daddy are together, only Daddy drives the car") are stronger than the overt messages ("You can be or do anything you want to").

● Insist that all children take equal responsibility in carrying out the jobs necessary for maintaining the classroom or center. Create rotating boy-girl helper teams to do each task, and appreciate them at circle times.

● If you use lining up as a method for organizing children's group movement from one place to another, invite children to make a list of all the ways they can line up other than "boys here, girls there"—then use these ideas!

● Model learning new skills and sharing tasks in the classroom. If you are not experienced in woodworking or cooking or science, join in that center and practice with the children, letting them know what you are doing and why.

● Ensure that girls and boys get equal opportunities to speak at group times, snack times, and the like. Support girls in talking about their ideas and skills. Be sure to give boys opportunities to express feelings if they often don't. Give equal opportunity to boys and girls to figure out for themselves how to handle difficult moments, rather than immediately going to their rescue. When children are choosing activity centers, ensure that centers regularly have spaces for both boys and girls; if this means particular children do not get their preferred center that day, assure them they will get to choose first the next day.

● Sadly, it is still common for classmates to tease and bully a child who does not conform to gender stereotypes (Gidney 2007). Do not allow teasing about "not acting like a [girl/boy]" to bully a child into acting as she or he is "supposed" to regarding gender roles. Work with the children to create and live the classroom rule "Everyone gets to be different! Everyone is safe here."

Build children's skills for thinking critically and taking action

Young children benefit from activities that provide them opportunities to explore their ideas about gender identity and to think about what is or is not "fair" with respect to gender. As preparation, find out what children actually think about what girls, boys, women, and men do—and are "supposed" to do. This can be quite enlightening.

For example, invite the children to complete the phrases "These are things that [women/men] do. . . ." After getting their ideas, ask some prompting questions, such as "Can a [boy/girl/woman/man] do [name specific activities that contradict what the children said]?" Write down all the children's ideas. Use this information to plan activities to broaden children's awareness of gender roles and activities people actu-

ally do. In each activity, be sure there is racial identity, ethnic/cultural, and economic class diversity, as well as images of people with disabilities. Here are some possibilities:

● Create a display of pictures of women and men doing the same "home" or "work" task—for example, in a meeting, walking the dog, cooking, carrying a child, and so on. Use this display to talk about the many kinds of tasks the children's family members do and about what kinds of tasks the children do now at home and would like to do when they grow up.

● Collect pictures and books that show males and females displaying various emotions. Tell persona doll stories that go beyond stereotypical gender behaviors. Invite the children to figure out strategies for responding to negative comments made by the dolls (e.g., "You are not a real [girl/boy] if you do that").

● Invite visits from adults whose work, home, and community activities will broaden the children's ideas about gender roles and challenge gender stereotypes (e.g., male nurse, female auto mechanic, male dancer, female firefighter, female soccer player, stay-at-home father, female Habitat for Humanity volunteer). Ask the visitors to tell the children about their work. Take photos of them, and later have children dictate what they learned from the visits. If possible, take field trips to watch these same visitors at their workplaces. Document what the children experience. Back in the classroom, again have children dictate about what they saw and learned; then post your photos and children's dictation. Make books for the classroom based on the children's experiences with the visitors to your classroom and your field trips to their workplaces.

After doing these activities, go back to the initial list of children's gender role ideas. Invite them to add to it, based on what they have learned since then. Point out what the children "used to think," and contrast that with what they now know about "what men and women do." Share the lists with the children's families. Ask the families to point out additional examples that can help create and support children's broadening gender views.

Ellen Wolpert, a longtime center director and anti-bias educator, describes a useful critical-thinking tool to counter children's use of stereotypes, which she calls the Fact or Stereotype game:

> Introduce the word *fact* as "something we all agree is true," and then the word *stereotype* as "something that isn't always true but that some people believe is true about a group." Then suggest that children test out some possible stereotypes. For example, you might use this one: "Some people say that boys run faster

than girls. Let's find out!" Take the children outside to take turns running with a timer, and let them see that their own behavior shows them that certain boys run faster than certain girls do, and certain girls run faster than certain boys do. Conclude together that "boys run faster than girls" is a stereotype! Play the game anytime you hear a child voicing a stereotype (e.g., "Only mommies cook"). Go around the room and find out whether any children live in families where someone other than the mother does the cooking: "Fact or stereotype?" Write down what you find out together.

Play this game often, using a range of stereotypes, so that children are able to investigate this kind of misinformation for themselves—it is very empowering. And young children love the big word "ste-re-o-type"!

Take action

ABE Goal 4 supports children in standing up for fair treatment for themselves and for others. Like all other learning, it requires small, ongoing steps to allow children to learn, practice, and deepen their skills. As they learn to recognize unfairness, children may be left feeling angry and helpless unless their learning is coupled with ways of changing unfair to fair. When we encourage children to take responsibility for making life better for themselves and others, they gain confidence in their ability to work with others to create positive change.

● Engage the children in discussing ways to handle hurtful or discriminatory behaviors. Here's a list from Julie's classroom: "You can say, 'Stop that'!" . . . "You can ask another kid to help." . . . "You can just do what you want anyhow." . . . "We got a rule, 'We all get to be different'!" Use persona dolls to help children practice their good ideas. Post the list of strategies that the children develop.

● Acknowledge and honor children when they stand up for themselves or for others.

● With kindergarten or school-age children, pay particular attention to their using terms of gender or sexual orientation as put-downs. Such slurs often reflect biases against people who are gay or lesbian; however, even teasing another child as being "girlie" or "acting like a boy" are hurtful. Young children may not understand the full significance of the words but do know they are put-downs.

● Celebrate International Women's Day (March 8) by honoring the important women in the lives of the program's children and staff, as well as women who have made and are making important contributions in the larger society. These women do not have to be famous, just important to the children. This activity helps to broaden children's ideas about the role of women as heroic, since most media heroes are men.

● Watch for incidents that could be springboards for action appropriate to the children's stage of development and for the local community. For example:

> In one urban preschool, the children like to take walks around the block. One day their teacher notices a "Man Wanted" sign in a store window. She reads it to the children, explaining what it means. When they get back to school, she helps them discuss the sign, and the children decide it is not fair to say "*Man* Wanted" and ask their teacher to write this down. The teacher takes the letter to the store owner, inviting him to visit their classroom. He does, and he tells the children they are right and he will change the sign to read "Man or Woman Wanted." Later the children send him a thank you card.

* * *

Limiting gender roles hurt children in all areas of their development. While gender role norms have become less narrow in some communities, there is still considerable pressure on children to shape and limit their learning behaviors according to gender. Paying attention to the diversity and equity in relation to gender identity creates a strong foundation for children to succeed in school and life—and to fully become who they can be. It is a vital part of anti-bias education.

Remember to do gender identity activities that cultivate all four anti-bias education goals

From Gender Bias to Gender Equity in Early Childhood Education Staff

by Bryan G. Nelson

"What benefits do fathers and male teachers provide children?" I am asked this question frequently, despite the existence of many studies that demonstrate that children *do* benefit from the involvement of fathers and other male caregivers in children's upbringing. On the other hand, I am never asked about the benefits of mothers and other female caregivers. That is a non-question—we just take it for granted that children need women.

So, why the question about men? I've come to the realization that asking that question is an indication of the confusion we have about children and men. It is one key way that sexism keeps men from being involved in young children's daily lives.

Instead, early childhood educators need to ask and answer questions such as these: "What can we do to support positive male involvement with children as parents, caregivers, and early childhood educators?" . . . "How can we make our program more welcoming to men?" When we change the questions, we change our focus from gender bias to gender equity.

In addition, we must uncover and overcome myths and stereotypes that get in the way. Here are some examples (adapted from Nelson 2004):

Myth: **Men do not apply for jobs to teach or care for young children**—They do, but often they do not get hired.

Myth: **Men are not wanted or needed to work with young children**—Most people want to have caring men involved in children's lives. In fact, in one survey, 98 percent of NAEYC members said they believed it is important for men to work with young children (Nelson 2002).

Myth: **Men who teach young children are gay**—Men who teach young children are a diverse group that includes men who are straight, bisexual, and gay, just like the group of women who teach young children and just like the population at large. In an inclusive profession that serves a diverse population of children and families, sexual orientation has no place in determining the appropriateness of a person to be a teacher of young children.

Myth: **Men are not nurturing or patient enough to work with young children**—Men have been caring for children as fathers, uncles, brothers, and grandfathers for generations. How they do this varies by culture and throughout history. So, too, have the ways women care for children varied.

Myth: **Men who work with young children will sexually molest them**—Of course we must keep our children safe. But suspecting every man, or instituting "no-touch" policies for male teachers only, does not protect children. Actions rather than suspicions are what protect children. These actions include carefully screening, recruiting, and supervising all staff and volunteers; providing staff training on preventing and recognizing child abuse; and building close partnerships with parents (NAEYC 1996).

Most people do believe that it is important for children to have men as teachers and caregivers. However, until we challenge the myths and stereotypes about male teachers, this is unlikely to happen. If we want male teachers to enter and remain in early childhood education, then the field must encourage, support, and accept them.

For further reading

Carlson, F., & B.G. Nelson. 2006. Reducing aggression with touch. *Dimensions of Early Childhood* 34 (3): 9–15.

Father Involvement Initiative. 2002. *The effects of father involvement: A summary of the research evidence.* Ontario: Author.

Nelson, B. 2002. *The importance of male teachers and reasons why there are so few.* Minneapolis, MN: MenTeach.org.

Nelson, B.G., & B. Sheppard, eds. 1992. *Men in child care and early education: A handbook for administrators and educators.* Minneapolis, MN: Men in Child Care Project.

Pruett, K. 2000. *Fatherneed: Why father care is as essential as mother care for your child.* New York: Broadway Books.

Sean, E., S.E. Brotherson, & J.M. White, eds. 2007. *Why fathers count: The importance of fathers and their involvement with children.* Harriman, TN: The Men's Studies Press.

Learning About Economic Class & Fairness

8

"Lookit! Lookit! I got new shoes! I was good, so Momma bought me princess shoes! Aren't they pretty!" says a 3-year-old at circle time.

"Jorge's mama smells funny. I don't like her," a 4-year-old tells the teacher, referring to a mother who arrives from picking lettuce in a field where insecticide was sprayed that day.

"Mrs. Fujimoto, you have got to get Ayumi here to school on time! It's too hard on her to enter the group after everything has started!" comments a teacher to a mother who brings her child to the center by bus.

Inequitable opportunities, privileges, and life experiences based on economic class deeply affect young children's lives. Although a family's economic resources do not determine how much they love their child nor how skilled they are at parenting, a lack of resources can make the fundamental necessities for their children's healthy growth and development—safe housing, nutritious food, and regular health care—very difficult or impossible to get.

Millions of children in low-income and working-class families are at risk, for any of several poverty-related reasons. Maybe they are not fully immunized or have untreated chronic illnesses. They may have low energy due to a poor diet or suffer from environmental poisoning (e.g., from lead paint in their homes or toxic waste in their neighborhoods). An increasing number of children are living in cars, on the streets, or in homeless shelters (Federal Interagency Forum on Child and Family Statistics 2009). While American Indian, Black, and Latino children are disproportionately more likely to be living in poverty, the data show that White (and Asian American) children are not immune. (See the table "Children Living in Poverty.")

Despite the large numbers of children living in poverty, class and classism are arguably the most overlooked and misunderstood dynamics of inequality in the United States.

Many poor people work very hard and remain poor. It is not unusual for adults in the family to hold more than one job, and even when both parents are employed, family income may still be below the poverty line. In fact, such "working poor" families make up the largest proportion of low-income families with children (Wolpert 2005). These statistics disprove one prevailing social myth—that people are poor because they choose to not work and are lazy. In the National

---

Children Living in Poverty

Percentage and number of young children under age 6 living in low-income families, by race/ethnicity

American Indian	68%	0.1 million
African American	64%	2.2 million
Latino	63%	3.6 million
White	30%	4.0 million
Asian American	24%	0.3 million

Source: NCCP (National Center for Children in Poverty), "Basic Facts about Low-Income Children: Birth to Age 6" (New York: Author, 2008).

Goals for Children

• Children will feel pride in their family's efforts to care for them and earn a living, regardless of the family's economic conditions. (ABE Goal 1)

• Children will appreciate that material possessions do not define them or anyone else, and that all people are valuable regardless of their material possessions. (ABE Goals 1 & 2)

• Children will be aware of the many kinds of work that family members do, paid and unpaid, both in the home and in the wider world. (ABE Goal 2)

• Children will recognize wasteful behaviors and will feel pride at their ability to conserve and recycle. (ABE Goal 3)

• Children will recognize unfair or untrue messages (including invisibility) about children and families based on their economic status. (ABE Goal 3)

• Children will stand up for themselves and others against teasing or rejection based on economic status. (ABE Goal 4)

Center for Children in Poverty's 2008 report, 51 percent of children under age 6 in low-income families (i.e., 5.4 million children) have at least one parent who works full-time year-round, and another 29 percent have at least one parent who works part-time or full-time for part of the year (Douglas-Hall & Chau 2008).

In addition to experiencing the effects of resource disparities connected to economic class, young children absorb value-laden attitudes and beliefs about themselves and others regarding where and how they live, what they do and don't own, how they travel, what they wear, and so on. They receive these messages about economic class directly (e.g., in comments from adults and other children) and indirectly (e.g., from what is misrepresented or invisible in media, from attitudes and behaviors they observe).

It is from all these sources that biases develop. Many preschoolers, for example, assume that rich people are happier and more likeable than poor people (Naimark 1983; Ramsey 1991). For example:

> A group of 4- and 5-year-olds is selecting magazine pictures of families for a collage. The teacher notices how frequently they select pictures of families in fancy clothes and with new looking furniture or cars, and that they are passing over pictures of families in garden clothes (with dirt), in crowded rooms, and in buses. She asks why the children are choosing the ones they are and is surprised that the answer is, "They look happy," even though all the family pictures have smiling people.

At the same time, preschoolers also often say that it is not "fair" that some people have more money than others, and they suggest that those who have lots should share with those who have less (Furby 1979; Ramsey 1991). As children get older, however, they become more likely to absorb and believe the stereotype that people who are poor get what they deserve (Leahy 1990).

Stop & Think: What messages have you absorbed about economic class?

■ When you were a child, what did you think about your family's economic status? Did you not think much about it? Was it a source of anxiety or embarrassment? of pride?

■ What lessons did your family teach you about the uses or value of money?

■ When did you first realize that some people had more money and others had less? How did you feel about that? What did you think was the reason for the difference?

■ What did you learn as a child or teenager about why some people are "successful"? Where did you learn those ideas?

■ What messages have you received about the comparative value of working with your hands—"blue collar" work (e.g., farming, trucking, carpentry) or "pink collar" work (e.g., cosmetology, working a cash register, waiting tables)—as compared with "professional" work?

■ If you or your family have ever received public assistance, what was that like for you? If not, what messages did you get from your family and teachers about people who receive public assistance?

■ What are your thoughts and feelings today about people who receive public assistance?

Children's experiences and understandings of economic class and fairness

Comparatively little has been written about how young children think about economic class, but observations by teachers and families, as well as a modest body of research, point us in some useful directions.

● **Children pick up social messages about the value and importance of different kinds of work, including the work that their family members do.**

Children learn about who is important enough to be visible and valued from sources such as children's books, videos and toys, and even their early childhood curriculum. These sources tend to emphasize the work of professional and middle-class people. For example, children's books and posters often depict families going to private doctors' offices (not clinics), shopping in malls (not at garage sales), traveling in shiny cars (not crowded buses), residing in detached houses with trimmed lawns (not in apartments or aging buildings), and living one family to a home (not in shared quarters with extended families). "Community Helper" units in some curricula tend to focus on only a few types of work, thereby ignoring the many other types that support a community's survival and quality of life (see the box "My Mommy Doesn't Work"). The work of waitresses, farm workers, store clerks, office staff, and bus drivers is rarely presented as being valuable in the way the work of doctors, nurses, firefighters, and police officers is.

"Princess, princess, I'm the princess," Celia sings as she puts on an elaborate costume in the dramatic play corner. "You can be the maid," she tells Emily. "You have to do everything I tell you." The teacher who hears this wonders what connections, if any, Celia is making between her play and the reality that her mother works cleaning houses for others.

● **Children receive messages that material things are proof of love and approval.**

Messages about the desirability of new possessions are pervasive in most children's lives. Children swim in an ocean of such comments: "Oh what a pretty new dress you're wearing." . . . "You can show your new truck at circle time." . . . "How exciting that your momma brought you to school in her new car!" Many children also regularly experience getting material things as rewards for good behavior, as solace for injuries, or as substitutes for time with loved ones. The underlying message is that "good" children have many new things and that families show their love by purchasing new things for their children.

Young children often respond by becoming competitive about who has the most new toys or certain clothing—creating a hierarchical order of who is better and who is lesser. Psychologists have expressed concern not only that children are learning to relate to physical objects, especially toys, in terms of *getting*

My Mommy Doesn't Work

Charlie, a teacher in a state-subsidized children's center, asks the children at circle time about the work their parents do. He is surprised to hear 4-year-old Katie reply, "Nothing. My mommy doesn't work." This comment bothers Charlie. Katie's mother is home during the day caring for a new baby, and in the evening she takes classes at the local community college while Katie's aunt takes care of the children. At circle time the next day, Charlie asks the children a few more questions and is surprised to find out that all the caregiving, homemaking, and life management that their parents do is invisible to the children.

At a staff meeting, the teachers decide to create a curriculum to address all the many ways family members work to support each other and maintain family life. They think it would be wonderful to have photographs of all the family members doing their part to keep their family functioning. One problem surfaces immediately: Where to get cameras so that all families can participate? Luckily, one of the parents works at a local chain drug store and is able to get the managers to donate 10 disposable cameras.

The cameras go home to half the families with the request that they use half the roll to take pictures of the day-to-day work of each family member. The teachers stress the special importance of the family taking a picture of their child doing something helpful (e.g., putting away toys, playing with the baby, dumping out the cat box). Sensitive to the possibility that some families may be embarrassed about their home, the teachers clarify that pictures do not have to be inside, but could be out buying groceries, taking the bus to deliver the child to school, playing with younger siblings at the playground, and so on. Once the first families return the cameras, the rest of the families are able to use the second half of the rolls to take their pictures.

The teachers make a series of classroom books with the photographs, called "Everyone Works in My Family." The children love the books, and the teachers use them to compare the different ways people contribute to family life. Each child receives a badge with the words "Family Hero" that also identifies the child's particular contribution (e.g., "HENRY. Family Hero. Picks up toys and puts them away"). At circle time, the children make charts showing which tasks all families share and the many ways families get their work done.

Source: Adapted from L. Derman-Sparks & P. Ramsey, *What If All the Kids Are White? Anti-Bias Multicultural Education with Young Children and Families* (New York: Teachers College Press, 2006), 84–85.

and giving instead of *using and enjoying* but also that children are learning to identify and judge themselves and others in terms of their possessions (Kline 1993).

The ideas described later in this chapter will help you create a learning environment that lessens the focus on material things and instead honors children for other aspects of themselves.

● **Children learn attitudes of entitlement and superiority or inferiority related to their economic class.**

Families with greater incomes and in professional or management work may directly or indirectly communicate to their children a sense of entitlement (e.g., that they have a greater right to the material resources of the world), as well as a sense of superiority over families with lower incomes (Coles 1977). Similarly, parents in low-paying jobs, wishing to help their children grow up to have a "better life," may directly or indirectly communicate that the type of work they do is unimportant and menial. They may add to that message a sense of struggle and frustration about not having higher paying employment or being able to give their children the things that families with higher incomes are able to provide. While the impact of such attitudes shows more as children get older, early indicators appear among preschool children. Teachers often report comments such as the following:

> "I got lots more toys than you did. I got a new trike and a new Candy Land game and two new dolls and lots more! What did you get for your birthday?"

> "You can't play with us because you do not have [the latest, expensive, well-advertised toy]!"

It is important, in a mixed economic class group, to be alert for signs that children from low-income families feel "lesser" than children from higher-income families because they cannot compete with the quantity of toys, clothes, or lavish birthday parties outside of school (see the box "Learning Class and Gender Shame"). Similarly, be alert for signs that children from affluent families feel that they are entitled to privileges such as not having to clean up, as did one child who told her teacher, "My maid does that for me."

● **Children do not yet have the skills to sort out advertising messages that tell them they "need" to have various material things.**

Through TV, films, videos, and in-store signs, advertising targets children with the message that they should want and *need* to have the latest film spin-off toy, clothing, sugary cereal, action figure, or doll. Young children lack the skills to sort out or resist these pervasive messages. Some children seek out peers who have coveted items. Although this issue grows as children enter elementary school, even preschoolers respond to advertising by pleading with their family to buy certain toys, feeling deprived at not having a new possession, or feeling superior when they do have the latest targeted objects.

> "But Mama, I want to be supercharged!" Rodney complains, quoting the advertisement for a sugary cereal. "I *have* to be supercharged. You gotta buy it, please!"

Adults in the family often succumb to the messages of consumerism, as well—even when they cannot afford to make the purchase.

Learning Class and Gender Shame
by Nancy k Brown, early childhood teacher, director, and consultant

Jessica comes to school every day in sturdy jeans and T-shirts, but as soon as she arrives she changes into the frilliest costume she can find in the dramatic play corner, stuffing her home clothes into the back of her cubby. As the day progresses, she staunchly insists that the costume is hers, clothes worn from home. And she begins taking clothing, usually pink, out of her classmates' cubbies, again tearfully insisting they are really hers.

Her worried teacher talks with Jessica's teenage sister, who brings her to school each day. The sister reports that at home Jessica plays happily with her two older brothers (whose hand-me-downs she wears to school). "We'd all like new stuff if we could get it," her sister says, "but Mom doesn't have money for that."

With that information in mind, the teachers begin paying closer attention to what is happening in the classroom. A number of the 4-year-old girls from affluent families show up every day in new, trendy, pink or lavender clothes and spend a lot of time swapping clothes, changing into and out of outfits, and playing in front of the mirrors. The teachers had jokingly labeled this group "the pink connection" and often complimented them on getting a new dress, how pretty they looked, or what lovely outfits they were wearing.

With a sense of shock, the teachers realize that the problem in the classroom isn't Jessica's—it is theirs. Jessica's sense of not being good enough, of class and gender shame, is coming from her experience at school, and it isn't a good environment for any of the girls. Very deliberately the staff set about changing their interactions with the children.

● **Children pay close attention to how adults interact, and they pick up key messages about class differences.**

Children are excellent observers of their world. Although they do not yet have words for the social dynamics between adults, they see them, interpret them, and feel them keenly. They pay attention to which staff member is in charge in the classroom, for example. Whatever we may say about showing respect to everyone, children notice when the cooks aren't considered as important as the center director, as this example shows:

> While eating her snack, 4-year-old Audra states, "I love Pooz (the center's cook). She's kind of the pretend mommy." "Pretend mommy?" the teacher asks. "Miss Helen (the center's director) is the real mommy of the school. Pooz is just pretend," Audra replies. "Why is Miss Helen the real mommy?" asks the teacher, perplexed. Audra replies, "She's the boss. She tells people what to do."

Children observe how staff and families make subtle but powerful distinctions in their interactions. Children notice that only some parents speak up with teachers, and they have no way of understanding how that might have been molded by a parent's own educational background and experiences. Children also pay attention to which families participate in the classroom, and they do not understand that it may depend on whether the family receives subsidized care or pays private tuition. For children from higher-income families, it may seem like their family "fits" or "is part of" the classroom world. Children in lower-income families may come to feel like outsiders as a result of their parent's absence in the classroom.

Working-class families often encounter extra demands in their lives that, in turn, inconvenience teachers. It may be hard on teachers, for example, when a child arrives late because her family has to take unreliable buses to school. Working-class families and those living in poverty may tell their child not to get his clothes wet at school, because they could lose their job if they miss work to tend to a sick child or have to wait hours in an outpatient clinic or emergency room. Sometimes, teachers have a hard time with these family requests—seeing them as too restrictive and putting the child in a position of having to choose between family and school activities. Even though the annoyance is indirect, children can feel the disapproval. Knowing and respecting the family's perspective can help the teacher overcome any feelings of resentment and can lead to positive, mutual solutions. (See the section "Strategies for Exploring Economic Class and Fairness" below.)

Conversely, higher-income families may make unrealistic demands for particular curriculum or supports for their child. They may be openly critical of low-income families and not want their child getting too friendly with those children. If a program is dependent on the financial contributions of the higher-income families, teachers may acquiesce to their demands, even when doing so reinforces family messages of entitlement and may conflict with what teachers' professional expertise tells them is best. This dynamic can also lead to teachers feeling resentful, which, in turn, can affect how they treat children.

As you consider these dynamics, be alert for lower-income families who feel isolated or uncomfortable because they are not part of the network of higher-income families. As with all families, build relationships carefully, talking to family members one-on-one and letting them know you respect how much they love their child and how hard they work to make a better life for their family. Be thoughtful and respectful about the limitations on time and resources that many families cope with. Find out what skills and interests the families have, and use that information to set up opportunities for them to support others (through clothing swaps, supplying meals to a family with a new baby, sharing interests at a family meeting, etc.).

● **Young children can (and do) develop resiliency and the skills to handle challenging economic realities.**

While it is necessary to pay attention to the harm that poverty causes families and children, it is also essential to recognize the coping strengths that the majority of families pass on to their children. This lovely anecdote (from Chafel et al. 2007) illustrates how young children learn such skills and resiliency:

> One winter morning, a new student, 5-year-old Cassie, arrived at the school [with] hiking boots. She could hardly contain her pleasure. "Look!" she exclaimed . . . "these ties are made of stuff that will not break and the tops will keep the snow off my socks." "They are amazing boots," I agreed . . . "Where did you get them?" "Backstreet Missions store," [Cassie] responded with pride. "My grandma said she hit it just right this time—my size and nearly new!" Other children immediately joined the conversation to discuss the best places around town to shop for shoes "other people hadn't used up yet." Several . . . told her they would remember the store the next time they needed new shoes.

Teachers need to learn about the strengths of each family and child, use those strengths, and build on them. For example, to enable them to cope with the challenges of limited resources, many families with low incomes teach their children to be thoughtful caregivers to younger siblings and to be highly competent at life management skills (dressing themselves, fixing cereal, etc.).

Strategies for exploring economic class and fairness

The following suggestions will help bring an anti-bias approach to economic class issues in your program.

Create a welcoming and equitable learning community

The learning environment hugely impacts children's experience of acceptance in the classroom and success in learning.

● Have the same high expectations for children from every family.

● Pay attention to each child's unique learning style, knowledge, and skills—often a function of his specific life experiences. Does the child tend to use words to show what he knows, or actions? Does the child expect adults to tell him what they want him to do, or to ask him (e.g. "It's time to set the table" versus "Would you like to set the table now?"). Instead of looking for what children *don't* know or do, adapt activities to support the *strengths* children bring into your program.

● Create beautiful environments for *all* children. Fresh paint, live plants, and clean, bright cushions do not have to be costly. Get contributions from neighborhood stores (surprisingly easy when they know it is for a children's program), and involve parents and others from the community in doing the work.

● Be mindful of families' concerns about clothing. Make or buy aprons for children to wear during messy play, and make sure the paints you use are truly washable. (Purple is often particularly difficult to remove.) Thrift stores are wonderful places to pick up men's long-sleeved shirts that children can wear buttoned up as smocks. Have children wear plastic ponchos during water play. Remember that it may be very difficult for lower-income families to purchase new clothes, and washing clothes can require spending many hours (and dollars) in Laundromats. Arrange an ongoing clothing swap, where families can donate clothing their children no longer use and take home what they need.

● Be cautious of introducing activities to "help poor people," which can unintentionally convey messages of the superiority of the helper and helplessness of the receiver. For example, asking children to contribute toys for "the poor" at Christmas may teach pity and lead children to question whether parents with low incomes really love their children because they do not buy them toys. In contrast, children act as allies when they contribute toys throughout the year to a toy bank.

● Use sensory materials that are not food. For many families food is a precious resource and is not for play (see the box "Food Is for Eating"). Children from families who have plenty can learn that food should not be wasted. For example, use birdseed rather than rice or cornmeal at a sifting table. Make finger paint instead of puddings or yogurt. String leaves and pods rather than macaroni.

Foster nonclassist interactions

As children are bombarded with messages that they need to have possessions in order to be valued or even to be noticed, early childhood teachers have a responsibility to children of all economic backgrounds to combat this harmful message of entitlement.

● Make a decision not to focus on children's new possessions during circle and sharing times. Encourage children to share information about *experiences* they had with their families. Or ask children to bring in their oldest toy and talk about how they still play with it.

● Encourage preschoolers to use toys and materials cooperatively. The approach employed in many early childhood settings—providing a quantity of the same item so children "won't have to share"—conveys the message that private ownership and exclusive use are important. For example, try intentionally limiting the number of the popular crayon colors at a table so that the children must share.

● Help children to work together cooperatively. Make whole-class murals out of handprints or drawings. Create a class quilt, with each child contributing a square. Ask pairs or teams of children to do specific tasks together (e.g., setting the snack tables, cleaning up the block area). Celebrate the important work they do in a class book called "We All Work Together."

● Create persona doll stories that help children recognize and challenge hurtful stories and behaviors that demean children from families who have lower incomes. Acknowledge family strengths and skills for handling difficult economic realities in these stories. If you do not know much about families who cope with great economic challenges, talk to people in the community who do!

Promote knowledge and appreciation of everyone's contributions

Everyone has important contributions to make, regardless of economic background. Help children to celebrate every contribution!

● Find books that honor the "invisible" work done by members of the families in your program and others in your community. Read books about waitresses, bus drivers, farm workers, secretaries, cleaners, cooks, and cashiers. Talk about how important their work is and about how it helps us all to live. Invite family members to come tell the children about their work (if they can arrange some time off). If they can't come in, ask if they could describe their work in a letter to the class, a tape recording, or a phone call with you so you can share the information with your group.

● Make a class book with photographs of all the support people who keep your program going (e.g., mail carrier, kitchen staff, garbage collector, janitor). Invite them to talk to the children about their lives and their work. Help the children dictate thank you letters to each person, and brainstorm with children ways to make the work easier (e.g., cleaning up after themselves, cutting down on waste).

● Work with children on recycling. For example, ask whether anyone has ideas about how to reuse the remaining puzzle pieces from a puzzle with missing pieces. Use rectangles cut from brown paper bags for

---

Food Is for Eating

Like many teachers, Marina enjoys creating activities where children make necklaces of macaroni and bean collages or play at a cornmeal table. One day three mothers ask to meet with her. Nervously, but firmly, the women inform Marina that they do not want their children playing with food. "Food is for eating," one says sternly, "not for wasting." Chagrined and a little embarrassed, Marina agrees to stop using food for curriculum projects. She also begins to consider the amount of wasted food at snack and lunchtime.

After a discussion among the center's staff—including the cook and the janitor—everyone decides to help the children limit waste and think about what a precious resource food really is. They start serving lunch family style so that children can control the amount of food they put on their plates. They make a worm compost box in the yard and encourage the children to scrape their leftovers into the compost. With the help of families, they build a series of planter boxes and use the compost to feed the children's new vegetable garden. The children find the project fascinating. Watching food scraps turn to dirt is as interesting to them as watching the seeds sprout. The seedlings also entrance everyone; the teachers have to set limits on the children's enthusiasm to water the plants. The children could hardly wait until the lettuce and carrots grew.

Meanwhile, it occurs to Marina that the garden might be a tie to a nearby community of Central American immigrant farm workers. After careful discussion with her co-teachers, she and the other teachers decide to expand the curriculum to "Food: Where Does It Come From?" The children go on field trips to see who plants and picks the strawberry fields. They also explore how the strawberries get from the fields to the store and who takes care of the food in the store. And of course, how do strawberries taste? Marina feels that things are going very well

until she hears Emmet say to Isaac, "We're going to visit those aliens again tomorrow!" Stunned, she asks Emmet what he thought an alien was. "You know," he replies, "those brown people from Mars who pick the strawberries." Checking with other teachers, she discovers that some of the parents have been uneasy about the field trips. There have been conversations about "illegal aliens" and some anger from parents whose family members lost their union jobs when the frozen food plant relocated to Mexico.

The teachers decide to address these issues directly and call a special family meeting. Marina leads a discussion about how people sometimes scorn and mistreat farm workers, who are often very poor. She names these attitudes and behaviors as stereotypes, misinformation, and social oppression. Some of the families had worked the fields themselves, and she encourages them to talk about the living and working conditions of field workers. Teachers help all the families find commonalities between their own economic struggles to support their children and those of the people currently working the crops. Not all the parents are convinced. However, when Marina begins to talk about the children's hurtful misinformation regarding the "aliens," most of the parents are concerned.

Together, parents and teachers identify ways that children have absorbed these biased assumptions from what they see (and do not see!) in their community and in the media. They then brainstorm ideas for challenging the negative images and conveying ones that are more accurate. Ideas begin to flow, and yet another new curriculum focus begins to emerge. And so the work continues. . . .

Source: Adapted from L. Derman-Sparks & P. Ramsey, *What If All the Kids Are White? Anti-Bias Multicultural Education with Young Children and Families* (New York: Teachers College Press, 2006), 145–46.

---

art activities (the color and texture is beautiful with tempera paints!). Create learning experiences around using old boxes, juice cartons, toilet paper rolls, and other reusable objects that families can collect.

● Create a theme on "Where we live." Include apartments, trailers, subsidized housing, and single-family dwellings. (Be sure to represent a range of races, cultures, and kinds of families in various types of housing. Don't fall into the stereotype of having all White families in middle-class homes and all families of color in low-income homes.) Talk about how loving families live in many, many ways. Include a section on homelessness.

● If your program celebrates or studies holidays, use them to emphasize gifts of the heart rather than purchased gifts. Ask children about what fun activities their family did together rather than what gifts they received. Better yet, create an ongoing class book about people being kind to one another, called "The Best Gift of All." Help children dictate stories for the book throughout the year, and read it frequently at circle times.

● Read children's books that tell stories about working-class people's efforts to improve their lives:

for example, *What to Do about Pollution* (by Anne Shelby); *Somewhere Today: A Book of Peace* (by Shelley Moore Thomas); *Subway Sparrow* (by Leyla Torres); and *Pearl Moskowitz's Last Stand* (by Arthur A. Levine). Learn about local people who have been or are activists for poor and working-class people's rights. Invite them to school or tell the children about them.

Supporting low-income families

Economic issues affect *all* children, and the objectives and activities just discussed apply to *all* children of all economic classes. However, as classism most profoundly injures children in lower-income families, it is important to critically analyze some of the biases these particular families face.

Uncover your own biases

Take time to uncover your own beliefs about low-income families, your own family, and about families of any income. Think about how the income levels of the children you care for affects your work and how you feel about that. Many people in our society hold some or all of the following misperceptions and attitudes.

Yucky Trash

In a private kindergarten program serving children of well-to-do professional and business families, teachers Lenore and Eddie become concerned about the children's wastefulness with materials and their assumption that materials will always be easily available to them. The children's constant competition about new toys and clothing is also upsetting. They decide to promote a closer connection with the natural environment and to foster appreciation of its value.

They extend the time children spend outdoors and use natural objects to teach concepts that they usually teach inside the classroom (counting trees, identifying leaf patterns). They bring natural materials into the classroom, using grasses as paintbrushes and twigs and small logs as blocks. They invite a local environmental activist to talk to the children about local problems with waste and conservation efforts. With his help, the children start to keep track of the amount of trash that accumulates in their classroom. Lenore and Eddie then encourage them to come up with ways to cut down on the waste, such as drawing and writing on both sides of the paper, using only one paper towel to dry their hands, making sure they carefully cover paint containers, and protecting all the outdoor toys from rain. The class also recycles classroom material.

Then, again with help from the environmental activist, the teachers extend the activity to the rest

of the school. They help the children write or dictate statements and draw pictures of what they are doing to conserve the environment. Children make copies of those for their families, asking them also to do more conserving at home. They also invite the principal to hear how they are cutting down on waste, and they ask if they can invite other classes to set up a school-wide project. Eventually, several other classes join.

In the 4-year-olds room, children walk to a local park as a regular part of their curriculum. One of the parents has the idea of having the children bring bags, wear gloves, and pick up trash in "their" park. Lenore asks the children to talk about how they feel about all the trash. "It's ugly," says Jacob. "I don't like it." . . . "It's yucky," say others. When Lenore asks the children whether they'd like to do a community service project by cleaning up the park, they are enthused (as well as enchanted by the new term "community service"). The parents and teachers make "trash collector" hats for the children and take pictures of the park before, during, and after the cleanup. Later the children make and put up signs: "Keep Our Park Clean" . . . "Don't Make a Mess" . . . "I Like to Play in a Clean Park."

***

Source: Adapted from L. Derman-Sparks & P. Ramsey, *What If All the Kids Are White? Anti-Bias Multicultural Education with Young Children and Families* (New York: Teachers College Press, 2006), 148–49.

Myth: Families with low incomes are unsupportive of education

Although families in low-income communities are generally strong supporters of education and teachers, they may not always show this support in ways that teachers recognize. The reality is that lower-income families are less likely to have the means to purchase educational materials, to be able to take time off from work to volunteer in the classroom, or to have as much time and energy to attend school functions. Also keep in mind that some lower-income family members may have had bad experiences with schools in the past and may not feel safe asking questions of teachers or even sharing their concerns. Do not take their silence as lack of interest in their child or a lack of support for your program.

Myth: People are poor through their own fault

The pervasive social belief that people will succeed and flourish if they work hard ignores the realities of low-income work and of class privilege in education, resources, and contacts. This belief implies that it is a result of laziness if a family is living in poverty—which is rarely true. It also implies that affluent families are wealthy due to their own individual hard work, even though much wealth is inherited and some members of rich families do not work at all. In reality, the single biggest predictor of economic success is the economic success of the family in which you were raised.

Myth: Families who are low income and working class are not as good at parenting

This classist idea comes from "cultural deprivation" explanations for why children from low-income families of all ethnic groups do not do as well in school as children from middle- or upper-income families. This notion takes off the shoulders of educational institutions and educators the responsibility to find ways to recognize and build on each child's strengths and to effectively support children's growth in early childhood programs regardless of their family's economic status.

Myth: Only low-income families contend with substance abuse and incarceration

Some lower-income families do have to contend with family members who use addictive drugs, but it is important to remember that substance abuse crosses all class, racial, and cultural lines. However, substance abuse in lower-income families is more likely to result in jail time than in treatment, and children are more likely to be placed in foster care as a result. It is important to support families who have members in jail, regardless of economic class lines (see the box "When a Child Has a Parent in Jail" in chapter 9). Moreover, teachers must be particularly aware of how bias about incarceration affects the family/school community.

Support families across economic lines

One of the most important ways you, as a teacher, can influence students and families is to provide equitable support regardless of economic factors.

● See yourself as a partner with *all* families, supporting their children's inherent strengths and building skills where skills are needed. Learn about the resiliency many lower-income families demonstrate.

● Have an open-door policy in your class, and plan ways to welcome and include family members when they visit. If children from more affluent families have nannies, find ways to include these caregivers in your program. Be sensitive to any discomfort and anxieties that may arise for adults uneasy in a school setting.

● Set up a family room and resource center. This area might include a coffee or tea pot, a lending library for children (books, tapes, paper, pencils, games), and a learning center/lending library for parents (typewriter, computer, tape recorder, books, articles, and audio recordings for parents who have difficulty reading, as well as materials on local adult literacy programs). Resources should address parenting issues and explain your program's philosophy, goals, and activities. The area might also include a material-making center and a place for workshops (you supply the material; they make toys for home and school).

● Find out what each family needs in order to participate in the classroom, conferences, and meetings; work to meet their requirements. The resources available to higher-income families that make involvement in their child's program possible are less available to lower-income families. Many workplaces do not allow employees to take time off during the day, which is allowed in many professional and upper managerial positions. Getting to meetings may involve taking a bus or two with small children—an enterprise that can add hours to the family member's already demanding schedule. Without provisions for additional child care, working-poor families may not be able to attend because they cannot afford to pay a sitter. It is helpful to set up meetings where the family is, rather than always making them come to you. If some families do not want you to come to their home because of their housing situation, be creative about

alternate locations (e.g., local church, library, community center, or coffee shop). Provide flexible times for conferences.

● Get to know the children's neighborhoods (e.g., shop, visit community centers, use the library, and attend events in the community). As you do so, collect resources for your class (e.g., photographs to turn into posters, books, puzzles, donated materials from stores; ideas for field trip sites; names of community members to invite to your class).

● Compile a listing of family support resources in the community, and always learn the names of specific people in these agencies. Ask families to help by letting you know which agencies have been helpful and treated them with respect. Build alliances between families by sharing this information with *all* families, regardless of need, so everyone learns what is and isn't available in your community.

Classism in our profession

No one is unaffected by economic class issues, including those in the early childhood profession. Class status deeply affects staff and programs. Inadequate wages, lack of benefits such as health care, and the low societal respect given to the field all have a negative impact despite the best intentions of early childhood teachers. Staff turnover is one serious consequence of inadequate salaries. When staff leave because they cannot afford to stay, it puts at risk deep bonds and consistent relationships with

children; ongoing, integrated curriculum; and strong family-school and inter-staff relationships.

The economic status of many early childhood teachers may also result in tensions with some of the families in the program who are more affluent than the teachers. In some cases, higher-income families may reflect social attitudes about income and professionalism and may not treat the staff with respect or recognize their educational background or their high level of skills.

Within programs, economic class distinctions among the staff may interfere with open, honest dialogue and shared growth. Some staff members from working-class or poverty backgrounds may self-limit their contributions at staff meetings, for example, because their earlier school experiences have taught them that their contributions will not be taken seriously. A hierarchy of authority may result, giving more status and respect to some teachers than to others, a dynamic that children pick up on and absorb. Sometimes this hierarchy also overlaps with racial and ethnic differences.

Addressing classism in your workplace is a significant part of anti-bias education and makes a difference to children and families as well as staff. Here are some suggestions:

● Work to create an atmosphere where you and your colleagues can openly share and discuss issues of economic circumstances and class, with the goal of creating rich, full participation from and respect for all the people who make the children's program pos-

Everybody Sleeps Somewhere

In the Parent Co-op Preschool program, the topic of the economic downturn is an ongoing one among parents. Some families have lost jobs, some families have taken on extra jobs at lower pay, several have moved in with relatives, and everyone is concerned. The teachers assume that the children are not paying much attention to these issues until two things happen on the same day. Walking to the post office with their teacher, a small group of children see a man sleeping in a doorway. Aaron says, "Look at the lazy guy," and Habiba says, "He's a bad guy. Good guys sleep in their own rooms." Later that same day, three other children are building a car with the big hollow blocks. "A big car," says Chen, "so we can go all the way to Lego Land!" Carl looks around, finds some cushions and a pillow, and puts them in the back of the "car," saying, "That's for when it's bedtime and we can go to sleep." "People don't sleep in cars," Chen says emphatically, "They sleep in beds." "Well, sometimes when we go camping, I sleep in the car," says Letitia, but Carl just looks worried and quickly leaves the game.

Later, when the teachers talk with each other about the two incidents, one of them discovers that Carl's family is, in fact, living out of their car and his parents had emphatically told Carl not to talk about it to anyone. The teachers also know that two of the children are now living with various friends and relatives, sleeping on couches, in sleeping bags, or on cushions on floors. If the children truly believe that only "bad guys" and "lazy guys" don't have their own rooms or their own beds, how were the children making sense of what was happening to their families?

After checking with Carl's family and assuring them that they will not single him out, the teachers make a plan for group time the next day. First the teachers begin a chart called "Everybody Sleeps Somewhere," on which the children help make a list of all the ways and places that people sleep. They put up pictures of children sleeping in hammocks, on mats, with grandparents, in shared beds, in cribs, in tents. They change the dramatic play corner from a kitchen setup to a camping setup, with a small tent, day packs, sleeping bags, and mosquito netting. "What," asks one teacher, "do you think people need to sleep comfy and happy at night?" The children have lots of ideas: a stuffed bear, a favorite pillow, Mommy to tuck you in, your dog sleeping on the floor, a clock that ticked (that one is controversial; some of the children think the ticking sound is comforting, others hate it!).

"Do you have to sleep in a bedroom to be comfy and happy?" the teacher asks. This is a new idea, but the children soon decide that the bedroom isn't what is important at all. Getting out a persona doll named Maggie, the teacher then tells a story about Maggie and her family sleeping in their car until her mom or dad could get a new job. "What," she asks them, "could Maggie's family do to be sure she is comfy and happy?" The children have lots of ideas (a special pillow, sing her a sleepy song, be sure she's warm), and to the teacher's delight, Carl joins in with a few good suggestions— even though he says nothing about his own family.

sible. At staff meetings or during staff development activities, take some time as a group to explore the questions in the Stop & Think at the beginning of this chapter.

● Celebrate and model complete respect for the work of each staff member. Be sure that all staff members are included and have a voice in decision making— not just the head teachers and the director.

● Share information with families about the real costs of quality early childhood programs. Let the community know how little early childhood staff people are paid considering their education and responsibilities. Keep speaking up about how the low wages of early childhood staff subsidize other industries by making it possible for parents to go to work.

● Work to create equal opportunity access to professional development. Develop a program policy that reimburses staff who choose to attend conferences, take courses, or engage in other professional develop-ment activities. This may require fundraising efforts, which can also serve as opportunities to educate the families and the communities about economic class issues within the early childhood profession.

* * *

While economic class has been relatively invisible in early childhood materials for both adults and children, many teachers are aware of its impact on the children and families with whom they work. Early childhood programs are an appropriate and important place to help children begin to sort out their ideas and feelings about themselves and others, gain accurate information, and learn to interact respectfully across economic class differences. We hope this chapter opens up more conversations, research, and practice.

Note
Special thanks to Dr. Patricia Ramsey for her help with key research findings.

Remember to do economic class activities that cultivate all four anti-bias education goals

Learning About Family Structures & Fairness

9

So no matter the age, no matter the stage, no matter how you came to be.
And no matter the skin, we are all of us kin, we are all of us one family.
—John McCutcheon, "Happy Adoption Day"

Family is central to the life of every child. It is through this earliest relationship that children come to view themselves and others and find their place in the world. To truly reach all children, early childhood educators must acknowledge, make visible in their programs, and respect all the family structures that are real in children's worlds.

The family structures of the children we serve are many and varied, and it is not uncommon for children to experience changes in their family's structure at different times over their lives. Today only some of the children living in the United States reside in the type of household that in the post–World War II era was held up by the dominant culture as the "normal" family (i.e., mother at home, father employed, biological children, and private home).

Young children most commonly understand *family* as "the people who live with you" or "the people who take special care of you." Validating each child's family requires creating and sustaining a learning environment that communicates this definition. To do this, early childhood educators may need to broaden their own concept of *family* to include all the different varieties and structures of families that exist in our society. We may need to examine any negative beliefs that we have about the worthiness of certain types of family structures and be willing to abandon such biases. Our professional ethics as early childhood educators require us to equitably nurture and support children from every kind of family.

It is also essential to remember that knowing the structure of a family does not reveal anything about how well that family functions. In any family structure, people may be living joyfully or in pain. The family may operate harmoniously or in discord. For example, don't let yourself assume that just because a family has a traditional structure that they do not need support and connection. You have to get to know the individual families to know what they are really like.

Stop & Think: Our own and others' family structures

■ What was the configuration of your family of origin? Your current family? How was/is it similar or different from other families in your community?

■ What did others (in school, in your community) communicate to you about your family? Was your family accepted or admired? Did you experience invisibility, teasing, or rejection?

■ What messages did you receive from your family about families with structures different from yours?

■ With what types of family configurations are you most comfortable? least comfortable? Why?

■ How might you be supportive of children with whose families you feel uneasy or uncomfortable?

Children's experiences and understandings of family structures

Young children take for granted the kind of family in which they live. They initially think that all families are like their own.

● **Young children have their own definitions of who is in their family.**

These definitions are unique to the child and may include every living creature in their household. For example:

> The 4-year-olds are drawing pictures of their families and telling their teacher about each member. "This is my mommy and me and my sister and Dar," says Tobias. "Dar looks like a dog," replies the teacher. "Yes!" agrees Tobias, "You said draw our family."

In the preschool years, it is fine to let children have their own definitions of family. At the same time, doing activities about families will gradually bring children to an understanding of family structures more in keeping with adult definitions.

● **Young children perceive their family as an extension of themselves.**

Children are hurt if their early childhood community does not validate their family. Because family is such a personal construct, it is critical that teachers allow each child to define his or her family and then support that definition.

> Maria's mother and stepfather have just had a new baby. She breaks down in tears when her friend Brittany says that the new baby brother is not Maria's "real" brother. Brittany, whose family includes half sisters, says the baby is Maria's "half brother." When Maria calls the teacher over, the teacher agrees with Brittany because she is technically correct. This leaves Maria unhappy and confused. However, another teacher comes by and adds, "Maria, your 'real' brother is the brother you love. Brittany meant that your baby brother has a different birth daddy than you do. But he's still your *real* brother."

● **Children discover and are curious about other people's families.**

As children have more experiences beyond their own immediate family, especially when they start to attend early childhood programs, they come in contact with children whose family structures differ from their own. Because children comes to preschool taking for granted their own family structures, their questions often take the form of wanting to know why another child's family is not like their own.

> Sherry's two sets of cousins and two neighborhood friends all live in households with single mothers. She asks her mother one day, "How come their daddies don't live with them?"

How parents and teachers respond to these questions lays the foundation for children to feel comfortable with the diverse ways there are of being a family. In the example of Sherry above, there may be several reasons those daddies don't live with their children: The mothers may be single by choice, divorced, or widowed. When children ask, give a simple, matter-of-fact explanation if you know it (or if you don't, say so). In all cases, what matters most is affirming that people choose different ways to be a family and that all kinds of families can love and take care of children. Adults can help children figure this out by encouraging them to explore the idea that there are many kinds of families.

Not only curious but observant, young children notice a great deal about each other's families. Their matter-of-fact statements about each other's families may require little if any comment from adults.

> Zachary is out on the playground. Another child runs by and says, "You have two moms. They're lesbians!" Zachary responds, "Yeah, I know." Both children resume their play.

Goals for Children

● All children will receive encouragement and language to define their own family from their personal experience and will see their family represented in the learning environment. (ABE Goal 1)

● Children will develop awareness and appreciation of different kinds of families beyond their own as well as the ability to talk about their own and others' families. (ABE Goals 2 & 3)

● Children will develop skills to recognize and question unfair depictions of families and the lack of depictions (invisibility), which is also unfair. (ABE Goal 3)

● Children will learn and practice language and actions to resist hurtful or biased messages about their own and others' families. (ABE Goal 4)

● **Children need information as they seek to understand variations in family structure.**

Children's questions about the configurations of their friends' and classmates' families may confuse or hurt the child whose family is the focus of the questions. That a child is asking questions does not necessarily mean she is showing any bias; she may only be trying to make sense of a family that is different from her own. Adults need to help children sort out their ideas, as well as support children who may be upset by another's questions.

> "Teacher, who's that lady?" "Which lady, Johnny?" "The lady who brings Natalie every morning." "Oh, that's her mother," the teacher answers. "Well, then who's the man, the one who takes her home?" continues Johnny uncertainly. "That's her father," the teacher replies automatically. "But they aren't the same." "That's true," says the teacher, suddenly realizing Johnny's confusion. "They have different skin colors, but they are still Natalie's mother and father." "Oh," says Johnny, "okay!" (adapted from Wardle 1992)

> Krista is describing her family's new apartment. Tamara listens closely and then asks worriedly, "But where does the grandma sleep?" "Tamara," asks her teacher, "where does your grandma sleep?" "In my room," Tamara replies. Krista looks confused until the teacher says, "You know, girls, some grandmas live with their grandchildren and some live in their own places. Isn't it interesting how different our families are!"

Children's attempts to make sense of family variations can result in ideas that can turn into pre-prejudice or bias. Adults may need to provide follow-up activities in addition to responding to teachable moments, in order to help children sort out their confusions about family structures very different from their own.

● **Children begin to absorb attitudes and biases toward various kinds of family structures.**

Initially, young children do not attach value to any particular family structure unless they learn to do so from those around them. Even if they ask questions about their friends' and classmates' family configurations, children tend to accept them. But, in many subtle and not so subtle ways, children constantly get value messages about various family configurations from the familial, cultural, and societal attitudes they encounter.

Sometimes those messages address more than just the concept of different family structures; a child's concerns also may reflect other social biases related to families to which the children are exposed, and addressing these biases is important, as well.

> Alonzo and Dorian, both 5, are conversing over snack. "My dad is buying me a dog for my birthday," says Alonzo. "I want a dog, too, but my dad says we don't have enough money," Dorian replies. "Doesn't he love you?" asks Alonzo.

In this situation, a teacher would confirm that Dorian's father loves him just as much as Alonzo's does. But also she would explain that families have different amounts of money to spend, and that fathers show their love in many different ways, perhaps mentioning an activity she knows Dorian likes to do with his father.

Despite the great range of families that children live in, many kinds of family structures are still largely invisible in early childhood books, toys, materials, and learning environments. In addition, media messages about families still tend to predominantly show the dominant culture image of families (mother and father, one or two children, house in the suburbs, etc.). Children risk coming to think that this image represents the "normal" family, even if it is different from their own.

These messages can have a harmful impact on young children's developing understanding of family and on their openness to accepting all kinds of families. As a result, it is more common to hear preschoolers question the validity of a family in which the child is being raised by a grandparent, an interracial family, or a gay/lesbian-headed family than the validity of a traditional nuclear configuration.

Strategies for supporting all kinds of families

Whatever the curriculum approach, quality early childhood programs already include the topic of families. Therefore, adequately addressing the topic of family diversity is not so much a matter of incorporating new topics as it is ensuring that existing activities are inclusive. Even if the families you serve are homogeneous, it is important that the children learn that many different kinds of families exist. The fundamental anti-bias concept that "We are all the same; we are all different" supports children in feeling pride in their own family and being open to other children's families.

Including *all* family structures

As discussed in chapter 4, experiences and activities that support all families and teach respect for family diversity should go on throughout the year. Although we now have many quality learning materials that focus on family diversity, there are still large gaps. It is still difficult to find books and other materials depicting working-class families, parents with disabilities, biracial and multiracial families, transracial adoptive families, gay/lesbian-headed families, and transnational families. You may have to look a little harder for these or make your own. And whenever you buy materials depicting families, be sure you state and pursue your strong preference for those that show all kinds of families.

● Create an inclusive environment by avoiding language that excludes some children's family members, such as, "Everyone take this home to your mom" . . . "Let's make an invitation for your mom and dad for the family picnic" . . . "Can you tell us where your family is going for vacation?" Instead, use inclusionary statements: "Take this home to your family" . . . "Let's make invitations for the family picnic; whom would you like to invite?" . . . "What kinds of things will you do this summer?" Always talking about "mommies and daddies" as an all-purpose statement about families leaves out many children. It would be like calling a peach or pink crayon "flesh-colored," ignoring that skin comes in a wide range of colors and tones.

● The material environment can too easily communicate a narrow notion of family. Make sure your environment amply reflects the many kinds of families within your program and also beyond your classroom. For example, purchase more than one set of small people figures representing various ethnicities, ages, and both genders. Put all these family sets together in one container so that children have enough figures to select those that best represent their own family.

● In the block or dramatic play area, support children's play, whether they are acting out their own experience with family roles or exploring other kinds of family structures. Use children's questions and conversations as "teachable moments," clarifying and expanding on their concepts about family. While children themselves should mainly introduce their own topics and roles in dramatic play, it is important to remember that the teacher has the power to create a climate of openness and diversity.

● During group/meeting times, be sure that all children take the opportunity to discuss the important people in their lives. Children's silence about their family can be a strong indicator that they do not feel that their kind of family is accepted.

● Make lotto, matching, and number games that show all kinds of families. Avoid creating a collection of family puzzles that shows only one or two kinds of families. Supplement your collection with homemade puzzles using photos or drawings if you cannot find diverse commercial puzzles.

● Purchase books that show as many kinds of families as possible and read these books frequently. Regularly read books to children about common family issues facing preschoolers that happen within all types of families. For example, *A Chair for My Mother* (by Vera B. Williams) is about a young girl in a single-parent, working-class family who wishes for a special birthday gift. *A Boy's Best Friend* (by Joan Alden) tells about a 7-year-old with asthma who wants a dog. He lives in a lesbian-headed family, but that is not the focus of the story.

● Use books flexibly. For example, if you read the popular book *The Runaway Bunny* (by Margaret Wise Brown), you can sometimes make it a father (or grandparent, etc.) bunny in the story in place of the mother bunny. Discuss how fathers also take care of children.

● Create language experience charts that ask questions such as "Who are the people who take care of you?" These questions give children an opportunity to define their own families as well as hear about others'. Math experiences can incorporate making a chart that shows the members of each child's family.

● Adapt familiar songs and make up new ones that allow children to sing about their own family. For example, change the lyrics to "The More We Get Together" to "Oh, we belong together, together, together. Oh, we belong together; we're one family." Each child who wants to can include his or her family members (e.g., "With Pedro and Papá and Abuelito and Chico. Oh, we belong together; we're one family").

● Help children develop critical-thinking skills about families. On Mother's Day and Father's Day, for example, encourage each child to make cards or a gift for whoever takes care of them. Ask, "Who would you like to make something for?" rather than "Let's make a card for your dad/mom."

● Introduce persona dolls that have varied family structures. Then create a game where children look for books that show the same family structure as you have given a favorite persona doll. If they cannot find a book featuring that family structure, ask the children how they think the doll might feel. Help the children compose a letter to a librarian asking for help finding books for all the persona dolls' families.

● Always intervene, as appropriate to the situation, if you hear a child teasing a classmate about her or his family. (Chapter 4 provides detailed guidelines for how to intervene in incidents of teasing, rejection, or exclusion.)

Including each child's unique family structure

Family structures vary across all lines of economic class, racial identity, and culture. A child's positive transition into an early childhood setting requires a sense of belonging. If the child's family does not feel welcome and comfortable, it will be difficult for the child to trust the environment, form strong attachments, and develop to his or her potential. From the beginning, staff must send clear messages that *all* families are welcome.

● An act as simple as hanging photos or posters of families reflecting diversity of structures as well as of ethnicity, culture, and ability on the walls in the director's office conveys a strong message.

● In your initial contact with families—when they visit your school to see whether they will enroll their child or during their intake interview—clearly state your program's commitment to diversity of *all* family structures. Specifically list different kinds of families, so people who might often feel isolated or unwelcome will not have to ask, "Do you mean *our* kind of family?"

● Stress how important it is for their child that program staff and families build strong relationships.

Showing this type of respect will help families feel open with the staff and help teachers to focus on each family's strengths and their capacity to support their child within whatever type of family they have. (Chapter 4 suggests many welcoming and supportive strategies.)

Including families facing extra challenges

While all family types must deal with challenges of one sort or another, some types face unique challenges from significant societal prejudice and discrimination: single-parent families, blended and extended families, adoptive and foster families, conditionally separated families, and gay/lesbian-headed families. Along with the general support we offer to *all* families, an anti-bias approach requires us to be thoughtful about how these families are affected in specific ways.

The following is a brief look at the relationships between bias and the day-to-day struggles of such families (also see "Supporting Children in Lesbian/Gay-Headed Families," following this chapter). Understanding how the issues are different for each family type makes it possible to adapt the fundamental approaches so we can be as thoughtful and supportive as possible.

Be Aware

Some adults mistakenly assume that teaching children about diversity in family structure devalues "traditional" families or promotes certain other family configurations. The purpose of anti-bias education is to enable teachers to support *all* children's families and to foster in each child fair and respectful treatment of others whose families are different from the child's own. Anti-bias education does not disparage or advocate any particular family structure—but it does adhere to early childhood education's fundamental ethic of positively representing and supporting every child's unique kind of family.

Single-parent families

Some children in your program probably come from single-parent families. (More than 28 percent of children in the United States lived in a single-parent household in 2000, and the numbers have been increasing [Annie E. Casey Foundation 2009]). It is important to recognize that children's experiences in these families vary widely—single parenting can be by choice or by life circumstances such as divorce or death. The other parent may have been part of the family at one time or not at all, or may still play a role but in a separate household. It is important to find out who plays a significant role in the child's life and what supports, if any, the single parent has in his or her life.

If the parents have a shared custody arrangement, you need to find out right away which parent is responsible for the child on which days, who picks up the child, and other details. In such a situation, it's important to encourage children to acknowledge both homes, never asking children to choose one as their "real" home.

Be on your guard against both your own and others' assumptions or value judgments. Never use derogatory terms such as "broken home"; intervene if you hear others do so. Be clear that there is no such thing as a "broken" family. Each family form is what it is—and *is* a family!

Blended and extended families

Some children may live in a blended family or be cared for by members of an extended family. In many cultures, and particularly in immigrant cultures where families have experienced serious dislocation, cousins may be as significant as siblings. Keep in mind that families may use a variety of terms for various family members ("my stepdad," "Gary," "Pop-pop," etc.) and have varying connections with extended family. Encourage children to show all of their family in drawings and make gifts for everyone if they want to on special occasions (if your program does that kind of activity). Invite those extended family members who play major socialization roles in children's lives to school events and conferences, and intervene if others deny their importance (e.g., a child says, "Mamas put you to bed—not your auntie!"). You can model to all the children your understanding that all family members are "real" and that all family relationships are important to the child.

Adoptive families

One major task for preschoolers and kindergartners who are adopted is coming to understand the facts and distinctions between their adoptive parents and their birth parents. This is partly a developmental issue; however, they also often have to cope with other children's confusion and questions about whether adoptive parents are "real" parents. Adults add to this confusion when referring to a child's parents of birth as "your *real* mom" or "your *natural* dad" instead of the more accurate "birth mom" or "birth dad." A child's adoptive parents are her "real" parents because they are raising her. Adults using terms that imply that adoptive parents are not a child's real family may cause her considerable anxiety. So, too, may

the doubting comments expressed by other children.

Another source of inequitable treatment can come from social service and education professionals who automatically assume that being adopted is the cause of any social or behavioral problems a child may be having. Sometimes the adoptive parents themselves buy into this stereotype. But as with all children, the cause(s) of problematic behaviors may be typically developmental or circumstantial or the behaviors may have deeper roots—adoption being just one possibility among many. After staff sort things out for themselves, we may have to help the family do so.

When adoption is transracial (i.e., a child and parent have different racial identities), young children have an added element to deal with in figuring out the core issue of adoptive versus birth parents. Other children often wonder, "Is this your mother/father?" when parent and child have different skin colors. In addition, families may encounter considerable confusion—and sometimes hostility. Because the difference is visible, many curious people, even strangers on the street, feel free to openly comment about whether the child "is yours."

Always reassure children that nothing they said or did is the reason they are living in a foster family. Teachers can play a significant role in clarifying for

When a Child Has a Parent in Jail

by Louise Rosenkrantz

Increasingly, early childhood programs are working with children who have someone in their family who has been incarcerated. Louise Rosenkrantz was the director of a children's center in a federal prison. She also experienced the incarceration of her own father when she was a child. The insights she presents here focus on incarcerated parents. They also apply for a child who has a sibling or other loved one who is incarcerated.

—Eds.

From 1976 to 1986, I worked with a nonprofit project called Prison MATCH (Mothers and Their Children). For six of those years, I was the director of a play-based, community-administered visiting program in a federal prison. It was there that I gained an enormous amount of experience watching how the unpredictable nature of the prison system could devastate a young child.

It's not surprising that many of the key issues for children are deeply emotional; shame, embarrassment, loneliness, uncertainly, anger, and confusion certainly form a beginning list. But in my experience, the most devastating issue is that of unpredictability.

> You think you're going to visit your mother, but you arrive at the prison and, for a reason that has nothing to do with your parent, visiting has been cancelled for the day. Never mind that you're 5 and have been counting on this visit all week, and you've even told other people you're going to see your mom. You're expected to just get back on that bus and travel another four hours home without complaining because, after all, everyone's upset.

As we know through both research and experience, the bond between children and their parents is extremely strong even in the most difficult of times. Our training in listening to children and responding honestly and nonjudgmentally can provide immense support to the young child with a loved one in prison.

Along with a myriad of emotions, children with parents in prison must deal with difficult questions (which we can start to answer):

• Why is this happening to me? ("It's not your fault. Nothing you did made this happen.")

• Does it happen to anyone else? ("Many children have someone in their family in prison.")

• Is my parent safe? ("Yes. And you are safe, too.")

• Do I still have a family? ("Of course you do! And they love you very much.")

Underlying whatever words you use is listening for the child's feelings and recognizing and affirming both the child's and parent's love.

> My youngest sister doesn't remember knowing much about my father's imprisonment until it was imminent. Then she remembers being told he was going to prison, and the picture that formed in her mind was of the gun towers and cement cell blocks she had seen on television shows. Since our dad was going to a less restrictive federal prison, it would have been comforting if someone had asked her to describe what she *thought* was going to happen—then she could have gotten details on the *actual* situation.

Children want and need basic, practical information. "Do people sleep, eat, or work in prison?" . . . "Can my mom call me on the phone?" . . . "When do I get to see Daddy?" Teachers can work with families to answer these questions and sooth some of the confusion and fear. At first

the child that his adoptive family chose him as their child, and they all are indeed a "family" who love and care for one another.

Foster families

Foster children may be in care for brief periods or for their entire childhoods. All of them will have suffered some degree of trauma by having been separated from their family of origin. They may be in limbo, not knowing how long their current living situation will last. They may also be in transition between one type of long-term family structure and another (e.g., their foster parents are in the process of adopting them, their grandparents will soon be awarded custody). For all these reasons, children in foster care need spe-

cial support, as they may face a great deal of confusion and pain surrounding issues of family.

Be particularly careful regarding family terminology. Children in foster care have two families. Use whatever terminology the child uses for the foster family ("Dad," "Michael and Edna," "Mama 2," etc.). Never ask children to choose who is most important to them. If the original parents are legally allowed and able to visit and they wish to come to the school, make them welcome.

Check with the foster parent or parents about what they have told the child about the absent family and the likelihood of reuniting. Also, once the child is comfortable with you, find out what the child understands—it may not be same as what the child has you might use generic answers, such as those suggested above. But, in continued conversation with the child, family, and community agencies, you will find concrete, specific answers for the actual experience of that child. Some jails allow physical contact, some don't; some prisons let you bring in presents or money, some don't. Until you know the specifics of the child's situation, it's best to keep the conversation supportive but general.

> My middle sister was in second grade when our father was sentenced to a year in federal prison. A well-intentioned adult did the math, subtracted the time for good behavior, and was pleased to tell my sister the good news that her dad would be home for her birthday. Unfortunately, this well-meaning adult did not know that at that time you didn't get time off for good behavior on a one-year sentence and that our dad would serve his full term. My sister didn't know that either—after all, she was only in second grade—and on her birthday she waited all day, thinking he would appear.

This experience still affects my sister's feelings about her birthday, and she's over 50 years old now. It's another reason why I place unpredictability at the top of the list of issues children of incarcerated parents grapple with.

Whether you're faced with the situation of a child who blurts out family information at circle time or a family whose "business" is all over the newspapers and the community, the first step is letting both the child and the family know that you treasure the child and want to support the family.

It's also important to talk to a family member about how they want the child to answer the inevitable question "Why is your dad in prison?" With that information, we can help the child to give a straight answer ("He took some drugs that were bad for him" . . . "He got mad and hit my mommy") or not ("I don't want to talk about that"). We can help a child practice the chosen answer over and over until it becomes comfortable. Parents, too, need to know that you recognize what a difficult time this is for the family and that you trust that they want the best for their child.

The issue of why a parent is incarcerated is always a difficult one. Other children may announce, "Only bad guys go to prison." When we imagine what it is like for a child to hear that someone they love is a bad person, our first response is clear: Ask the child how she feels about what she just heard; listen carefully; and remind her that whatever happened, she can go right on loving that parent. When the why question comes up, you can ask open-ended questions about what the child knows or has seen. You can assure her that even if the parent has been hurtful to the child or the family, the person *wants* to be a good parent, and wants her to be safe and loved.

Over the years of working with families as part of Prison MATCH, I found that consistently one of the first things inmates talked about was their concerns about their children. After checking to see whether contact is wanted by the family on the outside, a child's teacher is in a unique position to help parent and child keep in touch. Here are some:

• Those wonderful drawings that children make in class can be hung on the parent's cell wall.

• Photos of the child on a field trip give the parent something to talk or write about.

• Being remembered with a child-drawn birthday or holiday card is a great present.

• Dictations, with child-drawn pictures, give a parent a sense of how the child is growing.

• An audio recording of the parent reading a storybook is a great way to help a young child remember the parent's voice.

been told. The wonderful children's book *Kids Need to Be Safe* (by Julie Nelson) reminds readers:

> Sometimes it's hard for parents to take care of kids and keep them safe . . .
>
> Sometimes parents need help taking care of their children . . .
>
> Foster parents take care of children when parents need help . . .
>
> Parents love their kids, even when they need help taking care of them. (2006, 1–4)

Foster parents are in need of special support, too. They may or may not know much about child development and what to expect at various ages and stages. They may not have a community of people who understand what they are doing and why. Foster parents must cope with balancing their own feelings toward the child's original family with the need to help the child feel lovable and secure and safe. When early childhood teachers see themselves as allies to all three—the child, the original parents, and the foster parents—they can be a significant source of strength and help.

Conditionally separated families

It is always hard on a family when someone is far away for an extended period. But the issues are different depending on the reasons for the absence. When a family member goes to the hospital for a mental health condition or is incarcerated, families have to deal not only with the absence but also with strong social messages about shame and secrecy (see the box "When a Child Has a Parent in Jail"). When a family member leaves to serve in the military, there is fear for the person's safety as well as issues around differing political views about war. When a family member has stayed behind, a child who has immigrated feels tugs and pulls about where "home" really is. Whatever the reason, given their egocentrism, children are very likely to presume that the adult's absence is somehow proof that they are not sufficiently lovable.

Teachers can help the whole family by supporting their child during this difficult, emotional time. Making drawings, dictating letters or stories about recent experiences, and sending photos of favorite activities to the separated family member can help the child and the separated family member stay connected. It is important to regularly reassure the child that although the absent family member is not around, he or she is still the child's [father/mother, brother/sister, aunt/uncle, cousin, etc.]. It is helpful to families to reassure them that the way those at home talk about the reasons for the separation, and help the child remember the absent person, will have a huge impact on what the experience is like for the child.

Military families. In their article "Helping Children Cope When a Loved One Is on Military Deployment," Megan Allen and Lynn Staley (2007) stress the importance of careful listening and paying attention to a child who is living with the uncertainty and sense of loss that comes when a family member is sent far away because of military duty. Along with the supportive and respectful approaches mentioned above, they recommend that a teacher:

● Invite the child to share communications received (letter, email, care package, video conference).

● Without judgment or criticism, acknowledge (and provide language for) the child's loss of time with the person.

● Be honest about and help interpret confusing information (tell children the truth and clear up misconceptions or stories from uninformed sources, including other children).

● Be willing to say "I don't know"; avoid saying "Everything will be all right" or "I know how you are feeling."

● Create a class webpage, with updated pictures and summaries of class activities; be sure the family has the web address to send to the deployed person.

● Help child and family prepare for reunification; remind them that any change in family structure, even happy ones, can be stressful and that it takes time to feel easy and comfortable again.

● Plan a "Welcome Home" lunch when the returned family member can visit and observe the child at school.

Transnational families. A child can be part of a family living in two countries in various ways. He or she may have been sent to the United States in the care of grandparents while the parents stayed behind to work. Or maybe just one parent stayed behind. Or maybe the entire family moves back and forth; the child may even be cared for by different adults depending on where they are living.

For transnational families, not only might the family structure shift, but issues of cultural discontinuity may be very pronounced (more on discontinuity in chapter 5). Whatever the reason, however, the same principles and solutions apply as for the other kinds of conditionally separated families.

Connecting families with community support

While the early childhood program is often a home base of support for families, we can help make a difference by connecting families with larger circles of support in the community specific to their situations. Local advocacy groups, regional and national organization conferences, and publications can provide information and activities, not only for these children and families but also for the early childhood professionals who work with them. In many communities, local groups representing specific family structures provide opportunities for those types of families to share experiences, learn new approaches to supporting their children, and support one another in the face of prejudice and discrimination.

Strategies for learning about each child's family

Without information about each child's particular kind of family—its structure, needs, culture, and so on—a teacher cannot implement a strong, culturally responsive, anti-bias learning environment. Yet, too often families are a neglected resource. In some programs only the director talks to the adults in the family. In some, no staff time is allocated to family-teacher conversation. Some teachers who have access may think it is impolite to ask families about their home life.

In chapters 4 and 5, we suggest many ways for learning about each family in your program. All of the approaches depend on your first building a respectful relationship. Family structure is one more dimension of understanding and outreach that is needed to strengthen these relationships.

Plan on needing several conversations

Often the richest way to learn about and connect with a family is to make home visits. Meetings at school can also work, particularly if you keep them short, don't sit at a desk, and offer simple refreshments. Do not expect to learn everything you want to know in one conversation. It takes time and trust to really know someone. But as families and staff come to like each other, information and understanding transform the relationships.

Combine questions about the family's structure with questions about their values and beliefs: Questions such as "Who are the people who make up your family? In what ways do they care for Maia?" fit right in with "What foods does she like and not like?" . . . "What are her favorite games, toys, TV shows, and songs?" . . . "What are your family's favorite ways of having fun?"

Let questions flow. Remember that any question may be hard for some families, and let them know they do not have to respond to every question. You can always say, "We want Maia to be safe and happy here. Is there anything else you want me to know about her and your family?"

Many programs use a written questionnaire to ask questions about a family's approach to guidance, goals for their child, and holidays, but this is usually not an effective way to get useful information. It is almost always easier for families to discuss complex ideas than to write about them coherently. As we described in chapter 4, talking informally with family members at the beginning or end of each day is often the best way to hear about what is happening in a family. Respectful listening goes a long way toward easing the burdens of families.

Be sensitive to a family's fears

A family with an incarcerated member may want to keep that secret. A lesbian/gay-headed family or an immigrant family without legal papers may not feel safe in giving full information to the program. Often teachers jump to conclusions based on their own pre-vious experiences, without considering the possible motivation of a parent for withholding information. For example:

> Paul does not tell his child's teacher that he is gay because he is waiting for signals from the teacher that it is safe to do so. Then, in circle time, the children talk about their families, and his son Edwin says that he "lives with two daddies." The teacher feels hurt that the family did not tell her when Edwin first entered the program.

Ask questions about things you do not understand. Opening the lines of communication affords family members the opportunity to clarify their values, needs, and expectations.

Cherish every family just as they are

> Kyle's older brother has just returned from active duty in the military. While telling the teacher about his return, Kyle's mom begins to cry in relief. Kyle looks up at her soberly, and then says, "It's okay, Mom. We're at school. And it's in our rules—at Kinder-Cottage everybody's feelings are safe."

For many children, their early childhood education setting is the one of the first places they experience how the world feels about their family—and by extension, about them. To appreciate and support the bond between child and family is one of the core values of early childhood education (NAEYC 2005). Early childhood educators are ethically responsible to respect the dignity and preferences of each family and to make an effort to learn about the family's structure, culture, language, customs, and beliefs—then to bring those understandings into our program.

* * *

When teachers recognize the biases and difficulties each type of family and each family of that type faces, and when we assure families that we support and treasure their unique strengths and gifts, then we create a classroom community where children (and their families) are indeed safe.

Remember to do family diversity activities that cultivate all four anti-bias education goals

Supporting Children in Lesbian/Gay-Headed Families

by Aimee Gelnaw and Margie Brickley
(with a special thank you to Margie Carter)

Of all the many arenas of diversity in our society, homosexuality is often the most controversial because some feel that it directly contradicts their religious convictions. Nevertheless, many children in our early childhood programs are growing up in lesbian/gay-headed families. Their kind of family deserves recognition and support, like all other kinds. As Margery Freeman, former director of the Ecumenical Child Care Network, an organization of church-related child care providers, explained the issue:

> We are in a deep faith dilemma here, for people hold opposing beliefs about homosexuality. We believe it is important, especially for those of you who work in church-related child care, to distinguish between our beliefs—whatever they may be—and our commitment as anti-bias educators to support human and civil rights for all people, including gay men and lesbians. We also believe that children nurtured to appreciate diversity, to accept God's people as they are and to oppose bigotry, are being nurtured to love God and oppose evil. (1992, 2)

About gay/lesbian-headed families

Families in which the parent or parents are lesbian or gay are one example of how people form families based on love. There is no one gay or lesbian way of living, just as there is no one heterosexual or Hispanic or Black lifestyle. Gay/lesbian-headed families are formed in and across all racial and ethnic groups; and they take all kinds of forms, including single-parent families, two-parent families, and families with parents living in two different households.

Gay and lesbian people become parents in many different ways, too. Sometimes children are the result of a previous heterosexual relationship or marriage; some are adopted; some are conceived through insemination, with a known or unknown donor; some are carried by one of the parents, and others by a surrogate.

As with any family, gay and lesbian parents vary in how much information they might give their child about their sexual orientation and when to do so.

Some parents very openly self-identify as gay or lesbian, and proactively teach their child to identify as being part of a gay/lesbian-headed family and to be aware of and resist homophobia. Other families may not use this terminology with their child or offer much information unless the child asks questions. However they handle such issues, every gay/lesbian-headed family, like any family, wants their child to grow up with a positive self-identity, high self-esteem, and the feeling that his or her family is respected and valued.

Issues facing their children

We know that to develop optimally, children must have their life experiences, feelings, and thoughts affirmed and taken seriously. In contrast, when children's life experiences are invisible, and they hear

---

Myths about Gay/Lesbian-Headed Families

Some people believe some very hurtful and incorrect myths:

Myth 1: Under the influence of gay or lesbian parents, their children will probably grow up with a homosexual orientation.

Myth 2: Lesbian or gay couples follow rigid gender roles, one person always playing "masculine" and the other "feminine."

Myth 3: Children will likely get AIDS from gay or lesbian parents.

Myth 4: Lesbians hate or exclude men from their lives. Gay men hate or exclude women from their lives. They never let the parent of the opposite gender have contact with the children.

Myth 5: "We have none of 'those people' in our program or community, so we do not need to take up this issue."

Now ask yourself: Do I believe in one or more of these myths? If I do, how did I come to learn/know/accept the myth? What sources of information underlie it? What information counters it?

---

and see negative, stereotypical, or untrue representations of their lives, shame, confusion, and low self-esteem will likely result.

> The 4-year-olds are playing house. Michelle and Elizabeth both want to be mommies. Michelle says, "Let's both be mommies." Elizabeth responds, "You can't have *two* mommies." "Yes you can!" Michelle replies. "No you can't. My dad says two mommies is bad," Elizabeth insists.

> Adopted as an infant by a gay couple, Oliver's parents talked with him about his adoption. Beyond giving that information, they followed Oliver's lead, his questions and comments. He is a happy child with lots of friends and good self-esteem. But after his first week of school, Oliver came home exclaiming, "I hate it when we have to talk about families at school." Concerned, his fathers asked him why. "Because they keep asking me questions, and I don't know the answers. . . . Do I have to pretend I have only one dad?"

> At preschool, the children are making handprints on paper plates for Mother's Day. Lilly asks if she can have two. Her teacher tells her that each child gets only one plate. "But I have two mommies," Lilly argues. "You will just have to choose one," her teacher insists. Asked later why she felt she could not let Lilly make two plates, the teacher replies, "It is just too expensive!"

These actual vignettes illustrate challenges faced by young children in gay/lesbian-headed families, including biased practices and homophobia. Children need teachers willing and able to welcome and support gay/lesbian-headed families in their programs, to intervene when discriminatory incidents occur, and to help children understand and value many types of family structures.

Some people confuse teaching about different kinds of families with teaching about sexuality. But learning about a gay/lesbian-headed family is no more about sexuality than learning about a heterosexual-headed family is. Children's interest in "family" has to do with who lives in their home, who takes care of them, and who loves them—not the sexual life of the family's adults. For children their family is just a matter of fact. Often it is not until they enter into the larger world of child care or school that they notice differences in theirs and others' families.

Finally, children in gay/lesbian-headed homes are not the only ones who benefit from a definition of family diversity that includes gay and lesbian parents.

Children whose parents are heterosexual do, too. Throughout their lives they are very likely to have gay or lesbian people (as well as transgendered and bisexual individuals) among their siblings or other family members, neighbors, friends, coworkers, and/or faith communities. Moreover, given the consistent percentage of homosexuality in the population, every year some of the children in your program (regardless of the kind of family they live in) likely will grow up to be gay, lesbian, bisexual, or transgender. The early learning of respect for oneself and for others lays a healthy foundation for all.

A struggle for equity

A long history exists of individual and institutionalized prejudice and discrimination against people on the basis of sexual orientation. Many lesbian and gay people have been rejected by their own families and friends or have lost jobs or housing when their homosexuality became known. Gay and lesbian parents in many states live under the threat of having a custody suit brought against them as "unfit to parent," and many have lost contact with their own families and custody of their children. Many have suffered abuse and name-calling, while others have been physically assaulted, and even killed, in hate crimes.

As a result of more than 30 years of activism, some states, cities, and places of employment now specifically prohibit discrimination based on sexual orientation. Domestic partnership rights and benefits are beginning to be offered by some employers. Gays and lesbians can openly adopt children or legally marry in some states; in others, civil union or domestic partnership laws protect lesbian and gay couples in committed relationships. Gay and lesbian people do not seek "special rights" or privileges. They *do* continue to struggle for justice, civil rights, and protection from discrimination and physical attack because of their sexual orientation. If children grow up learning to reject homophobia and heterosexism, the world will be much further along toward embracing diversity and delivering justice and equality for all Americans.

> Four-year-old Kira was the flower girl at the commitment ceremony of two women. Suddenly she reached up and pulled her aunt Rebekah's head down to her and said clearly, "Bekah, don't ever be afraid to love somebody. It's what makes us happy!"

Strategies for Welcoming All Families

In addition to generic strategies for creating welcoming environments:

• Include specific mention of gay/lesbian-headed families in your philosophy statement and admittance forms.

• Use generic terms when writing to families, such as "parent" and "guardian" instead of "mother" and "father."

• Hang a rainbow flag or poster in the hallway with the written statement "everyone respected here."

• Never "out" a person as being gay, lesbian, bisexual, or transgender. Every person has the right to determine how they identify and to whom. Do not presume that because you feel fine about someone's sexual orientation that it is okay for you to discuss it with others.

• Find out from each gay/lesbian-headed family what they have told their child and what terminology they are using, so the program can support their choices. Find out what terms the child uses for each parent (e.g., "Daddy Paul and Greg-dad"). Do not ever ask, "Which is your *real* mom (or dad)?"

• If families in the program have homophobic fears or biases, listen respectfully. Then respond with clear statements about the program's commitment to welcoming and respecting all kinds of families and address parental fears with accurate, clear information ("Children don't 'catch' homosexuality by playing with the child of a gay father" . . . "It is not even *slightly* true that seeing pictures of a gay-headed family or hearing a teacher say that 'some families have two mommies' will affect your child's sexual orientation").

• Support families in a process of working through homosexuality-related fears, prejudice, unfamiliarity, or taboos. Ongoing family workshops can build relationships between gay/lesbian parents and other parents and go a long way toward forming positive relationships that ease tensions for everyone in the community—especially the children.

Learning About Different Abilities & Fairness

10

After participating in several activities about disabilities in her early childhood program, 4½-year-old Hannah explains to her mom: "It means that they can't do stuff, but they can still do the stuff you can do, but they can't do all the stuff you can, but they can almost do the stuff you can."

Young children are curious about many kinds of ability differences. They ask questions. They sometimes exhibit discomfort and rejection. They also have the capacity to understand that a child with a disability is able to do much of what most other children can do, even if it's done differently. This chapter explores the anti-bias issues of working with children in inclusive classrooms.

Since 1975, the federal Individuals with Disabilities Education Act (IDEA) has required that all children with disabilities receive appropriate education in the "least restrictive environment"—that is, they must have the opportunity to be included in regular (rather than special education) classrooms to the greatest extent possible. Such "inclusive" early childhood programs are now accepted practice, as is the principle that children with a variety of physical, cognitive, and emotional disabilities can and should learn together with their typically developing peers.

Contact among children with different abilities is, by itself, not enough to create an anti-bias—and therefore truly inclusive—classroom, and neither is simply teaching superficial acceptance and politeness (e.g., "Be nice." ... "Play with everybody." ... "We love *all* children". ... "We *will* get along"). Teachers

and other staff must use intentional strategies to create quality inclusive classrooms.

In an active anti-bias learning community, all children are equitably nurtured and everyone is responsible for everyone's learning and well-being. (A good resource on how to do this is Copple & Bredekamp 2009.) All children—including children with disabilities—need respectful teachers who know how to foster their competency, strengths, and modes of interaction with the world. All children need teachers who make sure that people with disabilities are visible in their learning environment: in pictures and posters on the wall, in toys and books, in program staff, and in their communities. All children—those who are typically developing and children with disabilities—need to be able to ask questions, get accurate information, explore their feelings, and learn positive ways to interact with their peers.

Children's early experiences and understandings of ability and disability

By preschool age, children's developmental task of figuring out how they are the same and different from their peers includes understanding what it means for someone to have a disability. As in all identity

---

Written with help from Carol K. Cole and Bill Sparks, program specialists and consultants in special education in Los Angeles. This chapter does not discuss the specialized methods for working with children with various disabilities and special needs. A leading provider of useful resources offering such information is the Council for Exceptional Children's Division for Early Childhood (CEC/DEC). Visit its website at www.dec-sped.org.

areas, children's questions, comments, and behaviors reflect the interactions among their specific experiences, stage of development, cultural contexts, and individual personalities.

● **Young children are curious; they want to know about what they see.**

The bulk of children's questions indicate curiosity. Don't assume too quickly that a child's question reflects anything more than that. Listen for tone and other expression of feelings to help you judge whether the question reflects any bias and requires more than a matter-of-fact response. For example:

> Lucy, the assistant teacher in a 3-year-olds class, has one arm shorter than the other and only two tiny fingers on the hand. She and the head teacher agree they will not make an issue of it, and she will talk to the children about her arm if and when appropriate. During circle time, the teacher notices 3-year-old Mia looking intently at Lucy. Mia reaches out tentatively and very briefly touches Lucy's hand.
>
> After the song is over, the teacher matter-of-factly says to Mia, "I saw you looking at Lucy's hand. It doesn't look like your hand. Do you wonder why her hand and arm are like that?" Mia nods. Lucy explains, "I was born with my arm and hand like this." Mia asks, "Does it hurt?" Lucy shakes her head. "Will my hand be like that?" worries Mia. "No," answers Lucy, "because you were born with your hand just like it is now. Do you want to touch my hand, Mia?" Mia feels all around Lucy's arm and hand. "Now, Mia," says the teacher, "why don't you show Lucy where we keep the juice, and you and she help each other get snack ready?" The two go off together.

Children are curious when they notice that a classmate sometimes receives one-on-one attention. They may ask about a child who leaves for part of the day to visit specialists. Often a simple response is enough. Explain that the child is going to see another kind of teacher who helps her learn to talk, to strengthen her muscles, and so on. Children may also ask about peers who require the help of an aide.

> "Why is Wendy always with Rosa?" Aaron asks their preschool teacher. Rosa, a child with disabilities, requires an aide (Wendy), who accompanies her throughout the day. The teacher explains, "Wendy helps Rosa play, learn, and move from place to place so she can be part of what we do."

● **All children need accurate information about what people with particular disabilities can and cannot do.**

Given the limited frame of reference about disabilities that most young children have and their early stage of cognitive development, it is understandable that young children might struggle to make sense of what they observe. Children may think that a child who uses a wheelchair is a "baby" and cannot participate in preschool activities; a child who is deaf cannot know what a hearing child knows; a child who is blind cannot be active ("She wouldn't know where to go, and she might hurt herself"); a child who is not yet speaking is stupid; or an adult who uses a wheelchair or who has a hearing or vision impairment cannot be a parent or a teacher.

Children who are typically developing need accurate information and opportunities to interact with people who have disabilities to counter their misconceptions. Children with disabilities, too, may have misconceptions about other children, and possibly about their own abilities and limitations. They also need accurate information, as well as positive role models who can show children how adults with disabilities function in their daily home and work lives.

Goals for Children

• All children will develop autonomy and independence (as they are able), as well as confidence and pride in their competence. (ABE Goal 1)

• All children will learn accurate information, appropriate to their developmental stage, about disabilities and special needs. (ABE Goals 1 & 2)

• All children will gain understanding about how their own abilities are the same as and different from others'. (ABE Goal 2)

• All children will learn to interact knowledgeably, comfortably, and fairly with each other, whatever their abilities. (ABE Goal 2)

• All children will learn how to challenge name-calling and stereotyping with respect to their own or others' abilities and will share ideas about accessibility in order to promote interaction and independence. (ABE Goals 3 & 4)

- **Young children have the capacity to appreciate their shared abilities and similarities.**

As children who are typically developing and children with disabilities play and learn together in quality, inclusive learning environments, they come to understand and appreciate each other's strengths and challenges.

> Four-year-old Tim, who has Down syndrome, is pulling the wagon around the playground, one of his favorite activities. His classmate, Elena, joins him and gets into the wagon. She announces to the nearby teacher, "He's a messy painter, but he's a good wagon puller."

> The Head Start teacher notices Miko, who uses a wheelchair, carrying blocks on her lap from the block area to the dramatic play center for two of her class-mates. Seeing their teacher watching her, Miko com-ments, "I can take more blocks than they can. They are the builders. I am the truck driver bringing the blocks."

- **A child with a disability needs information, words, and emotional support for handling ques-tions from other children.**

Children with disabilities are likely to be asked questions about themselves in and out of the class-room, and indeed throughout their lives. It is impor-tant they develop cognitive and emotional strategies to know what they want to say and be able to say it. This is something that anti-bias educators can sup-port children in doing.

First, find out how the family has explained the disability to their child and to others, including what terms they use. Ask them how they would like you to talk with the child and to the group about it. Try to do this either before or when the child first enters your classroom. After the child has had a little time to get used to being in your class, explain to her that she has the right to choose whether and how to answer questions from other children; for example, she can answer, decline to answer, or ask you to respond, depending on the question, the questioner, and her feelings. In addition, support the child's feelings about being asked questions. For example:

> "I know it's hard sometimes when other children ask about why you wear a brace and that sometimes you wish they wouldn't ask so many questions. When you feel tired or sad or angry about kids asking so many questions, let me know and I will help you."

It is important to help the child develop the vocabulary to express his feelings and answer ques-tions. Privately discuss with him what he wants other children to know—what he wants you to say, and what he might say. Sometimes a child will want you to respond to another child's question. Your choice of words and emotional tone models how children can handle questions about disabilities themselves. Sometimes a child may first want to practice with you, so he can later express himself clearly.

> "Why doesn't Miguel have to stay in the circle the whole time?" complains Taisha. Abram chimes in, "Why does he get to sit next to you all the time?" Their teacher checks with Miguel, "Do you want to explain, or do you want me to?" Miguel shrugs, but says nothing, so the teacher replies. "Miguel is learning how to sit still for the whole circle time. It helps him if he sits next to me while he learning how to do this. He also still needs to get up and do something else for some of the time." She then invites Taisha and Abram to recall things they could not do but now can.

- **Children may worry about "catching" a disability.**

Sometimes rejection can come from misplaced worry about "catching" a disability through contact with a child who has one or even with the child's equipment.

> The teacher has brought a child-size wheelchair to the class. Eduardo refuses even to touch it. His teacher asks, "Eduardo, you decided not to try the wheelchair. How come?" Eduardo backs away, "'Cuz it's too scary." The teacher probes, "What do you think will happen to you if you sit in the wheelchair?" Eduardo replies, "I won't walk." "You think that if you use a wheelchair then you won't be able to walk?" she asks. Eduardo nods his head.

> "When a person needs a wheelchair, it is because something happened to his legs before he needed the wheelchair. Sitting in the wheelchair will not hurt your legs, Eduardo. Let's ask the other children who wheeled themselves around in the wheelchair." Eduardo and the teacher check with the other chil-dren, who each show him that they can still walk. Eduardo gingerly sits down in the wheelchair for a few seconds, then gets up. "So you sat in the wheelchair. Let's see if you can still walk." Eduardo walks, smiles, and goes off to a new activity.

- **Young children may reject a child with a disability out of fear, impatience, or misconceptions.**

Children need adult help to deal with being rejected by other children. So, too, do the children who reject another child because of a disability. Sometimes, rejection might stem from the child being frightened by a particular disability. For example:

> Four-year-olds Patty and Selina are playing with blocks. Kathy (who has burn scars on her face and arms) tries to join in their play. Patty declares loudly to Selina, "I hate Kathy; she's ugly." Their teacher, Ms. Jacobi, intervenes, keeping in mind the steps for turning interactions such as this one into teachable moments (stay calm, state what you observed, set limits, explore

feelings, and take action that respects children's learning process).

Ms. Jacobi: Patty, I heard you say that Kathy is ugly. That is a hurtful thing to say. What makes you say it?

Patty: Because she has those things on her face. I don't like them. They're scary.

Ms. Jacobi: I know it looks different and scary to you. Kathy, do you want to tell Patty how you feel about what she said?

Kathy shakes her head no. The teacher puts one arm around Kathy and one around Patty.

Ms. Jacobi: Kathy, do you want to tell Patty and Selina about how you got your scars?

Kathy: You [delegating the task to her teacher].

Ms. Jacobi: Okay. Patty and Selina, Kathy has scars on her face and arms because she was in an accident when she was a baby. When Kathy was 2 years old, some very hot fat in a frying pan spilled on her and burned her. It hurt her very badly at first, and she had to be in a hospital for a long time.

Patty: Do they hurt?

Kathy: No, they used to itch, but not now.

Ms. Jacobi: It is okay to want to know about Kathy's scars, but it is not okay to say she's ugly or not let her play with you. Kathy, how did you feel when Patty said you were ugly?

Kathy: Sad.

Ms. Jacobi: What do you want to tell her about how you felt?

Kathy: Don't say *ugly*.

Ms. Jacobi: Remember that in our classroom I expect us all to work and play together. Let's you and me and Kathy and Selina play with the blocks together.

Sometimes children express anger toward a child who has an affective disability rather than a visible, physical one.

Rhea is a child who has greater than typical difficulty controlling her feelings of frustration and anger. She often expresses these feelings loudly or violently.

"I don't like Rhea," says Corrine emphatically as she watches Rhea with a teacher who is stopping her from throwing a puzzle. "Why not?" asks her snack teacher. "She's too noisy! And she throws stuff." "Yes," the teacher agrees. "She makes a lot of noise sometimes, and it can be scary when she throws things. Jim (another teacher) is keeping her safe, and in a little while she'll be able to play again." Corrine frowns and mutters, "I don't like her!"

The teacher responds, "I think some things are really hard for Rhea, like not being able to put the puzzle together. Then she gets so upset she throws things. Some day Rhea will learn that when she is having a hard time she can use her words instead of throwing. . . . Corrine, I remember when you first came to school and had a hard time pouring your juice. There were lots of spills, remember? But look how you learned; you sure are a good pourer now! And Rhea will learn, too. She will stop throwing things and use words to tell us when she needs help. I think she will learn how to be a good puzzle maker, too."

For more strategies about how to handle misconceptions and fears about disabilities, see the section "Responding to Pre-Prejudice and Discriminatory Behavior" in chapter 4.

Stop & Think: Responding to people with disabilities

■ What happens when you meet someone with a disability? How easy is it for you to initiate an interaction? How comfortable do you feel during it?

■ What did you learn as a child about how "visible" a person with a disability should be? Was it okay to look at the person directly? Did you know/interact with anyone with a disability?

■ What is your reaction when children ask questions about a person with a disability within the person's hearing range?

■ How do you evaluate when a person with a disability does or does not need help? How can you tell? How do you decide if a child with a disability is doing something dangerous or if it is safe?

■ When working with a child with a disability, how well could you (and do you) talk about what the child is like as a person (e.g., her capacities or interests)?

■ What opportunities do you have to reflect on how you feel as you work with a child with a specific disability or developmental challenge?

■ Who are some people you could approach to help you think about your feelings and skills when working with children with disabilities or developmental challenges?

Fostering an anti-bias, inclusive learning community

An inclusive learning community says in many ways, "Here everybody belongs, plays, and helps each other learn in her or his own time and way." All children feel nurtured, encouraged, and respected for their "whole" selves—by the staff and by their peers. The anti-bias concept "We are all the same; we are all different" holds as true for differences in ability as it does for other kinds of diversity.

Developmentally appropriate practice requires teaching in ways that cultivate each child's fullest learning. The following strategies well help you create and realize an anti-bias, inclusive program for the children in your group.

Be very thoughtful about the words you use

Words matter. Some people use *handicapped*, a term common on official government forms; some prefer the word *disabled*; and some people dislike both. What is important to remember is that all people are complex, full human beings—their disability is just one aspect of who they are. So instead of referring to a "deaf boy," it is more respectful to say "a child with a hearing loss" (which also leaves room for the great range of possible hearing losses children may experience). "Laurie uses a wheelchair" recognizes the power the child has, as compared with saying "Laurie is wheelchair bound."

Regularly assess how well you are meeting all children's needs

As in all areas of anti-bias education, ongoing assessment of your learning environment and practices in relation to children with disabilities is essential. Assessment enables you to identify where you can improve in meeting children's needs and also where you are already succeeding. When assessing your practices, consider the following:

● Do I regularly observe how children are interacting, intervene in negative incidents, reinforce positive interactions, and use my observations for planning further activities?

● Are children with disabilities and special needs able to participate in all activities in some way?

● Are there opportunities for all children to contribute to the group and to help each other learn and carry out activities?

● Does my teaching reflect respect for children's own timelines and ways of developing?

● Is my teaching appropriately individualized so that the entire curriculum is accessible to all children?

● Do I treat children's varying abilities, strengths, and challenges as *differences* rather than as reasons for competitiveness and hierarchy?

Support all children's sharing of thoughts and feelings

An anti-bias classroom encourages children to be open about their questions, ideas, and feelings about themselves and others. This openness helps you assess each child's cognitive and emotional development, thereby strengthening your ability to provide accurate information and to teach respectful ways of interacting. In turn, this creates a sense of community among the children.

To foster an open and safe environment, do not criticize children for noticing and asking questions about differences. Children's behaviors such as staring or pointing at a person with a disability are not uncommon and usually indicate curiosity. Even so, the behaviors are hurtful (and when done by adults, also very rude). Adults are often embarrassed by children's pointing or questioning and respond inappropriately: "Don't look, it's not polite!" . . . "It isn't nice to ask that question."

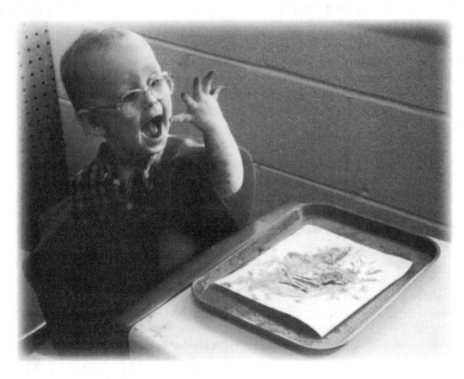

But these responses can imply to children that there is something "wrong" with the difference and can just teach them to stop asking questions. The adults also are communicating discomfort and tension. Without follow-up, children are left lacking the information they need to learn how to act comfortably and caringly and to ask questions respectfully. Instead, answer children's questions and, if possible and appropriate, invite the person with the disability to also respond. Afterwards ask, "Are you curious to know anything else?"

● **Do not deny that differences in physical, cognitive, or emotional abilities exist.**

For example, do not say to a child who can hear well that a child who is deaf is "just like you." This is confusing and does not give either child the information needed for interacting positively with each other. An anti-bias response helps the two children recognize how they are different *and* how they are the same:

> "You both talk but, Cassandra, you talk with your voice and Belinda talks with her hands. You can see what she says, but she doesn't hear what you say. So use your hands to show her what you want to do as you play together. I will help you learn how to understand and use some sign language."

● **Do not dismiss children's expressions of anxiety, fear, or rejection of disabilities.**

If a child says, "I don't like Susie; she can't walk," don't dismiss or ignore the child's concerns by making statements such as "Yes, you do; we are all friends here." Stopping children from expressing their negative feelings doesn't eliminate them; it just teaches children to stop voicing them. It also may lead to avoidance of the child with the disability because the fears interfere with getting to know her. Unresolved anxieties can fester, laying a foundation for prejudice and discrimination.

Also, do not try to handle children's anxiety by conveying that the child with the disability is to be pitied. For example, don't say, "We must be nice to Danny, because he cannot walk." Instead, the goal is for the children to see Danny as a member of the classroom community, all of whom contribute in their unique ways.

● **If you do not know the answer to a specific question, admit it.**

Be honest. Tell children you will have to learn more in order to answer. You can even involve children in going to the library or looking for other sources of information to research the answer together.

Interrupt hurtful language

By kindergarten and school age, some children have learned disrespectful terms for a person with a disability (e.g., *retard, dumb, cripple, spaz*). And they may use these and other terms to tease or put down another child, with or without a disability. While these children often do not know the adult meaning of the word they are using to tease or reject the other child, they *do* know that the word is a put-down. Regardless of whether the children know what the word means, put-downs and disrespectful words still hurt the targeted child. Preschoolers also hear these insulting words and may use them with no idea they are hurtful.

Considerately, yet firmly, interrupt any use of such language—as you would interrupt hurtful language in any other area of identity. Carefully address the needs of all the children involved in any name-calling incident. Make sure to follow up with activities that help children gain accurate information and terms for various disabilities, as well as activities that expand their empathy and skills for interrupting hurtful behavior. For children to truly develop understanding, empathy, ease, and respect for people with disabilities, it is essential that you introduce activities that promote all four of the anti-bias education goals.

Beware mistaking children's cultural or developmental variations for disabilities

Children with disabilities of any kind come from every cultural, racial identity, and economic background. However, a disproportionately high number of children of color end up in special education classes, which indicates that other factors besides disability are at work. The federal Office of Special Education and Rehabilitative Services warns that greater efforts are needed to prevent mislabeling children of color as having disabilities (see Posny 2007).

Researchers (see, e.g., Ladner & Hammons 2003; Skiba et al. 2005) find that schools identify greater proportions of African American children as having mental retardation and emotional disturbances than they do White children. More minority children are placed in special education classes than one would expect based on the percentage of minority students in the general school population. And schools with predominately White students and teachers place disproportionately high numbers of their minority students in special education.

Unexamined attitudes and assumptions and inadequate or inaccurate knowledge on the part of teachers or other school personnel can result in labeling as disabilities the cultural, racial identity, economic class, and developmental *variations* in how children learn and behave.

Mislabeling can come about under several circumstances. A teacher may not understand the learning style of a child if it differs from her expectations of how children learn. For example, a teacher may not recognize that a child is a kinesthetic learner who has considerable difficulty learning while sitting for any period of time. Or a teacher may misunderstand a child's struggle to communicate and learn in an English-only classroom. The child may withdraw and not engage, or he may appear not to know concepts that he actually does understand in his home language—if tested only in English, he may appear to be developmentally delayed when he is not.

A third source of mislabeling can stem from differences in guidance techniques between home and school. To a teacher who is unaware or unappreciative of these differences, a child may appear to have a "behavioral" problem because he doesn't respond to the guidance cues of the teacher's own culture.

● **Explore all possible sources of a child's learning difficulties.**

When any child exhibits a learning or behavioral problem, first consider whether factors in the classroom or center may be causing the difficulty. Ask yourself: "What in the school environment could be contributing to the child's not fitting in?" . . . "What in my teaching style and methods might not be a good match for the child?" Think about each question from developmental and cultural angles.

Then, observe the child's behavior in many different contexts throughout the day to identify when the learning or behavioral problem most often occurs. Talk with the child's family about how she acts in various family situations throughout the day. You may want to get some assistance from a special education specialist (if you are fortunate to have access to a person in that role).

● **Work to ensure cultural continuity between home and school.**

If a child seems unable to control her behavior, it may be an indicator of a possible cognitive or emotional disability, or it may be a reflection of the different guidance style she experiences in her own culture and family. Make a bridge between home and school by integrating some of the child's home cues in your classroom, while also teaching the child the classroom cues.

If this step yields no progress, then further developmental assessment of the child may become necessary, along with adaptations in classroom practice according to the results of the assessment. Making assessments and creating solutions will require working with the child's family so that both are culturally compatible with home and school. (One useful resource on this topic is the DVD "Building Culturally Responsive Relationships with Diverse Families of Children with Disabilities," from the National Association for Multicultural Education.)

● **If it becomes necessary to talk with families about their child's possible disability, be sensitive, caring, and patient.**

One of your more difficult, though essential, tasks as a teacher is letting families know when you believe that their child may have some kind of disability and requires further assessment to figure out how best to help him. Opening up this communication can be hard to do. This is one of the times when it is very important for teachers to know and objectively manage their own feelings. As Carol Cole, a longtime educator of children with physical, developmental, and emotional disabilities, explains:

> It can be heartbreaking for a family to hear for the first time that their child may have special needs, or in a parent conference to hear a teacher verbalize what they may have privately feared. So I get upset if I hear a teacher or administrator say that "the parents are in denial" or that "the family should have known there was a problem" or that "they should just accept it and move forward."
>
> Such statements deny a family's right to their particular process of acceptance and coping. They also risk undermining the relationship between program and family.
>
> Even if the pace of a family's process is frustrating at times, better to say to them: "I know a lot about young children in general, but you will always be the expert of your own child. So if we put our heads together and share what we each know, we can come up with the best plan." . . . Even better to truly *believe* this.

Strategies for teaching about abilities and disabilities

Here are a number of classroom-tested ideas to support children in developing an anti-bias understanding of people's differing abilities. As with other anti-bias education topics, these activities are designed to provide accurate information and images, respectful interactions, and empowerment for children regardless of ability level.

Introduce a variety of disabilities through pictures, books, and dolls

Choose materials that show children with disabilities being active in a range of contexts.

● Regularly read children's books that honestly depict children and adults with various disabilities. Invite children to express their feelings and ideas about the stories, then plan activities based on what they say—especially to counter any misconceptions or feelings of discomfort or fear. Choose books and pictures that show people as whole, competent human beings and that address both their disabilities and their abilities.

● Mount posters and photographs and make games that show people whose lives contradict children's misconceptions.

● Provide commercial and homemade dolls that have various disabilities. These help children develop familiarity and ease with disabilities, open up conversations, and play their ideas and concerns.

● Use persona dolls that have disabilities to tell stories that explore similarities as well as differences with the children in the class. Use the dolls to tell about the common trials and tribulations (e.g., getting used to a new sibling, dealing with a grandparent's death, making a trip to the doctor) and the joys (e.g., getting a new pet, going on a special family outing) that all young children share. Also create stories that help children understand the adaptations that people

with various disabilities need (e.g., a wheelchair, extra time during an activity, an aide).

Provide supervised times to explore adaptive equipment

Adaptive devices and equipment might include wheelchairs, crutches, braces, walkers, hearing aids, glasses, Braille print, canes, and prostheses. Handling and trying out such equipment can satisfy children's curiosity, help take the mystery out of specific disabilities, and provide the information and experience that foster understanding and comfortable interaction with people wearing or using them. Contact organizations that have equipment pools for people with disabilities or a medical supply store to inquire about borrowing or renting equipment. Be sure to get child-size equipment! If you do a curriculum with children's crutches, carefully fit them to each child for safety.

Caution!—Do not let the other children touch a classmate's adaptive equipment without first getting permission from the child's family and then from the child. If permission is granted, always supervise children while they are touching or holding the equipment; it may be expensive to fix or replace. This is a good opportunity to teach children to respect other people's things.

Help *all* children find ways to learn from each other

Through your actions as well as your words, always convey the message that although we are all different, we all contribute. Here are some suggestions for ways to create opportunities for children with disabilities and children who are typically developing to work together in a range of activities:

● Intentionally set up small groups for using the various activity centers. For example:

> It is the first month of preschool. Eight children want to play in the block area this morning, but there is room for only five at a time. The children and teacher agree to set up a schedule so that one group of four plays for a while and then the next group plays. The teacher creates the two groups himself, making sure that each group includes at least one of the three children with disabilities. He keeps an eye on their play and, when necessary, helps them figure out how to interact with each other.

● Model specific ways to interact. For example:

> The preschoolers are getting ready to dance the Hokey-Pokey. The teacher brings Melinda into the circle next to him and moves her wheelchair through the steps. (Melinda is not yet able to move her wheelchair

herself.) The next time the children dance the Hokey-Pokey, the teacher asks Ling to dance with Melinda. Eventually the children initiate involving Melinda on their own.

● Arrange partners or small groups to work together on a specific activity that draws on each child's abilities; children can then help each other. In the following example, the child with a disability has an *advantage* in an area pertinent to the activity (e.g., knowing the colors) and is therefore able to teach her typically developing partner:

> During another activity, the teacher teams Melinda, who knows many color and shape names, with Susie, who is just beginning to learn them. They play a classification game together and Melinda teaches Susie *red, yellow, blue, green, square, circle, triangle*, etc.

● Provide resources to help children with disabilities and children who are typically developing understand each other. For example, have an age-appropriate sign language dictionary in the room to which you and children can refer: Take pictures of a person signing the names of objects in the classroom, and post them next to the word labels on shelves and cabinets.

Plan learning experiences to counter misconceptions

Find out the children's ideas about what people with different kinds of disabilities are and are not capable of doing. Use this information to plan experiences that expand their awareness and understanding. For example, if you learn that some children think that a person who uses a wheelchair or has a hearing or visual impairment cannot be a mother or father, you can read a book or invite in a parent who uses a wheelchair, and so on.

● Invite people with disabilities to visit your program regularly. Ask them to tell the children about their families, their work, and their hobbies. Plan for them to interact with the children throughout ongoing activities (e.g., reading aloud, working on a craft project). Before they commit to coming, make sure the visitors will be comfortable with answering the very direct questions of young children and that they can do so in a developmentally appropriate way.

● Visit workplaces that employ people with special needs. Disability rights organizations are especially good places to visit because children can see people—those with and without disabilities—working together to improve the quality of their own and others' lives.

Teach children how to help in ways that also support the other child's competency

The objective is for children to know how to *offer* help, as well as how to actually provide assistance. Teach children to always ask *before* they start helping ("Do you want help?"). Remind children not to do for the other person something that she can do for herself, and to provide only enough help to enable the person to do it herself as much as possible ("Is this the way to help?"). For example:

> Juanita (age 4½) is working on a collage. Born with cerebral palsy, which causes her hand muscles to spasm, Juanita is having trouble with one of the pieces. She gets a lot of paste on herself. Jasmine (also 4½) says to her, "I'll do that for you." Juanita keeps pasting and ignores Jasmine. The teacher intervenes, "Juanita, do you want help now?" Juanita responds, "No. I do it myself."
>
> Their teacher explains, "Jasmine, I can see that you want to be a friend to Juanita. But it is important that you give her help only when she wants it. Next time, why don't you try asking first, 'Do you need help?'" To Juanita the teacher says, "I'm glad you are making the collage by yourself. You are really being independent."

If the other person does want help, find out what specific kind of help he or she wants or needs. (If the child being helped is unsure of how to answer, help the child find the words.)

Foster children's awareness and skills as allies

Anti-bias education includes fostering children's skills for taking action to make unfair situations fair on behalf of classmates who experience any form of prejudice or discrimination. Of course, activities should take into account children's experiences and abilities.

● As a class activity with the children, check the accessibility of your classroom, then problem solve ways to make it work better for any children who have disabilities or any who might join the class in the future. For example, you can rent a child-size wheelchair and let children explore whether the different learning spaces and materials in their room are accessible. Then they can make a list of improvements.

● Matter-of-factly talk with children about the different needs of specific children and the adaptive strategies you choose to use with them (see the box "When the Teacher Behaves Differently with Different Children"). When you explain it in a clear way, children can appreciate the reasoning behind individualizing your methods to meet specific needs.

- Use persona doll stories—to help prepare for the inclusion of a new child with a disability, for example.

A child with a hearing impairment is coming into their preschool program, so Kay decides to do a series of persona doll stories about "Samantha"—a persona doll who wears a hearing aid and communicates mainly through signing. After some introductory stories about Samantha, she asks the children, "How could you let Samantha know you want to play with her if you don't know sign language?" One child suggests, "We could talk loud in her ear." Kay explains that Samantha cannot hear voices, no matter how loud they are. The children think of other ways: "We can touch her." . . . "We can show her what we want." . . . "We can wave to her if she is too far to touch."

Kay ends by telling the children, "A new child named Ashley will be joining our class next week. Ashley, like Samantha, cannot hear voices. She also uses sign language. Samantha and I will be teaching you how to sign your names and other words so you can begin talking with our new classmate."

The next day, after a fire drill, Kay tells the children that Samantha had not heard the bell for the fire drill, and when everyone jumped up suddenly, she got scared. "What should we do the next time there is a fire drill?" she asks. From the children's various ideas, the group draws up a plan for next time.

- With kindergarten or school-age children, you can make a book together about the various unfair ideas people have about people with disabilities. (For example: "Some people think a person who uses a wheelchair cannot drive. We know he can because. . . .").

- Bring photographs you have taken of various adaptations around the community. Then take an accessibility walk around your school: Are there workable ramps and doorways sufficiently wide for wheelchairs? Are bathrooms, water fountains, and telephones accessible? Are there curb cuts on the streets near your school? Is there an identified handicapped parking space? Are there accessible pedestrian signals (APS) at the crosswalk nearest your school? If accessibility is insufficient, this can lead to an action project in which children, teachers, and families choose an issue to work on together.

* * *

A quality, inclusive classroom integrates anti-bias education into its daily activities. Helping children understand that "different is just how people are!" as one 4-year-old put it, is an important lesson for all children, regardless of their abilities or disabilities. For children with disabilities, a strong self-identity requires skills to stand up to stereotypes and biases that convey inferiority. For children developing typically, knowledge about and connection to people with disabilities reduces the likelihood of fear and discomfort when they inevitably encounter disabilities (or if they become disabled) in the future.

All children benefit from gaining accurate knowledge and caring, respectful skills for interacting with a wide range of people. And making friendships across ability levels brings joy to the whole classroom community.

Note
The discussion in this chapter stands on the shoulders of pioneers Merle Froschl, Linda Colón, Ellen Rubin, and Barbara Sprung and their 1984 book *Including All of Us: An Early Childhood Curriculum about Disability* (New York: Educational Equity Concepts).

When the Teacher Behaves Differently with Different Children
by Carol Cole

I had given Jesse a special chair and had him sit by me every day at lunch. Some children wanted a turn in that chair. "He doesn't do what he's supposed to, so why does he get to sit by you every day?" Some teachers felt I was reinforcing Jesse's negative behavior.

To the teachers, I explained that, given Jesse's background (he was born with fetal alcohol syndrome), it was important that he experience the predictable structure and the individual attention that the chair next to me provided. This support would not need to last forever. To the children, I matter-of-factly explained that Jesse needed help and that someday he would not need the special chair but for now he did. I helped them to recall things they could not do before but now could do. The other children joined in my plan, and began reminding each other not to sit in Jesse's chair. Within the month, Jesse adjusted to classroom expectations. He chose to sit by his new friend Robert instead of in the special chair.

Children generally are very receptive to explanations about why a teacher might use a different strategy with one child. They are more accepting than some adults are. Talking openly about one child needing help enables the rest to understand a teacher's rationale, and it lets them feel like part of the solution. Most important, the talk reinforces the idea that everyone sometimes needs help, and because their classroom is a learning community, when they are the one who needs help, someone *will* help.

Remember to do ability/disability activities that cultivate all four anti-bias education goals

Learning About Holidays & Fairness

11

We do not do holidays in ways that would exclude any children in our school. We make a distinction between everyone participating in an activity to learn about a holiday and everyone celebrating it.

—Rita Tenorio

Holiday activities can be an important part of anti-bias education. When grounded in anti-bias principles, holiday activities support children's cultural identity and enhance their and their family's feelings of belonging to the school community. Anti-bias holiday activities are also a tool for broadening children's awareness of our diverse world, adding to their enjoyment of its cultural diversity, and teaching them about people who make important social contributions across a range of civic and religious traditions.

There are, however, potential pitfalls to using holiday activities in the classroom. Focusing only on the holidays of one cultural group can marginalize children who don't share that same culture. It also can teach children from that one cultural group the false message that only those holidays—the ones they are already familiar with—are "normal" and therefore right for everyone. This most often happens with holidays of the dominant culture, because those are the ones historically celebrated in schools.

Another potential pitfall is using holiday activities as the only or the primary way to introduce cultural diversity (e.g., recognizing and learning about Mexican people only at Cinco de Mayo). This runs the risk of unintentionally sending children the message that a cultural group's special holiday clothes, foods, and rituals are what the people of that culture wear, eat, and do all the time. Stereotyping or oversimpli-

fying a culture's holiday traditions is a third pitfall. This results when teachers lack adequate knowledge of cultures different from their own or when they are trying to design engaging activities that young children can do easily.

All of these pitfalls reflect a "tourist curriculum" approach to diversity, which undercuts the goals of anti-bias education. (For more about tourist curriculum, see chapters 1 and 4.)

Many families (and teachers) have strong feelings about the holidays they personally celebrate—and the ones they do not. It is important to understand and respect these feelings, but many other factors also should be taken into consideration when developing curriculum. This chapter will help you to make thoughtful choices about how to use holidays in your classroom as part of an anti-bias education approach.

Underlying concepts for using holidays in anti-bias education

Experienced anti-bias educators vary in how they approach using holidays in their curriculum: Some don't include them at all, others create only "special school holidays," and still others choose and incorporate a diverse range of holidays. Educators in faith-based programs combine their particular religious responsibilities with anti-bias education principles. The topic of this chapter is not deciding "Do I or don't

I include holidays in my curriculum?"; it is how to ground whatever holiday activities you do in the following principles of anti-bias education.

● **Holidays are only one way to explore diversity.**

In programs using an anti-bias approach, holiday activities are a small part of the year's curriculum. They are included as learning activities to support the four core goals of anti-bias education and the specific goals for children of chapters 5 through 10.

● **There is a difference between learning about and celebrating a holiday.**

Celebrating a holiday engages children in holiday activities as full-fledged participants, as if they accepted the holiday's underlying purpose and meaning in the way that those who regularly celebrate it do. Celebrating a religiously based holiday is only appropriate in faith-based programs in which the holiday is part of a belief system shared by every family. Even then, it is essential to recognize that within a belief system, different families celebrate in different ways. Celebrating a secular holiday is only appropriate when all families' perspectives on that holiday are considered and addressed.

In contrast, *learning about* a holiday means teaching children about what the holiday means to the cultural or religious groups who honor it and the various ways these groups choose to celebrate it. With preschool-age children, the focus is on how the different families in the program (or the community) choose to celebrate specific holidays.

Information should always be developmentally appropriate for young children. Teaching about a holiday calls on teachers to communicate accurate information appropriate to the child's level of cognitive development in a clear and matter-of-fact manner. It also requires that teachers make very clear that we can enjoy learning about one another's holidays without having to accept ideas and participate in rituals that are not ours. Teachers may read a book to children or invite individual children and their family members to share what they do during a particular holiday.

● **Holidays are not universal.**

All cultures commemorate significant events, ideas, or people that reflect their history, religious beliefs, and values. Even within a group that celebrates the same holiday, the ways it is celebrated may vary. The beliefs and traditions of one group or family may conflict with or complement those of others. Knowing the purpose and world view underlying a holiday will help you to make decisions about what role, if any, you want that holiday to play in your program. (For example, did you know that in the United States, Mother's Day started as an anti-war holiday?)

● **Every holiday tradition deserves respect.**

Respecting cultural diversity means recognizing that everyone has the right to his or her beliefs and traditions, including holidays—and no family's traditions are disrespected. It is hurtful to children and families to impose the holidays of one group on all the children and staff, or to make the holiday traditions of some groups visible while others' are invisible. This is why it is so vital that you make choices thoughtfully and respectfully about whether and how to make visible the holiday traditions of any families in your program, recognizing that no family's traditions should be disrespected. It is also why we advocate the principle of inviting children to *learn about* other children's holidays, rather than asking them to *celebrate* the holidays in the classroom.

● **Holidays often have deep emotional meaning for the people who celebrate them.**

We first learn our holiday traditions from our family as young children—leaving us deeply imprinted by all of their smells, tastes, sights, sounds, and interactions among family members and friends. Some of these emotional memories may

Goals for Children

• Children will see their family's approach to holidays honored in their early childhood program. (ABE Goal 1)

• Children will become aware of and be comfortable with the reality that people happily celebrate different holidays or celebrate the same holiday in different ways. (ABE Goal 2)

• Children will learn that some people do not celebrate religious or national holidays but do have other ways of having family celebrations and traditions. (ABE Goal 2)

• Children will recognize misinformation and stereotypes associated with specific holiday traditions. (ABE Goal 3)

• Children will participate in celebrations that honor people's work for fairness and justice for all people. (ABE Goal 4) be deeply wonderful or strongly unpleasant. Fueled by commercial and media hype, so much expectation is built up around holidays that many children (and adults, too) can feel disappointment if their holiday experience is not the way they think it's "supposed" to be. Adults may try to "make up" for their own childhood holiday disappointments with the children in their lives now. For families with religious affiliations, how holy days are expressed and celebrated has especially deep and powerful meaning. Some families deliberately select a faith-based school so their child will learn the particulars of how they want their holidays practiced.

All these strong emotions can make holiday curriculum choices complicated. Most families—and many staff—want *their* particular holidays to be recognized in the program, and often want the holidays done the same way they do them at home. Not marking a holiday or doing it very differently can result in a person feeling disrespected or robbed of something important to them. Sensitive, thoughtful, and unhurried development of a holiday policy and activities, which includes all staff and input from families, helps to address everyone's feelings.

● **Each family has its own version of holiday traditions, including not celebrating.**

Don't make assumptions about any family's holiday traditions. Even when families celebrate the same holiday, each may celebrate it with different symbols and activities. In addition, the same holiday may carry significantly different meanings. Respectfully ask each family what holidays they celebrate and how.

If you do choose to teach about holidays, use what you learn from the families in your planning. Remember, however, the answers will likely change from year to year as new families enter your program and old ones leave. Be cautious in incorporating published information and commercial holiday materials; your curriculum should always accurately reflect the individual traditions of your *particular* families.

● **Holidays that have official status usually reflect the beliefs, perspective, and history of the dominant culture.**

Official holidays are those mandated as special days by local, state, or national authority, and they are acknowledged by the closing of schools, banks, and government offices; paid time off; and publicly funded celebrations. In the United States, most of our major holidays are celebrations that honor the historical events (e.g., Columbus Day, Thanksgiving, the Fourth of July) or religious beliefs (e.g., Christmas, Easter) of the dominant (i.e., White/European,

Christian) culture. In contrast, religious holidays of other faith traditions, such as Passover and Ramadan, are not official holidays, and people who follow those may have to choose between working and losing pay if they take off. And alternative perspectives on the historical events (e.g., Native American views of Columbus Day and Thanksgiving) are often invisible in the celebration.

Even when a family's home culture differs from the dominant culture, many want their children to *learn about* the major national historical holidays. Many immigrant families see such activities as part of learning about their new country. (This does not mean, however, that the families stop honoring the history and holidays of their culture of origin.) This is another reason it is essential to learn what the various holidays mean to the specific families in your program.

● **Secular or commercialized versions of holidays are not culture neutral.**

Denying that religious beliefs and traditions underlie some holidays (e.g., "Christmas trees and Santa Claus aren't religious, and they are fun traditions for everyone") is no solution. This approach to Christmas, for example, can feel disrespectful both to families and children for whom Christmas is a significant religious event and to families who do not celebrate it at all. Likewise, activities about Easter with bunnies and baskets of eggs are not neutral. Some Christian families see this approach as a pagan celebration that trivializes one of the two most important holy days of the year. For many families of other faiths, the activities are inseparable from Easter itself (it is, after all, the *Easter* bunny).

● **Changing how a program does holiday activities requires thoughtfulness, sensitivity, and patience.**

Coming to understand what a holiday means to you, your colleagues, and families in your program will help you work with others to figure out mutually satisfactory solutions. Some people will find changes to a particular holiday celebration difficult, as this Head Start teacher attempting an anti-bias approach related:

> Changing how I do Christmas was hard for me, because Christmas was and is a big thing in my life. It was hard for me to step back and realize that what I was doing in my class was for me. But I do not want to hurt any of my children, so I did accept that I had to make some changes.

Others will be delighted, as one Muslim preschool teacher was. She described how liberating it felt when her child care center changed its traditional Christmas celebration to one where each family and teacher shared his or her personal holiday story and tradition with the group.

Stop & Think: Looking back at holiday celebrations

- When you were a child, what holidays did your family celebrate, if any? What was important to your family about various holidays? What, if anything, did you especially like? What was hard?

- Did school holiday celebrations reinforce or conflict with what you learned about holidays at home? How, if at all, did they broaden your perspective?

- From what you know now, to what extent did school or family holiday celebrations teach you stereotypes or misinformation about the history or lives of various groups of people?

Develop a holiday policy

A holiday policy spells out your program's objectives and decision-making process in approaching holidays in the curriculum. There is no one right policy. Experienced anti-bias educators vary in what they do. What matters is that your holiday policy reflects the needs of the children and families you serve as well as the principles of anti-bias education and your program's philosophy. In addition, you may have to take into account any state or city requirements related to holidays.

Some programs have "No Holiday" policies or "Program Celebration Only" policies. In these programs, holidays belong to the families. Annual school celebrations (e.g., school picnics, potlucks, end of the year excursions) serve the function of marking the passage of the year and connecting children, staff, and families. This is certainly one valid option. Make sure that families with whom you work are clear about why staff consider this best for the children. Also be sure to communicate this policy to prospective families and new staff before they join your program.

There are other options beyond a "No Holiday" policy within an anti-bias education approach. Choices can range from learning about one holiday from each family, to focusing on themes that include holidays from different cultures, to children talking about how their family celebrated a holiday at home. These are just a few examples.

While it takes time to hold the necessary discussions between staff and with families to establish a holiday policy that works for your program, it is well worth the effort. Such discussions enable everyone to grow in their understanding of their own and others' holiday traditions and to tailor decisions about

holiday activities in the curriculum to each particular setting. One administrator related that for a whole school year, her school devoted 20 minutes in each of their monthly meetings to do this work. Now they continue to review their holiday policy each year, considering it in light of the new families and staff in the program. Their annual update goes much faster than the original year it took to create a policy.

Each program can create its own process. Taking enough time to do so is worth it. Creating a well thought out foundation helps families and staff to be comfortable and open about how the program will address holidays, and it decreases the time and effort required for adjustments as needs change.

As you develop your holiday policy, consider the following questions:

1. How would holiday activities serve each of the four anti-bias education goals? Would holiday activities:

- Support the children's family traditions and cultural identities?

- Support the program's own identity (e.g., as a neighborhood school, a faith-based school, a bilingual school)?

- Expand children's awareness and appreciation of others' cultural traditions?

- Create school traditions that children, families, and staff can share and that serve as marking points throughout the school year?

- Broaden children's understanding of people and events that express social justice values (e.g., Martin Luther King Jr. Day)?

- Acquaint children with national and other dominant culture holidays?

2. What process will you use among staff to make decisions about which holidays to use and how?

3. How will you work with families from diverse backgrounds to find mutually satisfying solutions to holiday issues?

4. How will you work with families who do not want their child participating in holiday activities?

If your program decides to use holidays as part of an anti-bias curriculum, staff and families should decide together which national, community, school, and family holidays the children will *learn about* and which are appropriate to *celebrate* in the classroom. Anti-bias education goals can be part of all your choices.

Guidelines for planning holiday activities

Once you make decisions about which holidays you will use in your curriculum, here are some guidelines for making activity choices.

Understand the context of the holiday

Considering the following questions will clarify what holidays you will teach children about and which are appropriate to celebrate with a particular group of children and families:

● Is the holiday a sacred/holy or a historical/secular event? From what ethnic/cultural group(s) does the holiday originate?

● What is this holiday really about? What story does it tell? What messages does it convey?

● What portion of your families celebrate it (all, some, none)? How do they celebrate it, if they do?

● Do any families find any aspects of this holiday offensive or difficult? If so, why?

● What can be wonderful about this holiday for children? What might be difficult for them? (Think developmentally!)

● Are there specific misconceptions or stereotypes associated with this holiday that children might pick up? If yes, how will you counter them in your activities?

● What, specifically, do you want the children to learn from the holiday activities? To which of the four anti-bias education goals would the activities connect?

Plan how to equitably respect everyone's traditions

Don't treat some holidays as "different" and others as "what everyone does." Make visible and respect differences in how each family celebrates a particular holiday. Encourage the children to share what they enjoy about how their family celebrates a holiday.

Help children understand when a staff member or child cannot participate in some part of a holiday activity. For example:

A mother brings a special lunch to school for her child's birthday. She does not realize it is Ramadan, when observant adult Muslims fast between dawn and dusk, and is upset when Omar, a student teacher, doesn't eat anything. She complains to the head teacher that both her and her daughter's feelings were hurt. The head teacher explains Omar's right to practice fasting.

She also tells Omar that the child was puzzled by his not eating the special lunch her mother had pre-

pared. Omar makes sure to talk with the child during that day, explaining why he hadn't eaten and assuring the child that he was happy for her birthday.

Don't let your own or other staff members' holiday preferences get in the way of showing respect to the traditions of the program's families. For example:

The kindergarten has spent a few days learning about Passover. During a discussion of the Seder ceremony, the teacher explains the meaning and tradition behind matzo. Esther, one of the Jewish children, states that she cannot eat leavened bread during the whole week of Passover. The next day a birthday celebration for another child includes cake. As the teacher is enjoying a slice, a student teacher gives Esther a piece, because he feels sorry about "depriving" Esther and worries she might feel left out.

Luckily, the teacher notices the conflicted expression on Esther's face and intervenes: "Esther, do you know that cake is made with leavened flour and that you can't eat it during Passover?" Esther nods her head. "Let's freeze your piece and you can eat it after the holiday." Esther relaxes, gives her cake to the teacher, and goes off to play.

Unfortunately, the teacher had not thought to check ahead of time with Esther's family when the birthday celebration was scheduled during the Passover holiday. If she had, she might have made a plan with them—perhaps that they would bring appropriate cookies for Esther or tell the teacher where to buy some herself, or that she would ask the birthday child's family to check with Esther's family about bringing a substitute for her.

Make room for children to share their own experiences

Inviting a child to help teach his classmates about his own family's holidays strengthens the child's positive self-identity. Learning about someone else's holiday traditions can foster children's awareness of and comfort with diversity. For example:

In the weeks before Christmas, the other 4- and 5-year-olds in Ashar's class begin talking about Santa Claus and asking him what Santa Claus is going to bring him. Ashar keeps calmly saying, "I don't believe in Santa Claus. I don't celebrate Christmas. I'm Muslim." His classmates are puzzled. That night Ashar tells his mother, "The children at my school do not know about Muslims. My teachers celebrate Christmas, so let's get them Christmas presents. I celebrate Eid ul-Fitr, so let's get them Eid presents, too." At school, Ashar begins talking with his classmates about what his family does for Eid, and he shares Eid food and a game with them.

Ashar tells his imam and his mother, "I need a bus to bring my class to my mosque." The teacher and Ashar's mother arrange for a visit, and Ashar's imam takes them around and reads stories to them. Ashar is thrilled that his classmates visited his mosque, and it is a lovely experience for everyone. Subsequently, other children also decide to tell their classmates about their family' religious practices—and an ongoing theme for the curriculum emerges.

Consider how to approach birthdays

Birthdays are also holidays and cultural events. Carefully think through how, if at all, you will recognize children's birthdays. (Adoptive families may choose to celebrate "adoption days" instead.) Pay attention to birthday celebrations outside of school, as well. They can pose problems, such as some children being left out of party invitations, or frustration for families who cannot afford or do not ascribe to commercial gift giving.

If families plan to include the children from your program in home birthday parties, talk with them about how to support anti-bias principles of respect and caring for each child and family. You may want to come to agreement that all children in the class are invited or that the family comes to school to celebrate with the child's classmates. At the least, make a policy that if all children are not invited, birthday invitations cannot be distributed at school. Raise with families the idea of agreeing on a policy that makes gift giving affordable for all families and that emphasizes caring rather than materialism.

Create unique class or school celebrations

In addition to or instead of using family holidays, some teachers create their own celebrations for various parts of the school year. This approach makes it possible for every child to participate in shared special days with the rest of the class. Celebrations can be respectful—for example, "Honoring Our Families" get-togethers; "Thanking the People Who Make Our School Work" (cook, janitor, bus driver, etc.) days; or occasions for "Recognizing Family and Neighborhood Heroes."

Celebrations can also be whimsical and playful—for example, "Bring Books Alive Day" (making and wearing costumes from books, eating foods from favorite books, acting out favorite stories); "Pajama Day" (wearing pjs and slippers to school, telling bedtime stories, sharing family bedtime rituals); or "Backwards Day" (wearing clothes backwards, doing things in reverse order of an ordinary day).

The Language of Religious Holidays

Paying attention to the language you use is an important element in children's learning about, rather than celebrating, a holiday grounded in a specific faith. This is especially necessary in publicly funded programs where religious teaching is not allowed by law. Your language choices also support or undercut the concept of religious diversity and each family's freedom of choice.

The challenge is to choose words that focus on the history of the special day and that also make clear the diversity of beliefs. For example, you might explain Christmas with words such as "Christmas is special to some people because it celebrates the birthday of the god they believe in. Some families celebrate the day with gifts and their family members eating a meal together." Phrases such as "Christmas is the birthday of the Lord" belong to Christian families in their homes, not to teachers in classrooms.

Likewise, telling the story of Chanukah could focus on how "Jewish people got together and fought to be able to practice their religion. Some Jewish families light candles for eight nights to honor the event and some give their children a present each night." Religious Jewish families might tell the story in their homes as "God sent a miracle and the temple's oil lamp burned for eight nights."

Plan ways to work with families who do not want their child to participate

When a family does not want their child to participate in classroom holiday events, which may include birthdays, teachers must respect their preferences—religious or other. The task is to work together to find a "third space" (see chapter 5) without suggesting or assuming how the family would prefer to handle the situation. The first step is to find out the family's specific concerns. Many families are comfortable with their children learning about other people's holidays if it is clear the holidays are not being celebrated in the school.

You may find that through committed, respectful dialogue with families, you can adapt how you do specific holiday activities to make it possible for all children to participate. Here's one adaptation:

As each holiday approached, the program had an ongoing circle time discussion with children to "talk about their holidays." One of the program's new Jehovah's Witness families does not want their child to attend. After talking with the family, the staff decides to continue the circle time—but to ask the children to talk about "special family time." This makes it possible for everyone to participate.

Another adaptation is choosing not to do holiday activities in your class and instead inviting the children to talk about how their family celebrated after the holiday has passed.

A third strategy was used in a program regarding the annual Columbus Day holiday:

> A small group of Choctaw parents and grandparents approached the staff, explaining that they were inclined to keep their children home during that week. After much discussion with the families and among themselves, the teachers decided instead to tell stories both about the bravery of Columbus's journey and about the indigenous people who already lived (and still do!) in his "New World." Over the next few weeks, staff also invited the Choctaw families to talk to the children about their daily lives and the special ceremonial events of the Choctaw year. This worked so well that these activities have continued each year.

The *last resort* is a child staying home or spending time in another classroom or with the director on the day of a holiday activity. Some families may suggest this solution themselves, and it may be the best you can all figure out, but never offer it as *your* best idea.

The October–December push

The three national holidays of Halloween, Thanksgiving, and Christmas are the ones that most often appear in early childhood programs. They bring pleasure to many families and staff, as well as to children. However, they also pose a range of challenges for many families. Whether or not to include any of them in your curriculum, and what activities to use if you do, requires thoughtful decision making. Here are some guidelines and strategies for teaching about Halloween, Thanksgiving, and Christmas, if you decide to teach about any of them in your curriculum.

Halloween

Many children have fun every year celebrating Halloween in their neighborhoods, schools, and early childhood programs. At the same time, however, its pagan origins and associations with witches, ghosts, and evil make Halloween problematic for some families, including some fundamentalist Christian, Jehovah's Witness, and immigrant families. Still other families do not like the traditional gorging on sugar that follows trick-or-treating, or they no longer allow their children to go out at all because of their fears about possible harm. Commercialism also has turned Halloween into a time when parents feel pressured to buy expensive candy and ready-made costumes that sometimes are inconsistent with their values or budgets. In addition, children under 4 may find some of the costumes frightening.

For one or more of these reasons, some early childhood programs decide not to include Halloween in their curriculum or to modify how they do Halloween activities.

Countering disrespectful and stereotypical messages

Teachers report that some young children equate elderly women with the "ugly witches" they see in Halloween decorations and costumes. Many commercial costumes and masks perpetuate cultural stereotypes, such as "red Indians" and "sexy gypsies" (the word *gypsy* itself is an insulting term for the Roma people), or racial stereotypes, such as blue-eyed, blond-haired "princesses" and dark-skinned "bad guys" and pirates. In addition, the black clothes and black cats of Halloween witches reinforce the unfortunate association between the color black and evil (and so does language such as "black mood" or "black magic").

As an adult you may be so used to such images and associations as part of Halloween that it may seem fussy to make this critique. Yet, it is important for teachers to counter such messages with young children because these negative associations are among the myriad microcontaminants in popular culture that can encourage the development of stereotypical thinking and pre-prejudice. Here are some suggestions:

● Contradict ideas of old women as ugly or scary. Find out children's ideas about how elderly women look and what they can do. Read children's books about the many different ways older women look and participate in life. (Consider reading the delightful *Our Granny,* by Margaret Wild.) Connect with a community group of senior citizens and invite some to spend time with the children doing specific activities. If there is a grandparent volunteer program in your community, ask its members to be a regular part of your program.

● Counter negative ideas about darkness. Invite the children to tell about black and brown objects they like. You may want to start them out by offering one or two of your own as examples (e.g., chocolate ice cream, "my black dog Jack," blackberry jam, licorice). List these on a chart. Later in the day, children who want to can find and paste on pictures of the objects listed on the chart. You can also create a class book (e.g., "Black and Brown Are Beautiful") of pictures and words for children to read. This activity and similar ones can be done at any point during the year, but are especially relevant around Halloween when connotations of dark colors as evil are most promoted.

Designing new ways to do Halloween activities

Take into account approaches and concerns of specific families, adapt your activities, or create new ones.

● Involve children in making Halloween masks (and perhaps costumes). Display the finished masks in the classroom or let children wear their costumes for a parade at school. Besides helping to reduce the emphasis on commercial costumes and masks, this activity is a way of lessening the fears many preschoolers have of the masked figures that appear on Halloween.

● Provide a Halloween substitute. If some families do not want their children engaged in any traditional Halloween activities, consider creating an alternative celebration. For example, substitute dress-up costumes that children put together from the program's costume and scarf box and have a parade. Here's what Debbie Ravaçon's program did:

> When I started as director, I wanted to change our traditional Halloween practice of taking the children in costumes around the college to get candy. Children got scared, some families kept their children home that day, and the quantity of candy violated the center's commitment to healthy eating. The staff struggled with what to do because they enjoyed the activity themselves. Eventually, we agreed on doing a child-made funny hat parade around the college, with no candy. We also let the whole college know why we made these changes.

Thanksgiving

Although Thanksgiving is a holiday widely celebrated by people in the United States, including new immigrants, it is not embraced by all. While many families use it to express thankfulness for family and for their current lives, Thanksgiving does raise challenging issues. Its story and traditions largely reflect the perspective of the European colonists, not the indigenous people who had been living on the continent for many thousands of years already. And while the holiday honors the social struggle of a group who immigrated in search of a better life and religious freedom, it does not recognize what the cost was to the Native Americans they displaced.

Unless teachers are well informed and thoughtful, Thanksgiving can become (even if unintentionally) a "unit" that teaches young children damaging misinformation and stereotypes.

Countering disrespectful and stereotypical messages about Native Americans

Some teachers choose to use the Thanksgiving holiday period to help children appreciate American Indian people as they are now:

> Native peoples are everywhere in the Americas. We number in the tens of millions; we speak hundreds of languages. We live in the hemisphere's remotest places and its biggest cities. We are still here. . . . We work hard to remain Native in circumstances that sometimes challenge or threaten our survival. We are still here. (Smithsonian 2007)

Most people in the United States have grown up surrounded by so much misinformation about and stereotypical images of Native Americans that it is essential to clarify our own thinking and to find out children's ideas about them before planning curriculum about these present members of our communities. Plan and carry out many activities before, during, and after the Thanksgiving period. A one-time activity is not enough to counter children's mistaken images or ideas.

Step 1. Take time to list what you think you know about Native Americans and what you need to learn in order to work with the children. (A good resource here is www.oyate.org, for dependable information about stereotypes and ways to choose children's books.)

Step 2. Find out what the children in your program think they know about American Indians. Ask questions such as these:

> Who knows about American Indians? . . . Where do you think they live? What do they do? How do they look? . . . Does anyone know a person who is an American Indian? Is anyone an American Indian themselves?

Make a note of children's misconceptions and stereotypes (e.g., "They all live in tipis . . . shoot bows and arrows . . . wear feather headdresses." . . . "Indians are all dead").

Step 3. Collect accurate, *current* images and information that counter the children's stereotypes and misinformation. Several available children's books (including some for primary-age children) and adult picture books offer authentic images. One teacher makes copies of the pictures and displays these. If your community has a museum about American Indian life, its gift shop may have useful materials. Focus on the daily contemporary life of specific Native American groups. It is best to choose a Native nation from your own geographic region. When you refer to the group, always use its tribal name (e.g., Hopi, Cherokee, Choctaw, Miwok).

What's in a Name?

What term(s) is most respectful to use for the peoples who occupied North America before Europeans arrived? According to *Do All Indians Live in Tipis?* (Smithsonian Institution 2007), a book of questions and answers from the Smithsonian's National Museum of the American Indian: "Whenever possible, Native people prefer to be called by their specific tribal [nation] name"—for example, Navajo, Ohlone, Pequot, Yurok. The book continues:

> In the United States, *Native American* has been widely used but is falling out of favor with some groups, and the terms *American Indian* or *indigenous American* are now preferred by many Native people. *Native American*, however, grew out of 1960s and 1970s political movements and is now used in legislation. Legally, it refers not only to the indigenous people of the lower 48 states but also to Native people in U.S. territories. As an adjective, many people now prefer to use simply *Native* or *Indian*. (2)

How do you know which term to use with a specific Native family? . . . Ask!

Source: Smithsonian Institution, National Museum of the American Indian, *Do All Indians Live in Tipis?: Questions and Answers from the National Museum of the American Indian* (New York: Collins, in association with the National Museum of the American Indian, 2007).

Step 4. Using an anti-bias approach, design activities about American Indians to use not only at Thanksgiving but throughout the year. Here are a range of suggestions:

● Make a class book with accurate, current images, and keep it where children have easy access. Be sure the class book helps children explore the contemporary life of American Indians in all its diversity—for example, in the country and in the city, in the Southwest and Northeast, and so on.

● Read children's books that accurately portray contemporary Native life. Examples include *Salmon for Simon* (by Betty Waterton and Ann Blades), *Two Pairs of Shoes* (by Esther Sanderson), and *On Mother's Lap* (by Ann Herbert Scott). Do not substitute traditional Native folktales for books about contemporary Native people. Folktales can be a delightful part of the curriculum, but only when used in conjunction with stories about Native peoples today.

● Tell stories with persona dolls about current American Indian life. As with all persona doll stories, be sure to use authentic-looking dolls and accurate information, and create a specific doll child and family who are from a specific American Indian nation.

Tell stories about different aspects of their daily life, as well as stories that strengthen both children's empathy for the hurt of experiencing prejudice and their skills for standing up to counter it.

● Invite Native visitors to talk about their lives and to interact with the children. Ask them to wear their daily clothing as well as to explain the use of traditional ritual clothing. Be sure to arrange multiple visits, not just at Thanksgiving. If there are no American Indian families, staff, or friends of the program available, sources of guests might be an American Indian center, bookstore, or crafts store or a Native studies program in a nearby university.

● With school-age children, you can use the topic of learning about American Indians as a catalyst to explore differences and similarities in more depth. For example: (1) Compare daily life with ceremonial activities; casual clothes worn for play or school with formal clothing worn to religious services. Discuss how these differences exist in everyone's life. (2) Compare daily life in the past with the present day. You might have children bring in photos of their own 19th century or early 20th century relatives to compare with how their family dresses now. If families do not have such photos, bring in pictures clipped from magazines or show books about that era. Then contrast images of Native American past and present dress. (3) Compare books that depict American Indians accurately with books that depict stereotypes. Talk about what is fair and unfair; "what helps us learn about American Indians, and what hurts their feelings."

Planning activities that recognize the newest immigrants to our nation

Many early childhood programs serve increasing numbers of recent immigrant children and families. Since Thanksgiving honors the Pilgrims (European immigrants who settled in what is now New England), the holiday is a good time to counter misinformation and negative attitudes children may have about today's "pilgrims." Here are some activity suggestions:

● Organize a "We Come from Many Places" celebration meal for all the families in the program. Children can help to cook and decorate the tables; immigrant families can be invited to show pictures and talk about their country of origin.

● Plan a song/story curriculum for the weeks around Thanksgiving in which the children learn a song or listen to a story from each of the countries the families in your program have immigrated from. For some children this will mean their immediate family; for others

The Hurt of "Cowboys and Indians"

Do not ever allow children to pretend-play being Indians. This is pretending to be a member of an ethnic group of people not your own, such as putting on "whiteface" or "blackface" to pretend to be White or Black. Such behavior is insulting to real members of the group. It is different when children pretend to be a specific role, such as father, doctor, truck driver, firefighter, and the like, as these cut across all (or many) racial identity groups.

Explain to children why pretend-playing being an Indian is disrespectful and hurtful, as it was to this Navajo-Laguna-Kiaoni-Pueblo girl:

> It makes me mad when children make fun of my culture. . . . When the children grow up I don't want them to think that Indians put feathers in their hair and dance around the fire. We don't do that. . . . One day I saw a kid running around with a feather in their hair and putting their hand to their mouths and making weird noises and I cried when that happened. So what I want you to do is to . . . learn about our real history.

Source: Oyate website (www.oyate.org).

it will mean grandparents or great-grandparents, and so on. For American Indian children, it means that their ancestors were here when other peoples first came. Focus on "how wonderful it is to have all these new songs and stories."

Planning activities to teach about the people who help supply our food

Since meal rituals are such a focus in Thanksgiving traditions, some teachers choose to do a series of activities that recognizes the foods children like to eat at home and teaches about honoring the people who grow, harvest, and deliver our food. With school-age children, this can be extended to learning about the variety of ways that people celebrate successful harvests internationally. Here are some suggestions:

● Find out what foods farmers grow in the area where you live. If possible, visit the fields with the children and meet some of the people who grow and pick the harvest.

● Ask families who celebrate Thanksgiving to let you know what seasonal foods they use for the holiday. Make displays and read books about the people who do the work of growing and harvesting those foods.

● Invite visitors who box, ship, load, or sell food in your community. Ask them to share with the children what they do. Help the children make the connection between the visitors' work and the foods their families buy and eat. Encourage the children to dictate thank you notes for the visits.

Christmas

Christmas is the biggest holiday of the year in the United States. Months before December 25th, that reality is visible in stores, the media, public decorations, and greeting cards. Although its rampant commercialization makes Christmas look as if it is a secular holiday, and some people celebrate it as such, Christmas is a profoundly religious event in the Christian religions.

In our multicultural society, Christmas, although important to many people, is still not everyone's holiday. For children and families from other groups—be they Jewish, Buddhist, Muslim, pagan, atheist, or anything else—Christmas can be a difficult time. For almost all families, the commercialization of the holiday, with its pressures to buy, decorate, and entertain, adds tremendous complication to already overloaded and busy lives. How can you address Christmas in your program in a way that is supportive and fair to all? Here is a range of approaches anti-bias educators use; you can adopt or adapt any of these strategies or invent your own.

Learning about each other's December holidays

Begin by finding out from families and staff members which December holiday(s), if any, they celebrate, and what they might like to share about their personal tradition. If the people in your program are culturally diverse, this could mean you will be learning about a number of different December holidays. In a more culturally homogeneous class, it could mean learning about the fascinating variety of ways families all celebrate the same holiday.

Make a plan for how you will teach about the various traditions in your classroom. For example, have a school party with every family sharing a special holiday food, song, or ritual. If family members cannot come into the classroom, ask them for a story or song that you can share with the children yourself. Help the children explore the similarities and differences among family holiday celebrations—whether it is the same holiday or different holidays. The aim is for children to understand that "Families are different. Each family's way of celebrating works for them."

If you use this approach, be very sensitive to children who celebrate differently from the majority of the children. Otherwise, it is easy for their holiday to sound like just a variation on the dominant culture's event. It is the teacher's responsibility (not the child's) to clarify the distinctions. For example, in one school, most of the children told stories about their Christmas holiday customs; the one Jewish child talked about Chanukah. Later, several of the children (and some adults) wished the child's family a "happy Jewish Christmas."

Countering holiday commercialization

Be sensitive to the pressures created by the commercialization of December holidays, especially on families with low incomes. The equating of love with expensive and numerous gifts has a strong influence on many children and their families. Challenge these negative pressures by focusing on meaningful ways to celebrate holidays without spending money. Encourage the caring and giving side of Christmas, rather than the material, gift-giving side. Talk about holidays as times when people who care about one another come together to appreciate and enjoy one another. Open up conversations with families about the pressures they might experience and ways they can counter these. For example:

● Family members might decide to only *make* gifts for each other, including offering help to do a specific home task or a favorite recreation activity. Your program could have a workshop where families can make books about their children to give as gifts. Families would bring snapshots to add to those the program already has, and the program would provide a scanner and printer and materials to bind the books.

● Depending on where families live, encourage them to create special "nighttime walks" to see lights on trees and the stars and moon.

● Invite families for a discussion about gift giving. Raise issues of commercialization and messages about consumption overshadowing the values of Christmas. Open up suggestions for alternative ways of gift giving, such as grandparents chipping in to buy one present for a child rather than many, or gifts of activities (e.g., a trip to the zoo, a children's theater performance) rather than things.

● With school-age children, extend these concepts to thinking about the ways that advertising and store displays make it look like the important thing about Christmas is to buy, buy, and buy!

Focusing on what children did over the break

If your program takes a Christmas or other winter break at this time, invite children when they return to tell about what they did, instead of doing holiday activities in class. Encourage children to identify the similarities and differences in the ways they spent their time. For example:

● Invite families to make a collage about their winter holiday—or about other family activities, if they do not celebrate holidays. (For this project each child gets a large piece of posterboard to take home at the beginning of December.) When school resumes, families bring in their collages. The array of collaged items is usually wide: family recipes, photos of family members and vacation trips, children in specific holiday rituals, and more. Hang all the collages in the same place so families and staff can linger over them, learning about the variety of celebrations in their school community (Bisson 1997).

● Make a wall chart or Big Book of stories that children dictate about their experiences.

Recognize celebrations to honor social struggle

Celebrations and special days that commemorate struggles for freedom, self-determination, justice, and peace are part of many cultures. For example, the Fourth of July commemorates the adoption of the American Declaration of Independence. Martin Luther King Jr. Day honors a man and a civil rights movement. Passover celebrates an ancient victory of the Jewish people over slavery. International Women's Day marks women's struggles to gain equality and decent working conditions. Mexican Independence Day and Cinco de Mayo commemorate Mexico's fights for independence from Spain and France, respectively. Earth Day honors the worldwide efforts to preserve the environment.

Even very young children can grasp the idea of honoring people whose work makes life better for others, even though children's understanding reflects their developmental stage, as this anecdote from family child care provider Bj Richards shows:

A few days after we did some Martin Luther King Jr. Day activities, the mom of one of my 3-year-olds emailed me: "As I was looking over the bank statement the other day, I asked my husband, 'Did you order some Doc Martens (as in the shoes)?' My daughter corrected me: 'Bj says we should call him *Dr. Martin Luther King.*' . . . Thanks, Bj, for teaching her about these important people!"

By age 4 children often can begin connecting activities about social justice holidays to their own experiences with unfairness and fairness. Although they cannot understand fully all the facts and complexities of history, young children can learn that many grown-ups have worked, and continue to work, to make the world a safe, fair, and good place.

As with all curriculum subject areas, it is important to research your subject, present accurate, factual information, and make sure the activities are appropriate to the developmental stage and cultures of the children you serve.

Read and discuss children's books

Child librarians can help you find books for young children, taking various approaches to justice issues. Here are several good ones:

● *Planting the Trees of Kenya* (by Claire Nivola) and *Wangari's Trees of Peace: A True Story of Africa* (by Jeanette Winters) are two wonderful picture books about Wangari Maathai, who was awarded the Nobel Peace Prize in 2004. *The Streets Are Free* (by Kurusa) is about a group of children wanting to turn an abandoned parking lot into a neighborhood park. *¡Sí, se puede!/Yes, We Can!* (by Diana Cohn) is a lovely, child-friendly story about an effective strike of mainly Latino janitors in Los Angeles. Books for young children also are available about Cesar Chavez, Martin Luther King Jr., and Rosa Parks.

● Eric Hoffman has two fine bilingual books about children taking action: *No Fair to Tigers/No es justo para los tigres* and *Heroines and Heroes/Heroínas y héroes*.

Involve children in an action project

Choose an issue that directly affects the children's lives and that relates to the social justice event or celebration. Engage in an action project related to the special day to help the children gain a sense of its meaning. For example:

The teacher talks with the children about the meaning of Earth Day and invites them to suggest actions they could take on that day. The children decide to "not waste food." They are already composting leftovers from lunch, but they decide to keep out "green things" to feed the chickens that one family keeps. And they decide to make signs (dictated to the teacher and decorated by the children) to put up in the building reminding people to turn off lights when they leave a room.

Be True to the Holiday's Meaning

In the United States, one of the most frequently recognized social justice holidays is Martin Luther King Jr. Day. In discussing such occasions with children, be sure to make clear what the holidays truly recognize, rather than perpetuating misconceptions or oversimplifying the meaning of the person's life's work.

Martin Luther King, for example, was trying to make the world a more *just* place—not just one where everyone gets along. As he articulated often, "True peace is not merely the absence of tension, it is the presence of justice." Rosa Parks (1992) also made clear that she sat down in the front of the bus not simply because she was physically tired from work but *because she was sick and tired of injustice.*

Make collages or class books

Activities related to a specific social justice event provide children with materials and ideas that last beyond the specific day or celebration. For example:

● For International Women's Day, ask children to bring in photos of women special to them. Add pictures of women special to the staff, including women active in social movements. Make a large collage, and then ask the children to tell about the women they chose (from Bj Richards).

● For Martin Luther King Jr. Day, make a book with the children about women and men in the children's families and neighborhoods who help make a better life for people. Ask families to suggest people. With their permission, get or take a photograph of each one and write a few sentences about the person. When you read the book to the children, invite them to add other sentences.

Invite visits from local activists

Talk to potential visitors *before* they come about their participation in a social justice action, to help them know what would be of interest to young children and to prepare them for likely questions. If you have your own experiences, tell developmentally appropriate stories about them, too:

> "This was something that I thought was very unfair, and I decided to do something about it. This is what I did. . . . This is how I felt. . . . This day has special meaning for me because. . . . "

Participate in community celebrations

Most communities have a local newspaper or website that lists community events. Pay attention to what is

going on around you, and find ways to include children and their families in community celebrations that demonstrate how we can work together to make the world better. For example:

> During National Book Month, a school sponsors a small parade around the public library. The children make hats that represent favorite books. They have so much fun that the next year, two other schools join them. The teachers prepare for the parade by talking about how people pay taxes and work together to support libraries and how librarians work to make books available. The following year, when library funds are being cut, the children join the local Friends of the Library group in a protest march on City Hall.

An additional benefit of this type of activity is that it broadens the sense of community for the families and connects them to others for mutual friendship and support.

*   *   *

Once you have a holiday policy in place, holiday activities can have a role in anti-bias education. However, effectively using holiday activities calls on teachers to be thoughtful about what you are really teaching and to consider children's developmental needs, cultural settings, and your anti-bias education goals.

Stop & Think: Holidays, this chapter, and you

- What feelings did you have as you read this chapter? Which topics or issues provoked those feelings?

- What parts of this chapter seemed most appealing and useful? most uncomfortable and challenging? Why?

- At this point in your thinking, how would you use the four anti-bias education goals to help you create holiday curriculum?

Note
The section in this chapter "Develop a Holiday Policy" is grounded in the work of Julie Bisson. To learn more about the process and issues to consider, read her book *Celebrate! An Anti-Bias Guide to Enjoying Holidays in Early Childhood Programs* (St. Paul, MN: Redleaf Press, 1997).

Remember to do holiday activities that cultivate all four anti-bias education goals

Anti-Bias Education with Other Age Groups

Throughout this book you have read about the observations and work of experienced anti-bias education teachers primarily of children ages 3 to 5. These last four Voices from the Field focus on anti-bias education with infants and toddlers and with school-age children.

Although the developmental issues at each of these ages are quite distinctive, the basic goals of anti-bias work still apply. These teachers have taken the principles and shaped them to the children's ages, the particular group settings, and the cultural dynamics of the children. Each of these glimpses into their work expands our understanding of how anti-bias education is adapted and shaped throughout the early childhood period, birth to age 8.

In the Beginning: Infants and Toddlers

by Janet Gonzalez-Mena

There are many reasons for taking an anti-bias approach in all infant/toddler programs. Babies are at the beginning of forming their identities. What they learn about themselves depends in part on what they see (and do not see) in their environment, as well as on the spoken and unspoken messages they receive from their caregivers. Specific actions can help or hurt infants and toddlers as they develop perceptions of equity about the world and as they incorporate feelings of superiority or inferiority into their identities.

Anti-bias work with infants and toddlers, however, is less direct than with preschool or older children. It is much less about what they are taught in projects, activities, or circle time, and more about what infants and toddlers absorb through relationships, direct experience, watching other people, and materials in their environment.

The physical environment

In order for infants and toddlers to see the world as diverse, pictures, books, fabrics, room decorations, play objects, and other learning materials need to represent all the children and families in the program and reflect their diversity. The physical environment should also incorporate the diversity of the children's larger community, beyond what they encounter in the program. This is a tall order, considering that too much "stuff" can easily overstimulate children at this age. One strategy to keep the stimulation level appropriate is rotating the assortment of materials, always keeping some familiar favorites available within each rotation. Another is selecting materials carefully, so they are simple, with clear images, and are easily used by very young children.

The social-emotional environment

Managing the social-emotional environment is more complicated than the physical environment, yet it plays a major role in anti-bias work with infants and toddlers. Authentic, respectful, and equitable interactions should span the types of differences present in your program. This includes people's age, ability, religion, sexual orientation, family structure, and cultural, racial, or ethnic background. Without caring and considerate relationships, having lots of diverse materials will not be enough to counter messages of inequity or disrespect—however unintended.

For example, hearing a staff member talk as respectfully to a teen mother as to a middle-aged mother gives a positive equity message. On the other hand, it will not work to *pretend* to respect a teen mother while really thinking of her as "less-than." Infants and toddlers are more likely to tap into the negative attitude than into the verbal message, or they will pick up a mixed message, which also has a negative impact. Infants and toddlers take in what they observe around them. Even though their communication is not as advanced as older children, what they are exposed to has a profound impact. Be sure that the experiences of these very young children do *not* include:

● stereotypes, prejudices, and negative images about any aspect of human diversity;

● interactions among adults that imply that one person or group of people is better than others; or

● personal interactions that demonstrate lack of respect to anyone.

Guidelines for Anti-Bias Education with Infants and Toddlers

1. Create an inclusive program where diversity of all kinds is accurate, visible, and welcome. Consciously work to counteract stereotypes about all people.

2. Put in place a process for building trusting relationships with families and for communicating with families about what they and you believe is best for their infants and toddlers.

3. Try to establish continuity with each child's home culture.

4. Find ways for staff to understand developmentally appropriate practice *and* to learn how to be sensitive and responsive to ideas that do not match our ideas about developmental appropriateness.

5. Aim for continuity of care so that infants, toddlers, and their families can establish and grow a close relationship with a primary and a secondary caregiver over time.

In sum

Adults working with infants and toddlers need to be vigilant about the verbal and nonverbal messages they convey. All children need outstanding models of adults who demonstrate effective and equitable interactions even in the face of conflict. Respectful care and thoughtful, loving relationships are the most powerful ways to give infants and toddlers an anti-bias, multicultural education.

Culture of the Program and Culture of the Home: Infants and Toddlers

by Bonnie Aldridge

A very young child's emotional and psychological health is primarily developed within a family context. Consistency of care between the home and the infant/toddler program supports a child's emerging sense of self, language, and relationships with others. All programs, including those for infants and toddlers, must understand and reflect the culture of every child's family to the best of their ability.

It is the caregiver's job to learn about how each family cares for their child. Before a child begins our program, we have a home visit, if the family is comfortable with that. Alternatively, we meet the family in a park or someplace else familiar to the child; we then are usually able to arrange a home visit for later. As guests in a family's home, we listen carefully to what they tell us about their baby and their family, and we make observations about the family culture and living space. We then convey these observations to the rest of the staff upon return from the home visit. Everyone helps think through how the family is reflected in the center environment and what changes might be needed to make them feel more included and at home.

Separation

It is human to feel some level of grief and anxiety around separation, and each of us develops behaviors that support successful transitions based on our culture and our individual needs. In our program we co-create a smooth process of separation, listening carefully to parents' thoughts and feelings. One family's needs may be very different from another family's. One father in our program preferred to read a story to his toddler with the caregiver close by, say a very clear and loving goodbye, and then leave. Another parent wanted a longer process; she said goodbye to her toddler at the door, and then the caregiver and toddler would walk to the window, and mom and son would kiss each other through the glass.

Primary care routines

In our program we talk about similarities and differences throughout the day—respectfully, matter-of-factly, and free of judgment. In every arena we pay attention to the anti-bias messages in our words. At this early stage, infants and toddlers are gaining a framework for future acceptance and comfort with diversity. This is especially true during the following common routines:

Diapering: We comment on all of the baby's gorgeous physical characteristics. With toddlers, we also discuss similarities and differences: "Look at our hands together. My hand is darker and yours is lighter . . . gorgeous, yummy brown and sweet, peachy cream."

Eating: We explain that some babies drink milk from their mommy's breasts, and some drink milk from a bottle. Let family preferences guide you. Rather than

---

The Home Visit
by Rheta Negrete-Karwin,
infant/toddler site supervisor

When we have a home visit, I remind the teachers that these are informal conversations, not interviews. We need to really listen and observe carefully with our ears and eyes. We sit and chat and pay attention. Do parents cradle their babies on their shoulders or on their chests? Facing in or out? What are the sounds in the home: music? quiet? lots of voices?

When we pay attention to the home culture, we are doing anti-bias work. We are leaving the comfort zone of our programs and our own culturally informed way of "doing it right." This is how we bring the families' cultures into the program. If a family puts their baby to sleep on his big sister's bed, we ask them to send us a blanket that his sister has slept on so the baby will smell his family while napping.

Their ways may not be how we do it in our own homes . . . but we learn a new way that incorporates and respects the practices of the family.

---

referring to all dairy as "milk," label each choice as "cow's milk," "soy milk," "rice milk," and so on.

Sleeping: Each family has its own expectations for their child's sleep. Is it a time for dependence or autonomy? What is the interplay between these two dynamics? Some children have always slept cuddled close to an adult, and some have always slept independently in their crib or on a mat. Learn about the family's practices and develop a sleep routine for each child influenced by what the family does at home. Sleep routines will often be different in a child care setting, but you can make adjustments to reflect the child's home practice, such as incorporating a special song or "lovey," being willing to rock some children to sleep, and putting some children directly into their crib, depending on each child's family practices.

Do not force a very young child to choose between your program's practices and the family's practices. When routines must differ, strive to create a safety net of sorts by naming the difference for the child and acknowledging that the way it is done at home is also good. When school and home communicate with and support each other, everyone usually can agree on modifications that will work for the child as well as broaden her or his experience.

Building family community

In our program we nurture a supportive culture of partnership by respecting the uniqueness of each family and the diversity of our center's community. What works for one family may or may not work for another. Culture, class, temperament, family structure, and values all influence parenting strategies. We encourage families to share their parenting joys and dilemmas with one another and to offer support, not judgment. As we become more intimately involved in understanding others' gifts, challenges, and values, a community forms. We become allies for one another.

Infants and toddlers can learn from the beginning that there are wonderful similarities and differences among all of us. With this strong foundation, it is then a natural progression for them (and their families) to move to anti-bias programs for preschool. Children and adults who value and love who they are—and value and love their friends—will speak up and advocate for equity.

For further reading

To develop your ability to create anti-bias programs for infants and toddlers: *Diversity in Early Care and Education: Honoring Differences, 5th ed.* (McGraw-Hill, 2008), by Janet Gonzalez-Mena.

An Example of Anti-Bias Education in a Primary Classroom: Exploring Arab American Issues

by Merrie Najimy

Growing up Arab American in the 1970s and 80s—not quite White, Semitic nose and lips, black hair galore—I felt like I lived in two worlds, "Arab"[1] and "American"—the former not to be shared in the latter, because of concerns about being different from the dominant culture.

My Arab world was my grandmother, aunts, uncles, and first cousins all living nearby, regular Sunday dinners at Sitto's (Grandmother's) house, her friends chatting in Arabic, the elders smoking fruit tobacco on the *argeelee* (water pipe). Women walking hand-in-hand and men arm-in-arm with no homophobic stigma attached. My cousins picking up the *tabla* (drum) and making powerful music, the beauty of the men dancing, and so much more.

I had many friends, yet felt like an "other." I made faces at Dick and Jane in the basal reader and scrib-

bled in the book because their lives were nothing like my life. They represented a life that I was supposed to emulate. When kids found out I was Lebanese, they often asked, "What's that?" which made me feel like my ethnicity was a disease. I now realize that the awkwardness I felt was due to the absence of a multicultural education—that is, an anti-bias framework. Now I'm a teacher myself, with experiences to share. I hope that my stories of doing anti-bias work with third-graders, in this case around Arab American issues, can serve as a positive example of what you can do with your students, whatever your cultural identity.

My educational framework

When creating learning experiences about people in a particular racial/ethnic group, I follow these guidelines and cautions. These principles apply to any identity:

---

[1] I am using the word *Arab* to include both Arab American and Arab identities.

- The issue of identity is always complex. Not all Arabs are Muslim. Not all Muslims are Arab. Some people of Arab origin identify as "Arab." Some identify only by national origin (e.g., Saudi, Lebanese, Tunisian), and to many Arabs who are devout Muslims, religious identity is the most relevant.

- Don't overgeneralize. Unfortunately, the majority of picture books available are set in the desert regions (e.g., Egypt, Morocco), but the Arab world is not all deserts. Search for photos from different regions to show children its geographic diversity. Help children to understand the diversity within Arab populations; for example, Morocco is home to Berbers, a non-Arab nomadic people, as well as to Arab people who have permanent homes in villages and cities.

- Do not look to the Arab children in your class to be "experts" or spokespersons for the entire Arab population. Instead, create a safe environment for all children to volunteer personal stories regarding culture or identity if they so choose.

- When reading books, do not project blanket assumptions onto Arab people and lifestyles. Talk about cultures and values of *individuals*; compare and contrast them to find commonalities and differences.

- If you have planned a lesson that will expose negative images and hurtful stereotypes of Arabs or Muslims, alert these children in your class in advance. Tell them what might come up in the activity, affirm their identity, and explain that you raise the stereotypes to help their classmates recognize the images as being unfair and untrue representations.

- Do not make assumptions about children's reactions to the materials or lessons you present. Work to understand their reactions by explicitly describing back to them what you observed about their behavior and asking them what their behavior indicates. You may often be surprised by their responses.

Stories from my classroom

Professor James Banks (Center for Multicultural Education, University of Washington, Seattle) defines a framework for curriculum planning to avoid the tourist approach. His notion is that when one knows, one begins to care; when one cares, one begins to do (or act). The "knowing" combined with the "caring" (or empathy) help to develop children who are intellectually and emotionally capable of "doing" (confronting racism and oppression). *Knowing* and *caring* relate to ABE Goals 1 and 2; *doing* relates to ABE Goals 3 and 4.

With this insight, I reframed my work under an umbrella theme of "Building a Class of Kids Who Care," building community while weaving culture and identity work into the fabric of my curriculum throughout the year. My point of entry for Arab culture begins with sharing my experiences with my students. (For non-Arab teachers, it might begin with sharing children's literature.)

Phase one: Building "knowing"

Day one, I embark on establishing a climate of validation, inclusion, and respect that fosters the transformation process. Moments after the children enter the room for the first time we gather in the circle and begin to generate norms to help us build a class of "kids who care." We build and maintain community through weekly class meetings. Throughout the year, in conjunction with cultivating the climate, comes the work through the curriculum.

Teaching the history of indigenous people of Massachusetts by using artifacts is central to our social studies unit and is a natural fit for anti-bias education. The concept of learning through artifacts allows me to bring in my own Arab cultural artifacts to do some storytelling of my Arab traditions. This often is my students' first positive exposure to anything Arab. The artifacts and my stories leave an impression on my students. They often refer back to them at different points in the year, particularly when we approach the media literacy elements in the curriculum (described later). The stories become the background knowledge that helps them to understand stereotypes and negative images of Arab people and to provide alternatives.

Our unit on families is inclusive, affirming the family structures of all of the children in our class, community, and the world. I use materials such as the movie *That's a Family!* (GroundSpark) and the *Families All Matter* book project (aMaze). During this unit, I bring in Arab culture and identity using my own stories about growing up Arab American, the year I lived in Lebanon as a child, and my visit to Lebanon and Palestine as an adult.

One book I use is *Everybody Bakes Bread,* by Norah Dooley. The people in the story are real people who live in the author's neighborhood, including a

One of the stereotypes prevalent in American society is that all Arabs are Muslim, and all Muslims are Arabs. The term "Arab" refers to the ethnicity of people who live in a large area, comprising many countries, in the Middle East and parts of Northern Africa. The term "Muslim" refers to members of the religion of Islam, which includes many sects and is practiced in almost all the countries of the world, including the United States.

Lebanese family who owns a restaurant. As I read the story aloud, I model how to make and use connections to understand people more deeply. *Looking for connections builds empathy; looking at difference builds understanding and appreciation.*

I talk about how my family's interactions are similar to the Lebanese family's interactions, sharing my remembrances of family, friends, food, and more. I explain how these connections between my own life and the story deepen my involvement with the characters. Then I ask: "What connections can you make to any of the characters?" and "How can those connections help you understand [that character or the story] better?"

Whatever your own background, find connections between yourself and your experiences that you can relate to the characters and story.

Phase two: Building "caring"

Following a constructivist approach to teaching, in this phase I use a set of guiding questions about the lives of Arab children across a series of read-alouds. With every book I find out, beforehand, what the children think they know and where they get their information. Afterwards, we examine images they did not anticipate would be part of the story. Finally, we analyze the values, traditions, and lifestyles of the characters.

As we explore these questions, the children begin to care about the lives of the children in the books. Again, I have my own stories, which allow me to further humanize Arabs. In this way the children construct their own knowledge and understanding of Arab people, making connections that build empathy and extend their understanding of Arab people.

A book such as *The Day of Ahmed's Secret,* by Florence Parry Heide and Judith Heide Gilliland, can be used to build understanding and empathy for the challenges others face. Ahmed, an Egyptian boy around 10 years old, is illiterate. Instead of attending school, he works delivering fuel throughout Cairo to help support his family. The story follows him through a day in his life, until he reveals his "secret"—that he is now able to write his name in Arabic.

Before I read the story, we discuss the children's expectations and assumptions about Egypt (e.g., "sand," "desert," "pyramids," "turbans," "white clothing," "hot temperatures," "camels," "old walls"). Inside the book they do see some of what they anticipate, such as some desert images. However, the children's perspectives are broadened by the beautiful and accurate illustrations. For example, many children are surprised to see the bustle of Cairo, with cars as well as donkeys transporting people and goods everywhere. They are especially affected by the fact that Ahmed has to work.

Because the Arabic language is central to the plot, I follow up by introducing the Arabic alphabet. (If you don't speak Arabic, I recommend the alphabet poster from Arab World and Islamic Resources: www.awaironline.org. It includes a pronunciation guide and describes each character's cultural significance.) My students are captivated by the Arabic script. But they repeatedly pronounce certain sounds with exaggeration, saying them over and over. This somewhat troubles me (are they making fun?), and I realize this is a moment to observe my own caution not to make assumptions about how children react to materials or lessons.

Not wanting to undermine the open learning climate I had worked so hard to build, I approach the situation carefully: "I noticed when I taught you the letters *kha, ayn,* and *ghayn* yesterday that you all started saying and exaggerating the sounds. I was wondering why?" To my surprise, they were curious: "We've never heard the sounds before, and they are hard to say!" . . . "It's interesting to see how other languages are written and pronounced." . . . "I always thought English is the main language everywhere, but people who speak another language probably think that *their* language is." . . . "It's nice to know about other languages so you can know about other people." Clearly the children were developing an appreciation and respect for Arab culture.

For many people, what they know and how they feel about Arab people is colored by political and cultural conflict. School-agers are old enough to hear about stories of conflict, presented in an age-appropriate, sensitive context. *The Librarian of Basra: A True Story from Iraq,* by Jeanette Winter, is a story that puts a human face on a people in the midst of war and shows that even then, individuals can work together to make a difference in their community. This book tells the story of Alia Muhammad Baker, chief librarian of Basra's Central Library. Set in 2003, just before the U.S. invasion of Iraq, Alia is worried about protecting the library's 30,000 books. Because the government refuses to help, she recruits friends to help her move the books into a nearby restaurant. The library is bombed nine days later.

One student asks: "Why go through the risk of trying to save the books?" I let them discuss and debate it as a group: "She wants to save them to remember the people." . . . "Books give info on how to stop trouble." . . . "Books give you relief so you can feel happier." While it may be beyond school-age children's developmental level to understand that books transmit history, culture, and identity to future generations, they can explain why books are important to *them*. They also can understand the bravery and resourcefulness of the librarian of Basra.

Phase three: "Doing" (media literacy)

By this point in the curriculum, the children have enough knowledge and are intellectually and emtionally ready to do critical analyses and engage in "ally" behavior. We now focus on critiquing images and information in the media—cartoons, news clippings, photographs, videos—that are disharmonious with their new information and empathy. By the time we get to examine media bias against Arab people, the children have had many classroom experiences challenging other types of bias, such as teasing, bullying, and gender stereotyping. Critiquing the Disney movie *Aladdin* is one example where the fruit of our previous anti-bias work became visible.

Although the children do not even realize the movie is about Arabs, they do see and can name its many negative images: "People chasing other people with knives." . . . "The tall guy is creepy, with red eyes, and snarls." . . . "The bad guys have darker skin; the good guys have lighter." One student's comment illustrates how insidious racism can be in the media: She explained that in the movie, "the darker skin people are the Arabs, and they are trying to kill the lighter skin people, who are not Arab"—however, she did not recognize Aladdin and Jasmine, who are light-skinned, as Arab. It was a terrific opportunity to explore the "light/good, dark/bad" stereotype. The children are further able to connect how dark-skinned African American characters are often the "bad guys" and how people from Africa get portrayed as "savages."

My experiences tell me that once you open a discussion like this, whether it is about gender, race, class, or something else, children get very passionate about the injustice they see done to themselves or to others. They begin to reject negative images about Arabs and to identify positive aspects: "The Arab people we read about are calm and generous." . . . "Arabs share things." They also reflect on the possible reasons the people who made *Aladdin* depicted so many stereotypes. Finally, the discussion moves to the potential consequences for Arabs who see themselves portrayed negatively: "Maybe Arabs who use violence do it because they get mad because of stereotypes." . . . "People might think their ancestors were bad."

Conclusion

In general, children have a deep desire for fairness. They want to be treated fairly, and they have a natural inclination to want the world to be fair for others. When children have the means to think about what they see, hear, and read (and have alternative information to counter negative images and messages from the media and elsewhere), they are more equipped to analyze their world. This is true for people of all ages. The children in my class learn how to think analytically; my wish is that they will apply these skills not only to issues about Arabs but also to those affecting people of all identities.

Anti-Bias Education in a Primary School

by Rita Tenorio

I used to believe that young children were "color-blind" and that the influences of American society took hold only when they got older. I thought it would be enough for early childhood teachers to teach that "Everyone is the same" and that we should "Treat everybody fairly." Then, when I realized that children were aware of differences among people, I thought that simply learning about acceptance together would help my students to become respectful of diversity. How naïve I was! I have come to see that those messages, while important and hopeful, were not enough. They ignored the very strong impact of racism and other "isms" on young children's development. I did not take into account the real experiences and ideas that young children bring with them to our classrooms.

Kindergarten and primary children may be too young to fully understand the complexities of racial identity, culture, language, and bias, but their behavior shows the influence of these factors. An English speaker might refuse to play with a Latino child because "He talks funny." On the playground, a group of White girls may not let their brown-skinned peers join their club. Many teachers wonder: Are young children really capable of discussing and processing these issues? The answer is yes! They have real ideas and opinions to share—and many, many questions of their own. The educator's role is to guide their ideas, teaching alternative messages that counter society's biases.

Focusing on listening

Our elementary school is a dual-language community that infuses a multicultural/anti-racist perspective throughout the curriculum. We are a multilingual, multiracial, multicultural community that includes Latino, Black, and White families. Our students come from a wide range of socioeconomic backgrounds, and we strive for a 50/50 balance of English and Spanish speakers. We value and nurture both English and Spanish, and find that English speakers need the help of their Spanish-speaking peers when the instruction is in Spanish, and vice versa. Working together across language groups serves everyone's best interests. Over several years, a series of activities and projects around issues of race and society evolved from our conversations, children's questions and comments, staff development workshops, and from sharing ideas on the Internet. We focus on teaching the social skills of communicating ideas and listening to another person's perspective.

Even in the earliest grades, teachers pose questions on issues of justice, hate, compliments, and put-downs. Examples include: "What is the meanest thing anyone has ever said to you?" . . . "Why do you think some people like to use put-downs?" . . . "Why do some people think that English is better than Spanish?" The children talk about a question with a partner. Afterward some are willing to share with the whole group; many have firsthand experience with immigration and prejudice. We might role-play situations and find ways to respond. The whole group works to solve challenging problems.

Other projects include making books about our families, remembering someone special, and writing bilingual poems. These activities deepen our conversations on social issues. For example, many of our students share stories about a family member currently absent from their lives because they remained in Puerto Rico or Mexico. Students and teachers build their understanding of how all families experience love, joy, pain, and sadness. As the children engage with these activities, they develop confidence for using their own voices and languages, sharing ideas, and learning about each other. By affirming their diverse backgrounds and the value of various perspectives and cultures, we also foster trust and respect.

Addressing racial identity

As the year proceeds, racial identity is specifically addressed in social studies. One of the first conversations I have with students on the subject focuses on the variety of skin colors we have in our group. At first, many children show amazement; the looks in their eyes and their hesitancy tell me this is a very personal topic. Some children may show discomfort describing the color of their skin—most often this is children with very dark skin. Many children indicate surprise when a classmate who self-identifies as Black is actually lighter-skinned than a Latino classmate. Some White kids boast about being "pink." The attitude that it is better to have lighter skin often underlies beginning conversations.

Another lesson focuses on whether children have ever heard something bad or mean about another person's skin color. The hands shoot up. "My mom says that you can't trust White people." . . . "My sister won't talk to the Puerto Rican kids on the bus." . . . "Missy said that I couldn't play, that I was too Black to be her friend." We talk about ways we have heard others use people's skin color to make fun of them or put them down and what to do in those situations. The children listen intently to teachers and to each other, and this conversation continues. As we discuss issues of racial identity, teachers pose further questions that intrigue and extend the children's thinking: "Do people choose their color?" . . . "Where do you get your skin color?" . . . "Is it better to be one color than another?" Many of our conversations revolve around a story or a piece of literature.

Recognizing the power of anti-bias activities

Families tell us about the positive effect these activities have on their children. They now have more ways to think about and describe themselves. They have a new awareness of racial identity and the diversity of their peers' lives, which they are not afraid to discuss. I want children to see themselves as true participants in this society and to recognize that they will help shape its future. I want them to gain the knowledge necessary for success and learn how to counteract the negative effects of racism and other biases. Beyond that, though, I want them to understand that they have the power to transform society! Intentionally and explicitly teaching with a multicultural, multilingual, and anti-bias approach helps ensure a bright future for all of our children.

Keeping On Keeping On:
The Anti-Bias Journey Continues

Keep in mind always the present you are constructing—it should be the future you want.
—Alice Walker

Each new generation of early childhood teachers carves out new, exciting paths as teachers adapt to the changes taking place in their communities, countries, and world. We hope the day will come when the "anti-bias" part of that journey is no longer needed because *all* children are growing up fully nurtured and able to be fully who they are, with no barriers of prejudice, discrimination, poverty, or war. Then learning about and valuing one another's diversity will be a natural part of growing up.

Until that day comes, we must keep on keeping on providing children strong, culturally appropriate anti-bias education and keeping faith in the possibility of positive change—in ourselves, in others, in our programs. We can also work with other adults to make positive change in our larger society—so that all children, everywhere, will have what they need to wholly thrive.

Expand your knowledge

Knowledge is power—or perhaps more accurately, knowledge gives you tools to act powerfully. It is important to keep building your understanding of the many diversity/equity issues regarding children, families, early childhood education, and the larger society—all of which inform anti-bias education work. New information, ideas and analysis of various aspects of diversity and "isms," appear frequently. While it is not possible to keep up with all of it (or even a good portion of it), you can try to stay current. (For links to some of these additional resources, see the "Anti-Bias" section of the NAEYC website: www.naeyc.org.)

Read

There are several ways to learn about new books and articles that will help you further your understanding and skills for doing anti-bias education. Ask for suggestions from colleagues or peers who do anti-bias education. You might want to start a monthly book club to share your reading and ideas. Get ideas from workshop presenters; they often mention specific books or provide a bibliography, and you can also ask them for suggestions. Check out publishers who carry books about adult diversity and equity issues; look for these publishers at conferences or on the Internet. Regularly check out the websites of groups that keep up-to-date on quality diversity/equity education materials. These websites often include listing of additional resources.

Attend workshops

Many professional organizations focused on young children offer workshops relating to early childhood equity/diversity education. Groups such as the National Association for the Education of Young Children (NAEYC), the National Association for Family Child Care (NAFCC), Zero to Three, the National Black Child Development Institute (NBCDI), the National Association of Multicultural Education (NAME), and the National Association for Bilingual Education (NABE) regularly include a range of useful workshops at their national, state, and local conferences. Some workshops may cover what you already know (which is affirming); others will introduce you to new ideas and information (which is enlightening!). Attending conferences is an excellent opportunity to connect with other educators and allies with whom you can share experiences and expand your knowledge.

Beyond the early childhood world, many other organizations offer conferences or training opportunities on anti-bias issues. These will give you a larger context in which to understand your early childhood education work. Unions, community groups, and religious organizations committed to social justice sometimes offer workshops and conferences focused on various aspects of diversity. Some organizations also provide training in community, institutional, and faith-based organizing methods.

Develop an ongoing support system

If you are like most people, being part of a support system will make all the difference in your anti-bias education journey. That has certainly been true for the two of us. When we have found ourselves in doubt (which all of us are at some point), stuck (which happens more often than we like to admit), or needing to share and celebrate a positive experience (which we often have to remind ourselves to do), we could always count on others for support. Indeed, this support has been vital to our work.

There are several types of support systems you can create or join. Each kind offers ongoing opportunities to reflect on your work with others, receive support and encouragement, learn from others' diverse perspectives and critical feedback, and get help in planning your next steps. When you are part of a support group or network, you have the constant reassurance that you are not alone.

Face-to-face support groups

Your support groups could consist of co-teachers, staff, families from your own program, other programs in your community, and/or fellow members of a local professional organization. Members usually get the most out of a group when its size is manageable (about six to 12 people) and when each participant commits to meeting regularly over at least a year. Some support groups stay together for several years. Support groups are most effective when they focus on self-reflection and growth, gaining new information and analyses, and taking action at work and in the larger community.

When arranging face-to-face meetings, the group should give thoughtful attention to practical issues such as child care, location, transportation, meeting times, and accommodating everyone's communication styles and languages. Members usually take equal turns facilitating discussion, working both from planned agendas and on emerging topics based on the group's needs.

Most support groups begin with time for each person to talk about a diversity/equity issue that has come up in his or her work or home life. After everyone has spoken, those who choose to may ask the group for ideas on how to address their issue and for support for the feelings that inevitably arise. Sometimes groups discuss an already agreed upon topic, and members may read about the issue in advance. The facilitator for that meeting presents the issue, and everyone has equal time to talk about possible causes, personal experiences, and potential plans of action.

The group should take some time to celebrate victories both big and small. Everyone should be encouraged to talk about strategies and techniques that worked. The lessons learned from our successes are just as important as those learned from our mistakes.

Email, blogs, and listserv networks

Many early childhood anti-bias teachers find that the Internet provides practical ways to maintain ongoing connections with colleagues both near and far. Some teachers set up a group email list or listserv and commit to regularly sending out information about whatever issues arise. Conversations are usually not predetermined and mainly arise from specific issues that come up in the course of members' own anti-bias work. Other teachers may facilitate their own anti-bias blog or keep up with others who blog about anti-bias issues.

Take part in anti-bias work in your profession

Never doubt that a small group of thoughtful, committed citizens can change the world. Indeed, it is the only thing that ever has.

—Margaret Mead, anthropologist

Anti-bias educators also strengthen their skills by working together within the early childhood field. We may choose to create or join diversity/equity committees within local organizations. We may choose to build city or regional networks that offer educational and action opportunities to other educators. As we gain experience doing anti-bias education in our own workplaces, it is both productive and exciting to look beyond our classroom settings. Taking part in anti-bias and other forms of diversity/equity work with colleagues not only contributes to advancing early childhood work as a whole, but it also expands our own understanding and helps us to feel linked to a broader network of people.

There are several steps you can take to make a contribution to the field:

Present conference workshops

Further your own and others' growth by sharing your experiences at local, state, or national meetings. Hearing about the work of colleagues is tremendously useful to other teachers. Consider co-presenting with other teachers, teacher assistants, and even children's family members to reflect your program's diversity. Conference workshops are usually one to two hours long. Highlight a few main ideas, with topics such as "How we build and use our library of anti-bias education books," "Building support and partnership with and among families for anti-bias education," "Using persona dolls to help children deal with their families loss of jobs and homes," and "Earth Day at our school."

Help set up/participate in a school-wide diversity/equity committee

Teachers who are part of a program in a larger private or public school or a community college can find it very beneficial to connect with the other teachers (and perhaps with families) in the school interested in diversity/equity issues, many of whom will teach other subjects or grade levels. It takes time and patience to build these relationships, identify common issues to address within the school, and agree on a plan of action. However, the time and energy invested are very worthwhile because this can result in a support system that gradually weaves anti-bias and other elements of diversity/equity education throughout the school or program.

John Nimmo, a director of a program with several classrooms, found that when his center established an anti-bias task force and its members attended workshops and conferences together that they became leaders in their classrooms. The task force allowed teachers to try out ideas, receive support, and learn new ways of thinking as they wrote a center-wide policy together.

Work within your professional organizations

Teachers can work in a number of creative ways within their local, state, and national professional organizations. Many local and state AEYC affiliates, for example, have diversity/equity committees. These committees develop strategies for increasing the diversity of their membership and leadership. They plan workshops on a range of diversity/equity issues to present at conferences. Committee members

also find support for their own education work. The National Association for Family Child Care includes diversity and equity as one of its core values in its national and local work. Zero to Three has a national policy network for those whose focus is infants and toddlers. Check with whichever professional organizations you have joined about ways to join with other members to do diversity/equity work.

Several state AEYCs also now have committees that set up anti-bias and diversity education centers at their annual state conferences. Members of the Washington state and Oregon AEYCs first used this strategy, and a network of educators in California has run a similar center at CAEYC's state conferences for more than 10 years. Currently called the Social Justice Advocacy Center, this center features exhibits that communicate ways to do social justice work with and for children and adults. It also hosts discussion groups (and joyful sing-alongs) on a range of topics. A small group of anti-bias educators in the Chicago AEYC set up an anti-bias commission to provide training, conference workshops, and networking support.

At the national level, NAEYC members can join together in Interest Forums and Caucuses to find support and to advance various diversity/equity approaches. These groups meet together at the Annual Conference and have links to their discussion boards on NAEYC's website (www.naeyc.org/community/interest_forums).

Join with other community groups

Ultimately, we cannot fully bring about change in our early childhood programs and in the lives of children and families without improving the economic realities and institutions of the larger society. Anti-bias education work has its own contribution to make, but it is not enough. If we want to see the full vision of anti-bias education come to fruition, then we must work with other community and national organizations to address a wide range of social and economic justice issues that affect children, their families, and us as their advocates.

One crucial equity issue is lack of decent wages and benefits for early childhood staff in family child care homes and group centers. Fair teacher compensation is one of the pillars of quality care. Many educators participate in the efforts of organizations such as the Center for the Child Care Workforce and its "Worthy Wages" campaign (www.ccw.org) or with various labor unions that seek to ensure appropriate compensation for early childhood professionals. Of course, there are many other social justice issues that are important to children and families. In many parts of the country, alliances and action networks come together to speak up for these needs. For example, NAEYC's "Children's Champions Action Center" network (http://capwiz.com/naeyc/home), which keeps members informed of legislative and regulatory issues in Congress, provides ways to speak out and connect with elected representatives.

Then there are more specific causes. Some early childhood educators, seeing war as an enemy of all children everywhere, join groups that seek to bring peace education to children and peace to the world. Other teachers, having become aware of the special hardships facing immigrant families, choose to join community groups focused on immigrant rights. Still others work within their faith-based institutions on social justice issues.

When we participate in the larger activism work of creating a more just society and world for all children, not only do we help change the world but also we deepen other people's understanding of the unique needs of young children and their families. We become allies and we gain allies, and like ripples in a lake, the impact of our actions and commitment keeps growing.

Step by step the longest march can be won, can be won
Many stones can form an arch, singly none, singly none.
                                                    —Labor song

Checklist for Assessing the Visual Material Environment

The toys, materials, and equipment you put out for children; the posters, pictures, and art objects you hang on the wall; and the types of furniture and how you arrange them all influence what children learn. What children do *not* see in the classroom teaches children as much as what they do see.

Rate each item:
N—not yet; S—still working on it; or Y—yes, we do this well

Posters, signs, photographs, puzzles, games, etc., that authentically reflect . . .

_____All aspects of identity of the children, families, and staff in the program (e.g., family structure; economic class; aspects of physical appearance such as skin color, hair texture, eye color, and body size; physical abilities; language).

_____Children and families from the major racial/ethnic groups in your community, city, and state.

_____Diversity in family structures: single parents, extended families, gay/lesbian-headed families, interracial and multiethnic families, adoptive families, etc.

_____Elderly people of various backgrounds doing different types of activities.

_____A balanced ratio of images depicting women and men doing jobs in the home and outside the home, and all different kinds of work (e.g., professional roles such as doctor or teacher, "blue collar" roles such as factory worker or truck driver, and community roles such as firefighter).

_____People of various backgrounds with different abilities and disabilities with their families and working. People with disabilities as active and independent.

_____Creativity of artists of diverse backgrounds and cultures (e.g., paintings, drawings, sculptures, weavings).

_____Images of important people, both past and present, including people who participate(d) in important struggles for social justice.

_____Balance and variety, so that there are no "token" images of any particular group.

Dramatic play materials that support . . .

_____The home lives of children, families, and staff in the program.

_____Diversity of gender role playing.

_____Diversity of cultures in your community, city, and state (supplementing the diversity of children, staff, and families in the program).

_____Economic class diversity.

_____Accessibility and special needs.

_____A variety of ways to care for a family, cook and eat, keep house, play, etc.

Language: Every day the staff support . . .

_____The languages that children, families, and staff speak through songs, labels and signs, stories, and interactions among children and with adults.

_____The ongoing development of children's home languages, and the development of English language skills.

_____Regular opportunities to engage with American Sign Language and Braille.

_____Children's different communication styles, giving everyone equal opportunity to voice their ideas and feelings.

Art materials are regularly available, including...

_____A range of skin tone paper, paint, crayons, markers, and playdough.

_____Mirrors for children to reflect on their own physical features.

_____Collage materials with images of diverse people and lifestyles.

_____Items meant for individual and for group art activities.

Dolls (purchased and homemade) that represent...

_____A fair balance of the physical characteristics of children, staff, and families in the program and in the community.

_____Diversity in the United States beyond what is represented in the classroom.

_____A fair balance of males and females, and also some anatomically correct dolls.

_____A range of different kinds of disabilities and a range of doll-size equipment that support people with disabilities.

_____A variety of types of dress (i.e., not just dresses for girls and pants for boys; not just dominant culture styles of dress).

Manipulatives that reflect...

_____Diversity in racial identity, ethnicity, gender, physical ability, and occupation (for all manipulatives, including puzzles, memory games, reading and number literacy games, and other small toys).

_____Diversity of skin tones, body shapes and sizes, physical abilities, clothing, and ages for play figures of people.

_____Accurate depictions of people in terms of current life in the United States, avoiding stereotypes of all kinds.

Children's books that contain accurate, non-stereotypical depictions of...

_____Physical characteristics and lives of the children, families, and staff in the program.

_____Different languages, especially those spoken by children, families, and staff in the program and in the community.

_____Diversity of gender roles, racial and cultural backgrounds, and special needs.

_____A range of occupations and income levels (that support and supplement the diversity present in the program).

_____Many different family structures, so there are no "token" books of any particular type of family.

Books that...

_____Present accurate images and information, with no overt or covert stereotypes.

_____Challenge unfairness and prejudice.

_____Encourage children to take action when faced with unfairness toward themselves or others.

Note: This list was compiled from the teaching work of Julie Olsen Edwards and Julie Bisson.

Anti-Bias Education

About the Contributing Writers

Bonnie Aldridge is a master teacher and infant/toddler specialist at Cabrillo College Children's Center in Aptos, California. She has worked in education since 1974, teaching in early childhood programs, in elementary and high school, and also as an adjunct faculty member in early childhood education at Cabrillo College. She enjoys photography, and her photos of children and families have appeared in many publications.

Julie Bisson has been teaching and learning in the field of early childhood education for the last 20 years. A graduate of Pacific Oaks College, she has been a preschool teacher and a director of child care programs. Author of Celebrate! An Anti-Bias Guide to Enjoying Holidays in Early Childhood Programs, Julie is currently a consultant, trainer, and college instructor. She was also a long-term member of the Seattle Culturally Relevant Anti-Bias Leadership Project and one of the co-creators of the Anti-Bias Education and Advocacy Centers at the California and Washington AEYC annual conferences.

Margie Brickley is a developmental specialist working in early intervention in New Jersey. She has written about ways to create welcoming environments for all children and families and how to talk to children about lesbian, gay, bisexual, and transgender (LGBT) people and their families. Margie has also presented numerous workshops at national and state conferences.

Carol Brunson Day is known nationally and internationally as a dedicated leader in the field of early childhood education. Beginning her career as a teacher of young children, she is currently president of the National Black Child Development Institute. Previously, Carol served as executive director of the Council for Professional Recognition for many years, and, before that, as a faculty member of Pacific Oaks College.

Tarah Fleming is codirector of iPride in Berkeley, California, an organization dedicated to mixed heritage family pride; director of its Multiethnic Education Program; and executive producer of the videos "My People Are . . . Youth Pride in Mixed Heritage" and "Serving Biracial and Multiethnic Children and Their Families." Her 20 years of teacher-training experience include addressing cultural competency, power and privilege, and developing equitable, inclusive curricula.

Aimee Gelnaw's advocacy for family diversity and lesbian, gay, bisexual, and transgender (LGBT) families spans 20 years. Executive director of Professional Impact NJ, the early childhood professional development center for the state of New Jersey, she previously served as executive director of the national Family Pride Coalition, which provides advocacy, education, and support for LGBT families. Aimee has written several published articles; coauthored a college text, Making Room in the Circle: Lesbian, Gay, Bisexual, and Transgender Families in Early Childhood Settings; and cotaught the Making Room in the Circle course at both Wheelock College and the University of North Carolina at Greensboro.

Janet Gonzalez-Mena is a writer, consultant in early childhood education, and former community college instructor with experience as an early childhood education practitioner. She has authored several college textbooks on early childhood education and various articles about infant/toddler care, cultural perspectives on discipline, and her own experiences of raising five children while working with and studying infant/toddler caregiving.

Luis A. Hernandez has worked as a public school teacher, Head Start trainer in multicultural curricula, director of the Miami-Dade County child care resource and referral agency, and adjunct professor of early childhood education at Miami-Dade Community College. Currently a training and technical assistant services (T/TAS) early childhood education specialist, he provides technical assistance, consultation, and training throughout the United States. Active in NAEYC, the National Latino Children's Agenda, NACCRRA, and the Center for the Child Care Workforce, Luis also serves on the boards of the Florida Children's Forum and the Parent Services Project.

Eric Hoffman has been working with young children since 1970 and has just retired as the program coordinator of the Cabrillo College Children's Center in Aptos, California. He is the author of the Anti-Bias Books for Kids picture book series and of the book Magic Capes, Amazing Powers: Transforming Superhero Play in the Classroom.

Lisa Lee has been a teacher, trainer, and advocate in early childhood and family support fields for more than 30 years. She was a founder and co-chair of BANDTEC (Bay Area Network of Diversity Trainers in Early Childhood). Lisa focuses on building the capacity of early childhood educators to work effectively with multiethnic, multicultural, and multilingual children and families.

Diane Levin, longtime faculty member of Wheelock College, is a leader in early childhood peace education and an advocate for nonviolent toys. Most recently, she turned her attention to the impact on young children of early sexualization by the media, advertising, and businesses. Diane is the author of many books, including So Sexy So Soon: The New Sexualized Childhood and What Parents Can Do to Protect Their Kids (with Jean Kilbourne).

Merrie Najimy began teaching elementary school in 1991 and is dedicated to integrating anti-bias, multicultural education into her daily curriculum and interactions with children. She has been a teacher trainer through programs such as Peaceable Schools and the SEED project. She has served as a building representative and president of her local teachers union, the Concord Teachers Association, and as the president of the Massachusetts chapter of the American-Arab Anti-Discrimination Committee.

Bryan G. Nelson has worked with young children, men, fathers, and families since the 1970s. Founding director of MenTeach, he is on the faculty at Metropolitan State University in Minnesota and is a co-facilitator of the World Forum's Men in Early Childhood Education project. He is a parent of two children (Otto and Emmett) and the recipient of a fellowship at Harvard University to research men, fathers, and children.

Bj Richards is a home child care provider in the Chicago area, where she has served diverse groups of young children for 20 years. Previously she founded a child care center in New York City and served as director for 11 years. A pioneer in adapting anti-bias education in the context of family child care, Bj looks forward to sharing a dialogue with other child care providers.

Louise Rosenkrantz has been involved in education and political activism throughout her career. She has been a preschool teacher, elementary school teacher, and literacy coach as well as a founding member of Prison MATCH (Mothers and Their Children) of North Carolina. While with Prison MATCH, she developed and ran a children's center inside a federal prison to address the needs of inmate parents and their children. Now semi-retired, Louise lives in Berkeley, California, where she works part-time as a staff developer for the Berkeley Unified School District's early childhood education program.

Nadiyah F. Taylor is a faculty member of the early childhood development department at Las Positas College in Livermore, California, and a former child development adjunct faculty member at Merritt College. Previously a preschool teacher, Nadiyah now provides professional development on best practices for high-quality early care and education, planning and facilitation of family child care leadership workshops, parent and provider trainings, anti-bias curriculum development and implementation, and partnering with families for a more culturally responsive program.

Rita Tenorio is an early childhood educator from Milwaukee, Wisconsin. She is one of the founders of Rethinking Schools and has written articles about anti-bias education. After many years as a kindergarten and primary teacher, Rita is the principal of La Escuela Fratney, a dual-language immersion school with a strong focus on multicultural, anti-racist education.

References

Allen, M., & L. Staley. 2007. Helping children cope when a loved one is on military deployment. *Young Children* 62 (1): 82–87.

Alvarado, C., L. Burnley, L. Derman-Sparks, E. Hoffman, L.I. Jiménez, J. Labyzon, P. Ramsey, A. Unten, B. Wallace, & B. Yasui. 1999. *In our own way: How anti-bias work shapes our lives.* St. Paul, MN: Redleaf Press.

aMaze. 1996. *Families All Matter Book Project.* Online: www. amazeworks.org/programs/fam/fam.html.

Annie E. Casey Foundation. 2009. *Race matters: Unequal opportunities for family and community economic success.* Online: www.aecf.org/upload/publicationfiles/fact_sheet7. pdf.

Banks, J.A. 1999. *Introduction to multicultural education.* 2d ed. Boston: Allyn & Bacon.

Bisson, J. 1997. *Celebrate! An anti-bias guide to enjoying holidays in early childhood programs.* St. Paul, MN: Redleaf Press.

Bredekamp, S., & C. Copple, eds. 1997. *Developmentally appropriate practice in early childhood programs.* Rev. ed. Washington, DC: NAEYC.

Brown, B. 2001. *Combating discrimination: Persona dolls in action.* London: Trentham.

Chafel, J.A., A.S. Flint, J. Hammel, & K.H. Pomeroy. 2007. Young children, social issues, and critical literacy: Stories of teachers and researchers. *Young Children* 62 (1): 73–81.

Chrisman, K., & D. Couchenour. 2002. *Healthy sexuality development: A guide for early childhood educators and families.* Washington, DC: NAEYC.

Coles, R. 1977. *Privileged ones: The well-off and the rich in America.* Boston: Little, Brown & Co.

Collier, V., & W. Thomas. 1997. General pattern of K–12 language minority student achievement on standardized tests in English reading compared across six program models. Washington, DC: National Clearinghouse of Bilingual Education.

Copple, C., & S. Bredekamp. 2009. To be an excellent teacher. In *Developmentally appropriate practice in early childhood programs serving children from birth through age 8,* 3d ed., eds. C. Copple & S. Bredekamp, 33–50. Washington, DC: NAEYC.

Crawford, J. 1991. *Bilingual education: History, politics, theory, and practice.* Trenton, NJ: Crane.

Cross, W.E. 1991. *Shades of black: Diversity in African-American identity.* Philadelphia: Temple University Press.

deGraff, F. 2006. *What a clash can teach us: A method to increase relations between parents and professionals in early childhood.* Amsterdam, The Netherlands: SWP.

Derman-Sparks, L., & C.B. Phillips. 1997. *Teaching/learning anti-racism: A developmental approach.* New York: Teachers College Press.

Derman-Sparks, L., & P.G. Ramsey. 2006. *What if all the kids are white? Anti-bias multicultural education with young children and families.* New York: Teachers College Press.

Derman-Sparks, L., & the ABC Task Force. 1989. *Anti-bias curriculum: Tools for empowering young children.* Washington, DC: NAEYC.

Dinan, K.A. 2006. *Young children in immigrant families—The role of philanthropy: Sharing knowledge, creating services, and building supportive policies.* NCCP Report. Online: www.nccp.org/publications/pdf/text_661.pdf.

Douglas-Hall, A., & M. Chau. 2008. *Basic facts about low-income children: Birth to age 6.* New York: National Center for Children in Poverty, Columbia University Mailman School of Public Health.

Espinosa, L. 2008. Challenging common myths about your English language learners. *Foundation for Child Development Policy Brief, Advancing PK–3* 8.

Federal Interagency Forum on Child and Family Statistics. 2009. *America's children: Key national indicators of well-being, 2009.* Online: www.childstats.gov.

Freeman, M. 1992. *Between us: Beginning a dialogue with our readers.* Ecumenical Child Care Network 10 (6): 2.

Furby, L. 1979. Inequalities in personal possessions: Explanations for and judgments about unequal distribution. *Human Development* 22 (3): 180–202.

Garcia, E. 2006. Keynote address. National Association of Multicultural Education Annual Conference, Phoenix, AZ, November 9–12.

Gidney, C. 2007. Bullying. In *Early childhood education: An international encyclopedia, vol. 1 A–D,* eds. R.S. New & M. Cochran, 91–94. Westport, CT: Praeger.

Hakuta, K., Y. Goto Butler, & D. Witt. 2000. *How long does it take English learners to attain proficiency?* Santa Barbara, CA: Linguistic Minority Research Institute.

Jiménez, L.I. 1999. Finding a voice. In *In our own way: How anti-bias work shapes our lives,* eds. C. Alvarado et al., 23–50. St. Paul, MN: Redleaf Press.

Katz, P., & J.A. Kofkin. 1997. Race, gender, and young children. In *Developmental perspectives on risk and pathology,* eds. S. Luthar, J. Burack, D. Cicchetti, & J. Weisz, 51–74. New York: Cambridge University Press.

Keyser, J. 2006. *From parents to partners: Building a family-centered early childhood program.* St. Paul, MN: Redleaf Press; Washington, DC: NAEYC.

Klein, S., B. Richardson, D.A. Grayson, L.H. Fox, C. Kramarae, D.S. Pollard, & C.A. Dwye, eds. 2007. *Handbook for achieving gender equity through education.* New York: Routledge.

Kline, S. 1993. *Out of the garden: Toys, TV, and children's culture in the age of marketing.* London: Verso.

Ladner, M., & C. Hammons. 2003. Special but unequal: Race and special education. In *No dream denied: A pledge to America's children,* ed. National Commission on Teaching & America's Future. New York, NY: Editor.

Lamm, C. 2007. Anti-bias perspective seminar. Unpublished manuscript. Fullerton, CA: Early Childhood Education Department, Fullerton College.

Leahy, R.L. 1990. The development of concepts of economic and social inequality. *New Directions for Child Development* 46: 107–20.

Levin, D. 2003. *Teaching young children in violent times: Building a peaceable classroom.* 2d ed. Washington, DC: NAEYC.

Levin, D., & J. Kilbourne. 2008. *So sexy so soon: The new sexualized childhood and what parents can do to protect their kids.* New York: Ballantine.

Martin, Jr., B. 1970. *I am freedom's child.* Glendale, CA: Bowmar.

MacNaughton, G. 2004. Learning from young children about social diversity: Challenges for our equity practices in the classroom. In *Young children aren't biased, are they?! How to handle diversity in early childhood education and school,* ed. A. van Keulen, 65–76. Amsterdam, The Netherlands: SWP.

NABE (National Association for Bilingual Education). *Why is bilingual education controversial?* Online: http://www.nabe.org/b_ed_politics.html.

NAEYC. 1995. *Responding to linguistic and cultural diversity: Recommendations for effective early childhood education.* Position statement. Washington, DC: Author. Online: www.naeyc.org/positionstatements.

NAEYC. 1996. *Prevention of child abuse in early childhood programs.* Position statement. Washington, DC: Author. Online: www.naeyc.org/positionstatements.

NAEYC. 2005. *NAEYC early childhood program standards and accreditation criteria: The mark of quality in early childhood education.* Washington, DC: Author.

NAEYC. 2009. Developmentally appropriate practice in early childhood programs serving children from birth through age 8. Position statement. Washington, DC: Author. Online: www.naeyc.org/positionstatements.

Naimark, H. 1983. *Children's understanding of social class differences.* Paper presented at the Biennial Meeting of the Society for Research in Child Development, Detroit, MI, April 21–24.

NCCP (National Center for Children in Poverty). 2008. *Basic facts about low-income children: Birth to age 6.* New York: Author.

Nelson, B. 2002. *The importance of male teachers and reasons why there are so few.* Minneapolis, MN: MenTeach.org.

Nelson, B.G. 2004. Myths about men who work with young children. *Exchange* Nov/Dec: 17. Redmond, WA: Child Care Exchange.

Nelson, J. 2006. *Kids need to be safe.* New York: Free Spirit Publishing.

Parks, R., with J. Haskins. 1992. *Rosa Parks: My story.* New York: Puffin Books.

Pierce, C.M. 1980. Social trace contaminants: Subtle indicators of racism. In *Television and social behavior: Beyond violence and children,* eds. S. Withey & R. Abeles, 249–57. Hillsdale, NJ: Lawrence Erlbaum.

Posny, A. 2007. *Memorandum to state directors of special education: Disproportionality of racial and ethnic groups in special education.* April 24. Online: www.state.nj.us/education/specialed/memos/042407disproportionality.pdf.

Ramsey, P. 1991. Young children's awareness and understanding of social class differences. *Journal of Genetic Psychology* 152 (1): 71–82

Ramsey, P. 2004. *Teaching and learning in a diverse world: Multicultural education for young children.* 3d ed. New York: Teachers College Press.

Shonkoff, J.P. 2007. Emotional & cognitive development linked. *NIEER's Preschool Matters.* Online: http://nieer.org/psm/index.php?article=233.

Skiba, R.J., L. Poloni-Staudinger, A.B. Simmons, L.R. Feggins-Assiz, & C.G. Chung. 2005. Unproven links: Can poverty explain ethnic disproportionality in special education? *Journal of Special Education* 39 (3): 130–44.

Smithsonian Institution, National Museum of the American Indian. 2007. *Do all Indians live in tipis?: Questions and answers from the National Museum of the American Indian.* New York: Collins, in association with the National Museum of the American Indian.

Sprung, B. 2007. Gender and gender stereotyping. In *Early childhood education: An international encyclopedia,* eds. R. New & M. Cochran, 382–86. Westport, CT: Praeger.

SRCD (Society for Research and Curriculum Development). 2009. Young Hispanic children: Boosting opportunities for learning. Written by E. Garcia & B. Jensen. *Social Policy Report Brief* 23 (2).

Tatum, B.D. 2003. *"Why are all the Black kids sitting together in the cafeteria?" and other conversations about race.* New York: Basic Books.

United Nations. 1989. *Convention on the rights of the child.* Document A/RES/44/25. Online: www.hrweb.org/legal/child.html.

Van Ausdale, D., & J.R. Feagin. 2001. *The first R: How children learn race and racism.* Lanham, MD: Rowman and Littlefield.

Van Keulen, A., ed. 2004. *Young children aren't biased, are they?* Amsterdam, The Netherlands: SWP.

Wardle, F. 1992. "Building Positive Images: Interracial Children and Their Families." In: *Alike and Different: Exploring Our Humanity with Young Children,* rev. ed., edited by B. Neugebauer, pp. 98–107. Washington, DC: NAEYC.

Whitney, T. 1999. *Kids like us: Using persona dolls in the classroom.* St. Paul, MN: Redleaf Press.

Wolpert, E. 1999. *Start seeing diversity: The basic guide to an anti-bias classroom.* Video and guide. St. Paul, MN: Redleaf Press.

Wong-Fillmore, L. 1991. Language and cultural issues in early education. In *The care and education of America's young children: Obstacles and opportunities. The ninetieth yearbook of the National Society for the Study of Education,* ed. S.L. Kagan, 30–49. Chicago: University of Chicago Press.

370.117
D435

128600

LINCOLN CHRISTIAN UNIVERSITY

More Resources from NAEYC

Recommended reading for early childhood educators on successfully developing an anti-bias classroom.

A World of Difference: Readings on Teaching Young Children in a Diverse Society

Carol Copple, ed.

The articles in this collection of readings from *Young Children*, NAEYC books, and more provide the current knowledge base as well as thought-provoking discussion on a wide range of issues—culture, language, religion, inclusion, socio-economic status—with emphasis on building respect and understanding. Useful both as an independent resource or as collected readings to accompany other course materials.

Item #: 261 • List: $17.00 • Member: $13.60

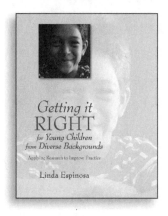

Getting It RIGHT for Young Children from Diverse Backgrounds: Applying Research to Improve Practice

Linda Espinosa

Grounded in real-life experiences and guided by rigorous research findings, this resource provides the tools practitioners need to meet the challenges of educating all young children. The author summarizes the latest scientific evidence on the development and school achievement of English language learners and children living in poverty to offer classroom and program recommendations. *Copublished with Pearson.*

Item #: 793 • List: $30.00 • Member: $24.00

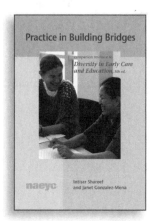

Practice in Building Bridges

Intisar Shareef & Janet Gonzalez-Mena

This collection of activities, discussion topics, stories, and ideas for journaling is designed as a companion resource for those using Janet Gonzalez-Mena's book *Diversity in Early Care and Education* (Item #2011).

Item #: 2012 • List: $10.00 • Member: $8.00

For a complete listing of resources on diversity and anti-bias, please visit **www.naeyc.org/store** or call **800-424-2460**.

3 4711 00221 7653

Prices are subject to change.